POLITICS WITH
BEAUVOIR

POLITICS WITH
BEAUVOIR
FREEDOM IN
THE ENCOUNTER

LORI JO MARSO   Duke University Press / Durham and London / 2017

© 2017 DUKE UNIVERSITY PRESS / All rights reserved
Printed in the United States of America on acid-free paper ∞
Cover designed by Heather Hensley.
Interior designed by Courtney Leigh Baker and typeset in Minion Pro and
Trade Gothic by Graphic Composition, Inc., Bogart, Georgia.

Library of Congress Cataloging-in-Publication Data
Names: Marso, Lori Jo, author.
Title: Politics with Beauvoir : freedom in the encounter / Lori Jo Marso.
Description: Durham : Duke University Press, 2017. | Includes bibliographical
references and index.
Identifiers: LCCN 2017004439 (print) | LCCN 2017012720 (ebook)
ISBN 9780822372844 (ebook)
ISBN 9780822369554 (hardcover : alk. paper)
ISBN 9780822369707 (pbk. : alk. paper)
Subjects: LCSH: Beauvoir, Simone de, 1908–1986. | Feminism—Political aspects. |
Feminist theory.
Classification: LCC B2430.B344 (ebook) | LCC B2430.B344 M37 2017 (print) DDC
194—dc23
LC record available at https://lccn.loc.gov/2017004439

Cover art: Granger

CONTENTS

ACKNOWLEDGMENTS

I first started reading Simone de Beauvoir when I lived in London and was attracted to a table in the London School of Economics bookshop. Beauvoir's picture was in the center and several of her books were prominently (and I thought beautifully and enticingly) displayed around the photo. I bought *The Mandarins*, devoured it, and from there started *Memoirs of a Dutiful Daughter* and breathlessly read through her four-volume autobiography. I didn't think about it at the time, but as I look back now, I suppose her books were all over the shops that spring of 1986 because she had just died on April 14. The fifteen months I spent in London were formative for me politically, intellectually, and personally. Encountering Beauvoir that day in the bookstore made a significant impact on the person I have become.

I have been reading and learning from Beauvoir for over thirty years. Every time I read and teach her writings, as I age and change and have diverse experiences, or in conversations with students, I see something new. I wanted to write my PhD dissertation (and my first book) on Beauvoir's political thought, but at the time I was counseled that it would be more prudent to write on a figure securely in the political theory canon. My idea for a second book began after revisiting Beauvoir's autobiographical writings, and it expanded to include other feminist thinkers and writers. Later, with my dear friend Patricia Moynagh, I coedited a book of essays on Beauvoir's political thinking. But I have always wanted to take the time and space to say just what it is that I find so compelling about Beauvoir's unique political vision, formed in her moment and in conversation with her contemporaries but still urgent for us today. As I see it, Beauvoir's writings, read in encounter, and in and out of context, can open us not only to intimate others but also to collective transformative projects and to the world. With her we might embrace freedom and joy whenever and wherever possible while supporting political struggles that seek to make space for the same for others.

Reading Beauvoir has taught me that freedom is experienced only in encounter and that political commitments emerge from communities formed within agonistic and affective interactions. True to these insights, this book is not mine alone but has developed out of multiple conversations of all sorts—exhilarating, friendly, polite, angry, careful, clarifying, humbling, passionate, difficult, and many that were imaginary—in encounter with my own universe of enemies, allies, and friends. Here I name only allies and friends and keep the enemies (some dead, some living, some characters in books or films) to myself, although both Beauvoir's enemies and my own play a not insignificant role in this book.

I am finishing up this project at what seems to be an especially dark moment for our planet, for non-whites, queers, immigrants, women (in particular for "unbecoming" women), the poor, and everyone marked by difference. Beauvoir's political thinking inspires my own political commitment to keep fighting, keep moving, keep living, and with others to keep making space for freedom. I could not keep that possibility open in my political life, nor could I have written this book, without my political theory friends, many but not all of whom I name in these acknowledgments. My students at Union College have also taught me; our collective thinking in several classes has left their mark on these pages.

It is gratifying to single out some of the friends who have thought with me, sharpened my arguments, and pushed me to be bolder about my claims. Bonnie Honig brainstormed titles with me, listened to me talk about each chapter (and read most of them), and volunteered her always brilliant provocations. The final result is no doubt much richer because of her attention to my work, and also because of mine to hers, in particular my teaching of her *Antigone, Interrupted* in my Cassandra, Medea, Antigone seminar. Torrey Shanks and Laurie Naranch read the entire manuscript before I sent it to Duke University Press for review, and our reading groups about new work in the field and our own projects has sustained me for several years. My former student Perry Moskowitz deserves my deep gratitude for their super-smart senior thesis on Beauvoir, which extended to an interest in my project and fueled many a conversation over coffee that year and beyond.

Many of my chapters are extensively revised versions of published articles, conference and political theory workshop presentations, or invited lectures. I am indebted to anonymous reviewers, audience members, co-panelists, participants in workshops, and journal editors who generously gave their time and talents to improve my writing. Before I knew this project was a book I wrote an article that I hoped might bring attention to the political thought of

Beauvoir by putting her in conversation with Hannah Arendt. I was teaching an advanced undergraduate seminar at Union and was struck by the many ways Arendt's and Beauvoir's theories intersected, not only because of their historical moment but also because of some shared concerns and methods. I presented drafts of this paper in several iterations, each time receiving comments that improved the manuscript. The first time was on a panel celebrating the fifty-year anniversary of the publication of *The Human Condition* at the 2010 American Political Science Association Meeting. Patchen Markell was one of my co-panelists, and to my delight, he encouraged me to continue the comparison. I am grateful for Patchen's work on Arendt, for his generous comments on that early paper, and for reading this manuscript in its entirety and giving me brilliant advice.

In March 2011 Roger Berkowitz asked me to deliver this paper at the Arendt Center at Bard College. My son, Lucas Lobe, was a student at Bard at the time, so I was especially happy and proud to be invited. I also work-shopped the paper with the University of Albany political theory group where I received great comments from Torrey Shanks, Laurie Naranch, Mort Schoolman, and Peter Breiner. My friend Leroy Meyer invited me to present it as the keynote lecture at the Realia Philosophy Conference in August 2012 at the University of South Dakota. Leroy died suddenly and unexpectedly in December 2016 and he is greatly missed. Linda M. G. Zerilli graciously read this chapter and helped me refine its central contributions on the question of judgment, as did Don Herzog. Amy Elman also read it with her sharp critical eye. The article was published in *Political Theory* in 2012 as "Simone de Beauvoir and Hannah Arendt: Judgments in Dark Times." Editor Mary Dietz offered impressively detailed comments and advice and found wonderfully engaged reviewers. The essay won the 2013 Iris Marion Young and Susan B. Okin Award, no doubt due to the excellent input I received along the way from these (and other) interactions. Substantially revised yet again, this paper appears here as chapter 2.

Chapter 1, "(Re)Encountering *The Second Sex*," began as a panel presentation with Lisa Disch and Kathi Weeks at the conference titled, "A Revolutionary Moment: Women's Liberation in the Late 1960s and Early 1970s," at Boston University in March 2014. A condensed version of this work was printed online in 2015 in the *Oxford Handbook of Classics in Contemporary Political Theory*, edited by Jacob Levy, whom I thank for his comments. I expanded the paper to present it at the Cornell Political Theory Colloquium in the spring of 2015. I thank my hosts Alex Livingston and Vijay Phulwani, my discussant Kevin Duong, as well as Jill Frank and Jordan Jochim for all the fun I had with them and for their contributions to what has become the first chapter of this book. Jason Frank could not be at Cornell for my talk, but his work and our friendship have shaped my thinking over many years.

Chapter 3, on the Marquis de Sade and Lars von Trier, was initiated during a dinner with Bonnie Honig where we discovered our mutual fascination with von Trier's films. Together we edited a special issue of *Theory & Event* called "Breaking the Rules: Gender, Power, and Politics in the Films of Lars von Trier" that was published online in March 2015. Prior to publication, I delivered this essay twice in the fall of 2014: at the American Political Science Association Meeting and at a conference Bonnie and I organized at Brown University. A revised version of the article was published in Bonnie's and my coedited volume, *Politics, Theory, and Film: Critical Encounters with Lars von Trier* (2016), and I have revised it yet again as chapter 3. I thank Bonnie for all our energizing conversations and for the tremendous fun we had working together. I thank Bonnie again and the contributors to the von Trier volume for their generous insights, especially Davide Panagia, Michael Shapiro, Miriam Leonard, James Martel, Joshua Dienstag, Victoria Wohl, Rosalind Galt, and Lynne Huffer. Lynne's writing on *Nymphomaniac* in particular, and her 2013 book, *Are the Lips a Grave?*, were influential as I completed the final draft of this book.

Chapter 4, on Fanon and Boupacha, was delivered on an American Political Science Association panel in Chicago in 2013, where I benefited from the savvy insights of Lawrie Balfour as well as Vicki Hsueh, our discussant. One section of this chapter was drafted as a contribution to the *Wiley Blackwell Companion to Simone de Beauvoir* titled "Simone de Beauvoir on Politics and Violence." I thank Nancy Bauer and Laura Hengehold, coeditors of this forthcoming volume, for inviting me to participate and for their excellent ideas for revisions. My friend Kathy Ferguson, coeditor for a *Theory & Event* symposium in June 2012 on the new translation of *The Second Sex,* and our contributors, Linda M. G. Zerilli, Diane Rubenstein, and Sally Markowitz, helped to shape my evolving thinking on Beauvoir. I also thank Sonia Kruks for her groundbreaking work on Beauvoir. I have been in conversation with Sonia (in person and on the page) over many years.

Chapter 5 was published in an earlier version in *Contemporary Political Theory* under the title "Solidarity *sans* Identity: Richard Wright and Simone de Beauvoir Theorize Political Subjectivity," 13, no. 3 (2014). Editor Sam Chambers found sympathetic readers and offered his own smart comments. I also presented it in the University of North Carolina political theory workshop in spring 2013, which sparked a productive conversation with Susan

Bickford, Jeff Spinner-Halev, Michael Lienesch, and their graduate students. Thanks to this extensive airing of the argument prior to publication and some good luck, this essay won the 2014 *Contemporary Political Theory* Award. Chapter 6 began as a lecture at the invitation of my friend Jodi Dean to the Fisher Center for the Study of Women and Men at Hobart William Smith and was published in an earlier version in SIGNS: *A Journal of Women in Culture and Society* as "Perverse Protests: Simone de Beauvoir on Pleasure and Danger, Resistance and Female Violence in Film," in June 2016. I thank Jodi, members of the Hobart community who attended my lecture, especially Paul Passavant, and the anonymous reviewers from SIGNS for helpful comments on this article, revised here for inclusion in the last section of the book. Chapter 7 was first written at the invitation of Toril Moi for the Hannah Arendt symposium for Duke University's Center for Philosophy, Arts, and Literature, presented under the title "The Bechdel Task: Arendt, Von Trotta, and Representing Women's Lives," in April 2015. Toril's inspiring work on Beauvoir has long been an example for me. I thank Toril for inviting me to this lovely event, and Ella Myers, my copresenter, for her comments and conviviality. I also thank Kathi Weeks, who hosted me at her home in Chapel Hill. As the Alison Bechdel rule stipulates, we were two (named) women talking to each other, not about men! This chapter was later presented at the American Political Science Association conference in fall 2015, where I was on a panel with Davide Panagia, Mort Schoolman, Mike Shapiro, and Torrey Shanks. They and the audience members, in particular James Martel, Kennan Ferguson, and Terrell Carver, played a role in shaping this published version of chapter 7.

In addition to all the people I've mentioned, I also need to single out Michaele Ferguson, my coeditor for a book about the gender politics of the Bush Administration that we called *W Stands for Women* and published with Duke in 2007. Since beginning that book in 2005, Michaele has been a constant and provocative interlocutor on feminist theory, politics, and life in the academy. Many other of my political theory colleagues and friends also read parts of this manuscript and offered their wisdom, including Çiğdem Çıdam, Guillermina Seri, Lida Maxwell, Nancy Luxon, George Shulman, and Elizabeth Wingrove. At Union College I am very lucky to be surrounded by a group of colleagues with whom I can share ideas, a laugh, frustrations, a cup of coffee, a glass of wine, or some combination thereof. Courtney Berger, of Duke University Press, has been a partner on this project from the start. I so appreciate Courtney's commitment to me and to the book. The entire team at Duke has been incredibly professional and supportive. I am forever in debt to two brilliant readers. The careful attention these insightful and generous scholars lavished on my manuscript and their spot-on suggestions for revisions greatly improved the final product.

My father, Tom Marso, died in February 2017 as I was finishing the page proofs for this book. My dad devoted his life to public education in a small town in South Dakota. He was the superintendent of schools for twenty-eight years (a tenure largely unheard of) where his humor and inclusiveness made him the good friend of most everyone. I loved seeing my dad take pleasure in my accomplishments, and I often turned to him for help when I stumbled. I am immeasurably grateful to him, and to my mom, for the example they set and for their faith in me.

Guthrie and Geoff Gray-Lobe, Danielle Powell, Rita Fellers, Jeff and Lynn Marso, Jim Lobe, and my extended family in New York City—May Parsey, Jonah Lobe, Eli Clifton, Mei Yee Mak, and Julia Kaye—all deserve a shout-out. Some of them are even eager to talk with me about Simone de Beauvoir, Lars von Trier, Alison Bechdel, or Chantal Akerman! My children, Lucas and Luci Lobe, now adults, are also (sometimes) willing to converse (or patiently listen to me talk) about the figures and themes in my writing. No matter what the topic, however, Lucas and Luci continually challenge and change me, and enrich my life beyond measure. Lucas's technical skills have been crucial, as he has helped me capture screen shots and bring the images up to specifications for publication. Luci's desire for happy endings inspired me to be willing to embrace my own feminist optimism in the conclusion. Seeing Lucas's and Luci's pride in my commitments, and watching them (often nervously but always on their side) as they move in fits and starts along their sometimes surprising and sometimes rocky paths, brings me enormous joy. Tom Lobe, my unfailing, critical and kind, ever agonistic but always loving life partner, plays an outsized role in everything I do, say, think, and write.

INTRODUCTION
OUR BEAUVOIR

Simone de Beauvoir is lauded as *the* exemplary feminist (indeed, as the "mother" of feminism) or lamented as typical of everything that is wrong with feminism.[1] She is celebrated or condemned for advancing a liberal individualist form of feminism.[2] She is denounced for thinking that socialism will automatically liberate women.[3] She is taken to task for not saying she was a feminist soon enough.[4] Her work was ignored by philosophy departments for decades on the grounds that she merely applied Sartre's framework to women, but feminist philosophers have rehabilitated her as the real brain behind Sartre's pen.[5] She is reprimanded for not paying attention to racial and class divisions among women and for caring only about middle-class white women.[6] She is rebuked for disavowing the body or, contrarily, for magnifying the importance of unseemly bodily functions.[7] She is admired for disdaining motherhood, housework, and other "feminine" activities or reviled for the same.[8] She is chastised for advancing gender as an essentialist category or for not paying enough attention to *l'écriture féminine*.[9] Although her famous insight, "One is not born but rather becomes a woman," has been taken up by trans and queer feminists as a rallying cry for the plasticity and hybridity of gender, she is considered by many to be thoroughly passé.[10]

These readings each claim Beauvoir as their own: to be loved, lamented, or disavowed. But they tend to miss what I will argue is at the heart of her feminism, which is also what makes her politics of interest to an audience beyond feminist theory.[11] To my horror, as I was finishing this book, a feminist theory colleague said to me, "There's nothing new to say about Beauvoir!" I show in this book there is not only something new to say, but there is much that feminists, literary theorists, and philosophers, all parsing "our" Beauvoir, have not seen.[12] What has been obscured, in spite of so much excellent scholarship, is the way Beauvoir's feminist politics are exemplary of her political thinking about freedom in encounter.

ENCOUNTERS: BEAUVOIR'S POLITICS

I interpret Beauvoir as a theorist of encounter. As recorded in her autobiography and novels, sometimes in frustration but other times in acceptance or even exhilaration, Beauvoir recognized that there is *always* an "other" in relationship with oneself. Sarah Bakewell (2016, 326) characterizes Beauvoir's multivolume autobiography as depicting "herself and Sartre and countless friends and colleagues as they think, act, quarrel, meet, separate, have tantrums and passions, and generally respond to their world." This is the Beauvoir I was first drawn to in a London bookshop, and the one whose way of doing and thinking politics is urgent for us now.

For Beauvoir, to encounter others is not only a fact of existence; it is also the *only* way to produce and experience freedom. Being with others is a foundational quality of freedom. Ambiguity, contingency, situation, and nonsovereignty characterize encounters, and each produces, diminishes, or destroys freedom. Beauvoir ([1949] 2011, 6) doesn't use encounter as a theoretical framing, but her language of "duality between Self and Other" hints at the dynamic that I develop and demonstrate is central to her political practice. In the introduction to *The Second Sex* she says, "No group ever defines itself as the One without immediately setting up the Other opposite itself" (6). When she talks about the duality of Self and Other, however, she is not advocating a Hegelian mutual recognition or reciprocity, or a struggle to the death between two subjectivities. Nor is she simply noting that Self and Other (or Master and Slave in Hegel's parlance) are each *simultaneously* self and other, although she is doing that too.

Emphasizing ambiguity, Beauvoir insists that to understand how freedom is grasped or missed, we must bring the bodies of the parties into view. Emphasizing situation, she adds that we must consider the structural, social, historical, and political conditions in which the embodied Self "looks" and whether and how the embodied Other "looks back." How the two negotiate the encounter influences individual and collective agency, as well as whether freedom itself will be produced, diminished, or denied. What happens here between the two will sway whether and which actions might be taken, whether and how freedom will be grasped, or if the opportunity for freedom will be squandered. In the encounter between men and women that Beauvoir describes, she says that cast in the role of Other, women don't make a reciprocal claim.[13] "Why do women not contest male sovereignty?" she asks ([1949] 2011, 7). What she seeks for women is not victory (in the battle of subjectivities) nor mutual recognition or reciprocity.[14] Noticing that women are trapped in their position as other, she says they don't struggle to overcome it. Devoid of this agonism, freedom is missed for both parties. Without struggle, *sans encounter*, freedom cannot emerge.

I foreground the language of encounter to supplement that of situation and ambiguity, other pivotal terms in Beauvoir's lexicon, because it better describes what is at stake in her advocacy for collective freedom. The language of situation speaks to the fact that freedom is not best understood as ontological or ethical. Focusing on ontology or ethics is too abstract and mischaracterizes the role of human will and consciousness. By highlighting situation and structure, we can see that freedom is linked to circumstance but that we still have agency. Structure does not eclipse our capacity to move; it situates and makes it possible. With others, and in situations we have not chosen, people still act and choose: within complex, sometimes violent, often diminished or challenging circumstances of multilevel and crosscutting agencies and forces, enacting change and acting in concert are still possible.[15] Choices are never fully autonomous but are crafted by our grasp on the world: our body, history, situation, power, and absolutely unbreakable bonds to others.

While situation speaks to the constraints of structure, ambiguity highlights the lived experience of embodied subjects. Ambiguity is for Beauvoir a kind of "twoness." Our lived experience is as subject and object, transcendence and immanence, freedom and body, choosing agents and trapped objects. She insists that ambiguity is an ontological fact of existence, an accurate description of our embodied perspective on the world, as well as an ethical guide for how to navigate the world without turning others into inanimate things devoid of agency.[16] Bodies also have *political* meanings, however, that mark them in relationship to other bodies, to structure, to history, to nature. Thus while ambiguity is ontological—we are all exposed and vulnerable to each other— ambiguity is also political: some are disproportionately vulnerable, marked as other, doomed to immanence and denied transcendence.

What using the language of encounter captures that the language of situation and ambiguity does not is the ontological and political fact that our lives are always entangled with others. Situation and ambiguity describe an individual's constrained and embodied grasp on the world in a quest for individual (or group) agency. Within the language of situation and ambiguity, we begin from the perspective of the individual or the group subject. To speak of encounters, we must acknowledge the social and political constraints of situation and the ethical imperative to acknowledge ambiguity, but we also see struggle and plurality. We move swiftly and decisively from the position of individual or group subject and land in encounter: *with* an other or others, *within* community, *within* the world, politically engaged. When we foreground encounters we notice that individual subjectivity and individual or group agency do not exist prior to but rather *emerge from* encounters. There are *always two or more*: responsiveness and judgment from other(s) limit and drive us as political subjects. How we maneuver and what we do within this entanglement constitutes political freedom. Our actions here enhance or diminish freedom for the two or for a larger collective.

I emphasize throughout this book that freedom cannot be experienced elsewhere than in encounters; it is completely meaningless (in fact impossible) for freedom to be experienced alone. This is what I highlight with the phrase *freedom in the encounter*. While situation and ambiguity define the potential for individual and group autonomy, agency, and action, freedom itself is possible only within encounters. We are in the world, always acting within (unchosen) structures—within nature, historical events, class (caste or group), the shifting political meanings accorded to bodies in terms of age, ability, race, sex, and gender. Our freedom, however, is not defined or measured by how much autonomy or agency we achieve against or from these situations but rather is only ever possible in relationship to others.

The encounters Beauvoir brings to our attention range from the smallest and seemingly insignificant (the praying mantis and its mate) to the intimate (between lovers, between parents and children), the explicitly political (gendered and raced colonial encounters), the aesthetic (reader and text, spectator and film), and the psychoaffective and somatic (the aging woman and the standards of beauty stamped within the consciousness of those she encounters). We do not grasp freedom in spite of encounter. Freedom emerges or is lost within collectivity: friction, movement, cooperation, care, and struggle characterize encounters between two or more.

Encounter is at the heart of everything Beauvoir wrote, but it can easily be missed when she is read solitarily. When we read her in dialogue with others, as thinking with and against others, it is harder to miss what so many have ignored when they focus on her feminism in isolation from her relationship to other thinkers and her other leftist political commitments. Beauvoir was deeply affected not only by reading philosophers such as Hegel, Heidegger, Bergson, Descartes, and of course Sartre, but also by Marxism and other socialist traditions. She was a voracious lover of films and novels. Collette was one of her favorite authors, but she also admired Americans including Faulkner and Hemingway and of course Nelson Algren, with whom she fell in love in Chicago in 1947 and had a relationship lasting several years. To advance Beauvoir as a thinker of encounter, we also must consider her commitments to feminist, antiracist, anticolonialist, and anti-imperialist projects and movements.[17] She responded to and theorized from within historical-political circumstances during her life in France, particularly Occupation, the war in Algeria, and the 1968 worker and student movements. When we read her work as *engagée* and in dialogue with others about social and political questions, the contributions she makes to political thinking, as well as its tight links to her feminism, suddenly come into view.

This book is inspired by my attraction to Beauvoir's habit of seeking out the company of diverse others (in books, in films, and in her imagination, as well as in her life) to talk about and puzzle through urgent political questions. For example, I highlight and extend conversations in which she was involved, such as with her allies Richard Wright and Frantz Fanon on questions of antiblack racism, decolonization, and forging new solidarities. Historical events are their own kind of collective encounter within this text, and they provide the context for encounters made possible within them. I retain the context of these conversations as occurring within and because of significant historical events, but I extend them to include new interlocutors who speak more directly to contemporary dilemmas.

I also attend to conversations with interlocutors Beauvoir loathed or who drew her perverse curiosity, such as the fascist Robert Brasillach and the Marquis de Sade. Beauvoir was present at Brasillach's trial for treason in 1945, but she did not meet him. She was compelled to be there, she said, to see with her own eyes a "conscious author of genuine evil" ([1949] 2004, 248). Because Hannah Arendt traveled to Jerusalem fifteen years later also to "expose" herself to an "evildoer," I invite these two thinkers into conversation.[18] Even though Beauvoir and Arendt share theoretical proclivities, philosophical influences, and the same historical moment, sadly for us they never met nor even engaged in conversation.[19] The conversation that I construct between them, however—on the trials of Brasillach and Eichmann, and then in the last chapter on Violette Leduc and Rahel Varnhagen—illuminates new interpretations on the judgment of evildoers and on feminist friendship.

Inspired by Beauvoir's insatiable curiosity and her willingness to pursue even severely discomfiting encounters, I imagine conversations that force us to confront unconscious desires for sadism, abuse, violence, and masochism. To this end I put Beauvoir's writings on the Marquis de Sade, a writer she called "imperious, wrathful, headstrong, extreme in all things" ([1952] 2012, 44), into dialogue with the films of the contemporary avant-garde *provocateur* Lars von Trier, also known for his dark and (some say) misanthropic vision.[20] Contrarily I create conversations that feature relationships of mutual recognition and care. Just as in *The Second Sex* Beauvoir creates surprising encounters between real and fictional women across generations, races, history, and location, my encounters move across time and genres and include characters from the films of Chantal Akerman, Martin Provost, and Margarethe von Trotta and the graphic art of Alison Bechdel.[21]

I am drawn to Beauvoir's way of showing how our lives are *always* interlinked with others, often in uncomfortable and dangerous ways, and that this is the stuff of politics, the place and moment where we grasp or deny freedom. She shows us (in theory, in history, and in fiction) that when we wish for unfettered sovereignty, we are mostly delusional.[22] But some of us *do* have more space, power, influence, and freedom than others, and she shows us this too. She is eager to condemn right-wing thinkers, for example, for the ideologies they manufacture to create and justify inequality,[23] and she spends all of volume 1 of *The Second Sex* demonstrating that motivated by their own fear of vulnerability, men who write and propagate myths about women make this language and these myths into material reality. Women really do have a circumscribed space of freedom due to the dominance and preponderance of male myths about femininity, and poor people really do have diminished life expectations because of the way ideologies of privilege create and sustain material conditions that trap whole groups of people in positions of material and psychological submission and hopelessness. Beauvoir notices that women get psychologically and materially invested in adopting and performing the myths of femininity, practicing daily habits that transform biological and historical contingencies into political and social destiny.

ENCOUNTERS: DEFINED

Theorizing politics as the process and result of encounters foregrounds the primacy of relationships, but Beauvoir never assumes these are sites of comfort, ease, safety, or peace. In relationship there is never direct, unmediated, transparent communication: there is always the inability to absorb or possess; there is a distance, an appearance of the foreign, forbidden, unfamiliar, unknowable, and threatening. What happens in the time and space of this gap is the key political moment. The distance Beauvoir insists we maintain (as well as struggle within) is akin to the Arendtian notion of the "in-between": the space between us where freedom lives, grows, diminishes, or might die. We disavow this gap and erase the in-between when we proclaim allegiance to god, infinity, humanity, nature, or articulations of collectivity that refuse to recognize distinction and diversity. These identifications deny the very possibility of encounter, effacing difference, foreign bodies, and unknown but (ethically) equal others. According to Beauvoir, the quest for plenitude and possession is foolhardy, even dangerous, and it results in oppression. When desire for wholeness, for appropriation or possession holds sway in the wish to diminish the anxiety and ennui of existence, hierarchical relationships are established. When the gap is affirmed in its ambiguity a different orientation can be nurtured. As Beauvoir (1948, 12) sees it, the space of the encounter is one of "excruciation" (we cannot possess the other) but also of "joy" (we can and should take pleasure in the fact of this impossibility). In either outcome, the encounter is a *political* moment: what we *do* in this space and in this moment, or what we unconsciously do or neglect to do, whether we enhance and affirm or deny or diminish freedom, reflects and generates our political orientation to the world. In these ways, and as I show, Beauvoir's work on encounter goes far beyond what has been characterized as "the ethical turn" in political thought. Parting ways with theorists who limit their focus to the behavior of individuals within encounter to observe or advocate an ethics of individual responsibility or choice, Beauvoir is attentive to the way encounters themselves are made possible by historical and political circumstances. She adds that individual subjectivities are themselves formed within encounters (beginning with the mother/child dyad) and that we each bring our situations and experiences to subsequent encounters.

Published in 1947, just two years before the appearance of *The Second Sex*, *The Ethics of Ambiguity* underwrites my choice to highlight the language of encounter to bring Beauvoir's political thinking into view. Although later Beauvoir said the book was dissatisfying to her because it was too "abstract" and lacking in concrete examples (that is to say, she thought it needed more examples of encounters), her goal for the piece was to claim that existentialism, which was seen as a "philosophy of the absurd and of despair" (1948, 10) indeed has an ethical vision.[24] But she also wanted to show that existentialist ethics is grounded in the "human world established by man's projects and the ends he sets up" (11). Rather than remaining, like the "Hegelian system," on the "plane of the universal [and] the infinite," Beauvoir commends a politics "experienced in the truth of life," where one can "live in the midst of living men" (158–59).

Wresting existentialism away from teleology and philosophical determinism, as well as from an absurdist philosophy of absolute contingency, the dilemmas Beauvoir explores in *The Ethics of Ambiguity* are always located in the conflict between at least two parties, themselves shaped by their encounters with history, structures, and the political meanings of their bodies. Nevertheless she pushes us to exercise agency and seize freedom where and when possible. One of the key features of Beauvoir's thought that distinguishes her from several of her contemporaries is her attention to the mundane and everyday encounter with the same penetrating analysis she gives to encounters with obvious historical significance.[25] In Beauvoir's analysis the personal truly becomes political! She draws out the political significance of repetitive, banal, habitual activities (housework, shopping—the activities that qualify as labor in Arendt's *The Human Condition*); she foregrounds intimate and unthought encounters (sexual, in dream-worlds) to penetrate how they sustain and nourish or have the potential to undo oppressive material and psychic webs of oppression; and at the same time, she gives due attention to the way structural forces inhibit and condition these smaller, seemingly insignificant moments of friction or affability. Her attention to sensory, somatic encounters interwoven within and in the context of structural, historical, and larger forces of biology and history helps us to enlarge our sense of how several kinds of encounters overlap in politically salient ways. In my interpretation of Beauvoir, history itself is revealed as a series of encounters, some purposeful and others aleatory, becoming a site of possibility rather than a predetermined trajectory. Some encounters seem marginal and others appear epochal, but none is determined or necessary, and meaning changes when circumstances change. Often an encounter's significance is not understood until after the event, and it is never *finally* understood at all.

The language we employ to describe even the natural world and biological processes takes on the force of a material reality itself that must be affirmed, altered, or undone within encounters. As Beauvoir ([1949] 2011, 26, 33) puts it in the chapter "Biological Data" in *The Second Sex*, for example, physiologists and biologists "ascribe meaning to vital phenomena," but "seeing in these facts the harbinger of the 'battle of the sexes'" is a political act, which in this case circumscribes the freedom of women by saying the female is, at one and the same time, a "danger" to the male of each species but also "naturally" suited for caring for children. We can recognize animals, machines, and material objects as demanding our ethical attention or as having strange forms of agency (such as the grotesque animals and trees and the chestnuts in von Trier's *Antichrist*, or boiling pots of potatoes in Akerman's *Jeanne Dielman*), but humans alone are choosing (and thus politically responsible) subjects.

Politics with Beauvoir, a politics wherein we make decisions together, wherein we choose to affirm freedom *for all* within conditions we do not and have not chosen, wherein we carve out freedom from within tight spaces and impossible choices and make that freedom grow, is the kind of politics we need right now. Of greatest urgency for Beauvoir, as I read her, is the fact that within *each and every* encounter there is a "contra," a meeting of adversaries, wherein a chance to expand or diminish freedom occurs. Beauvoir acknowledges that life is facticity and contingency, but she insists that there is room for freedom, for reflection, and to make meaningful choices that prioritize our shared world. As she insists, "It is because there are real dangers, real failures and real earthly damnation that words like victory, wisdom, or joy have meaning; nothing is decided in advance, and it is because man has something to lose and because he can lose that he can also win" (1948, 34).

ENCOUNTERS IN CONVERSATION: WITH ENEMIES, WITH ALLIES, AND WITH FRIENDS

Beauvoir acknowledges our often intense desire for unfettered freedom to do as we please, and she understands our (often collective) fantasies of sovereign action and the will to dominance. She also admits to her own ambition to win at every conversation.

She lived her life in the midst of multiple conversations, most of all with Jean-Paul Sartre. Poignantly, at the beginning of *Adieux: A Farewell to Sartre*, Beauvoir (1984, 3) laments:

> This is the first of my books—the only one no doubt—that you will not have read before it is printed. It is wholly and entirely devoted to you; and you are not affected by it. When we were young and one of us gained a brilliant victory over the other in an impassioned argu-

ment, the winner used to say, "There you are in your little box!" You are in your little box; you will not come out of it and I shall not join you there. Even if I am buried next to you there will be no communication between your ashes and mine.

Beauvoir seems to say that death marks the end of her almost lifelong journey with Sartre. But she undoes this very claim when she directly addresses her dead partner. Even in the failed space of death, she attempts a conversation. As I demonstrate, Beauvoir loved boxing with words—with intimates like Sartre, but also with those she saw as enemies, those she reached out to as allies, and those similarly situated but as yet unrecognized as friends. Although this conversation with the dead Sartre is seemingly pitched as a win–lose battle ("There you are in your little box!"), Beauvoir deliberately puts herself into her little box as well. Her conversations, sometimes practically but sometimes fantastically, seek something beyond the appointing of a winner. They seek confrontation and conversion—of ourselves, of others, and of material reality—into something that looks more like freedom.

Beauvoir's practice of staging encounters within texts and seeking them out with her peers shows how conversations situate (and can reveal) interlocutors as bearing power and determining meaning (or not). These conversations shift fields of meaning, help us see and say things we previously could not, and move us toward converting material realities. This book demonstrates that for Beauvoir conversations are not pluralistic or neutral dialogues between equal or equally situated partners, and their mechanisms and effects are not abstract. Instead they are sites of affective and agonistic struggle and potential transformation, able to create material reality or diminish space and possibilities for agency or, contrarily, to nurture a desire for collective freedom and create new coalitions and sites of potential solidarities. Even in failed or negative spaces, Beauvoir's work shows, encounters occur and freedom can be seized, denied, encouraged, or discouraged within their space and moment.

Beauvoir's love for the promiscuous, risk-taking, provocative, boundary-breaking, agonistic, and raucous battle of words situated her in relationship to her contemporaries and merits our attention now, more than thirty years after her death. I have organized the chapters to echo my discussion of the architecture of *The Second Sex* in the first chapter: confronting and hoping to convert enemies and ourselves, engaging and learning with allies, and seeking to connect isolated individuals in friendship. The conversations I extend and stage take seriously Beauvoir's observation that politics is located first in agonism and affectivity. After "(Re)Encountering *The Second Sex*," the chapters follow Beauvoir's conversations with two kinds of enemies (fascists and bourgeois taxonomies), extend her conversations with allies (Fanon and Wright) about colonial violence and racial hatred and discrimination, and, in the final section, take up her call to solicit and nurture connections between isolated women in need of feminist friendship.

My organizational motif—naming enemies, allies, and friends—itself makes a political intervention by invoking and reworking Carl Schmitt's friend/enemy distinction so fundamental to modern states. Like Schmitt, I focus on questions of power and antagonism as central to all political conversations, and yet I do not reinforce his logic of the political as governing how we should practice politics or do political theory. Encounter takes the place of decision and mutuality the place of sovereignty. Repeating but transforming the invocation of friends and enemies and triangulating it with the addition of allies introduces fluidity within boundaries and underlines the fact that encounters often discomfort and surprise us. They also can alter our moods and make us rethink our definitions and proclivities.

Each chapter is also an opportunity to bring diverse modes of thought into conversation with each other: antiracism with anticolonialism and antisexism feminisms, affect theory with structuralism and psychoanalysis, film with literary studies. My practice of following through on multiple levels and kinds of conversations about historical and political catastrophes and everyday habits helps us to think these approaches together in relationship rather than as isolated methodologies or as hierarchical choices that must be made (to focus on gender rather than race, for example, or name and isolate identities and measure suffering).

My first chapter, "(Re)Encountering *The Second Sex*," makes a case for reading *The Second Sex* as an encounter with enemies (the men who create myths about women, who also are put into encounter with each other by Beauvoir in volume 1), an attempt to find allies (diverse women sharing accounts of their "lived experience" in volume 2), and an appeal to create friends (readers of the text who heed the appeal and can begin conversations). *The Second Sex* serves as a repeated point of reference throughout the book. While I bring less prominent essays by Beauvoir into view and work with them extensively, *The Second Sex* never drops out and indeed plays a central role in this book. In this first chapter I situate my extended reading of Beauvoir's most well known text by putting it in conversation with one of the lesser-known essays, "Right-Wing Thought Today" from 1955. While some Beauvoir scholars have said "Right-Wing Thought Today" merits only historical attention, I argue that considering *The Second Sex* together with "Right-Wing Thought Today" illuminates Beauvoir's sophisticated parsing of the relationships among ideology, affects, and material reality in *both* texts. Each is transformed by the other such that we can newly understand why and how Beauvoir theorizes material reality as brought into existence, as well as potentially transformed, by ideological and affective dynamics and processes. These relationships will play a central role in how this book unfolds as I move from different registers of scale—from the conversational or dialogic encounter to the collective movement and from the individual symptom to the diagnosis of social and political pathologies.

My book's structure mimics what I have discovered Beauvoir's to be in *The Second Sex*. Part I, "Enemies: Monsters, Men, and Misogynist Art," features two encounters with enemies, one in a chapter on fascists and the second in a chapter on bourgeois taxonomies. In chapter 2 I explore why Beauvoir broke with her intellectual allies in 1945 to call for the French state to execute Robert Brasillach, a fascist journalist on trial for treason. In her little-read essay "An Eye for an Eye," she confronts an enemy and says she wants to see him die. (She refused to sign the petition circulated by prominent French intellectuals and writers to limit state sovereignty over death.) Doing so she asserts the primacy of her own political judgment and claims the right to make judgments that ally with victims. Following her down this road I discuss Beauvoir in relation with Arendt, who, reporting on Eichmann's trial in 1961, wanted him to be executed. But unlike Beauvoir, Arendt sought to silence victim accounts of suffering and shift the focus to Eichmann's deeds. Wondering whether these men are "monsters" and what makes them so, the two differently theorize how to make reflective judgments on when and how collective freedom is threatened and how the embodiment, suffering, and voices of the victims might matter in making judgments.

Chapter 3 takes up another neglected text of Beauvoir's and treats it in relation to Trier's 2009 film *Antichrist*, a work that at first glance appears to further misogynist stereotypes of women as witches and bad mothers. Drawing on Beauvoir's 1952 essay on the Marquis de Sade (thought by some to also be a monster, certainly a misogynist), "Must We Burn Sade?," I consider how feminists might capaciously encounter an aesthetic object that seems positioned in enemy territory. Bodies and body parts, monsters, and foreign tongues dominate the lexicon of these two chapters in the "Enemies" section, and the grisliness of body parts that is mostly excised from Beauvoir's and Arendt's essays on the trials returns to haunt us in von Trier's film. In their trial reports, neither Beauvoir nor Arendt is able to fully confront the *jouis-*

sance of torture and the lure of evil. Though they attended the trials in part for the chance to see evildoers, their essays bring us to the brink, but stop just short, of a close encounter with the devil. Not so with von Trier. He delivers the devil and more. Maybe too much more? Our desire to control, destroy, and violate, and the question of what we *do* when we confront the foreign, the object, part-objects, and body parts, is central to both Sade's and von Trier's worlds.

Like Sade before him, von Trier has a reputation for trafficking in body parts and for doing so in a particularly misogynist way. In a 2015 interview in response to the statement "It is not absolutely necessary in order to make a good movie that someone gets the clit cut off!," von Trier responds, "But it is a start!"[26] That "someone" would be a woman, and it is one of the grisliest moments in *Antichrist*. Is this film an enemy to feminists, and how do we judge? The reflections on judgment that emerge from Beauvoir's encounter with Arendt remind us of the necessary risks involved in political judgments when we are not following rules, as the two thinkers together insist on our willingness to run these risks. Arendt's careful parsing of the distinction between morality and aesthetics mirrors Beauvoir's capacious encounter with Sade, whose work she admires for targeting "bourgeois taxonomies" as our real enemies.[27]

Having located and named the violence of fascism and patriarchy as born from abstract categories, general rules, and liberal platitudes, in part II, "Allies: Antinomies of Action in Conditions of Violence," I follow Beauvoir's quest to develop collective efforts to challenge the ills of capitalist, patriarchal, and colonial violence, forms of violence that are themselves buttressed by ideologies that spring from, create, and defy material conditions all at once. This section also introduces Beauvoir's concern with antinomies of action. She asks, for example, how we can best make political choices while acknowledging that each choice is vexed, that our encounters are not only relational but also inherently unequal, and that we sometimes inadvertently create new forms of violence even when hoping to minimize it. Nevertheless action must be taken, choices made, failures enacted, and possibly even violence employed and freedom denied to some. As she wrestles with Fanon and Wright, allies on the Left, she sharpens her opposition to racial and colonial violence and its visible and invisible wounds on bodies and psyches. With these two she struggles to move oppressed peoples from wounds and perversions to agency and collective action, searching for insight into how to form alliances in solidarities beyond identity.

Confronting enemies makes us face up to the fact that while we must always seek to minimize violence, it is always too proximate and ready to erupt: the other (even within ourselves) often appears as a "foreign existence" and seems like an enemy. Choices made in encounters set off further reactions that diminish or enhance freedom. Talking to allies pushes these insights into new territory for Beauvoir. She met Fanon only once, arranged by their mutual friend (and Beauvoir's seven-year lover) Claude Lanzmann, to discuss whether Sartre might write the preface for *Wretched of the Earth*. By this time Fanon was dying of leukemia, but Beauvoir was impressed by his passionate alliance with the oppressed. His ideas made it into her work, and hers had certainly influenced him, though he never acknowledged as much.[28] In chapter 4 I extend Beauvoir and Fanon's exchange on colonial and decolonial violence by including Djamila Boupacha. Boupacha was an Algerian militant tortured and raped by French authorities. Although Beauvoir never met her (in a controversial decision she declined to do so when asked to by Boupacha's French lawyer, Gisèle Halimi), she wrote a bold article in *Le Monde* calling attention to how the French refined their torture techniques in the Algerian War and insisting that French citizens are responsible for perpetuating and condoning these violations. In captivity Boupacha was raped with a bottle by French soldiers and forced to admit to crimes (she later claimed) she did not commit. In the context of Boupacha's ordeal, reading Fanon's work on socioaffective ailments in encounter with Beauvoir's writings on the same shows how racialized and sexed bodies register pathologies (sometimes as perverse signs of protest) and how women's changing roles in anticolonial struggles set new gendered conflicts in motion.

What takes center stage within Beauvoir's encounter with Fanon and Boupacha are the intersections of gender and race, and the affective and often pathologized responses to structural and physical violence that spring from political meanings imposed on bodies. These same issues are discussed in Beauvoir's conversation with Richard Wright, but here I more directly tackle the question of whether and how it might be politically strategic to embrace identities born out of structural and physical violence. Wright was the most well known African American author of the mid-twentieth century due to the success of *Native Son* (1940) and *Black Boy* (1945), but he exiled himself to France in 1947. He had met Beauvoir the year before in Paris and then again when she came to the United States in early 1947 on her four-month "existentialism" tour, and he and his wife Ellen were her hosts in New York City. Beauvoir and Wright became fast friends in the United States, and Beauvoir cites Wright's work multiple times in *The Second Sex*. But Wright didn't engage as carefully with Beauvoir's work or think as much about the intersections of gender and race as he might have. Reading Wright in light of the conversation I created among Beauvoir, Fanon, and Boupacha puts Wright's work on race, and Beauvoir's on gender, in a new light. Here the conversation moves outward from the diagnosis of the individual symptom and toward collective action by looking to the situations of Kwame Nkrumah's Ghana and American Jim Crow racism. Wright and Beauvoir together show why and how identity categories limit the potential for encounters of solidarity across borders and across identities.

Part III, "Friends: Conversations That Change the Rules," focuses on isolated women who need to speak to someone, preferably to each other, on subjects other than men. Like the Algerians whom Fanon treats in his clinic, and like black Americans such as Wright who search for collectivity and home in "returning" to Africa, the women of *The Second Sex* are products of histories of diminished expectations, failed aspirations, and structural and bodily violence. One of the most enduring and difficult questions of *The Second Sex*, one that many feminists turn away from, is the question of how wounded subjects might choose freedom and enact change rather than repeat the same patterns and languish in what Beauvoir, with Sartre, calls "bad faith." Wright was worried about these questions too, which might account for Beauvoir and Wright's long friendship and the many resonances between their work. Wright saw the embrace of *négritude* as a troubling move for black subjects, and Beauvoir was discouraged to see women embracing femininity, even if it meant they turned *toward* other women.

Alison Bechdel's "rule" (often called the "Bechdel test") for feminist film specifies that in order to be considered feminist, a film must feature more than one (named) woman, and these women must talk to each other about something other than men. Having learned from Beauvoir and Arendt that determinative rules belie the risks of judgment, I refigure Bechdel's rule as my interpretive task in my section "Friends" to create conversations that *change* the rules or, better yet, get rid of them altogether. As it turns out, Beauvoir and Bechdel have a lot to talk about: Beauvoir too wants women to talk to each other about something *other than* men. Returning to insights gleaned from *The Second Sex*, in chapter 6 I introduce Chantal Akerman's classic 1975 feminist art house film, *Jeanne Dielman*, to interpret two contemporary films, each that sits uncomfortably with feminist audiences: David Fincher's 2014 *Gone Girl* and Lars von Trier's 2013 *Nymphomaniac*. In my reading the films present the unconscious desires of isolated women who misdiagnose their personal ailments, dissatisfaction, and acts of murderous violence as individual symptoms rather than political effects. Beauvoir's literary practice, extended here as a film analysis, creates what she hopes will be an affective response on the part of readers and spectators to realign our senses. Generated by the text or film, this new arrangement of the senses might inspire something like a longing for freedom.

Chapter 7 reignites the conversation I began between Beauvoir and Hannah Arendt in chapter 2. Here I argue that the gesture of feminist friendship, enacted and extended between differently situated women, might be not only life-affirming but also movement creating. I work with three texts in this chapter: the 2014 film *Violette*, which features the encounter between Violette Leduc and Simone de Beauvoir; Hannah Arendt's 1944 (auto)biography of the nineteenth-century Jew Rahel Varnhagen; and Margarethe von Trotta's 2012 biopic, *Hannah Arendt*. We will see how feminist friendship, or the gift of feminist consciousness, creates new encounters to change our ways of seeing, saying, and (re)making collective conditions. My conclusion is a happy ending. It's not the happy ending of Disney movies, romantic comedies, or Thai massages, but it does induce optimism and keep the body in view in terms of both its political situation and sensual possibilities. This happy ending calls upon us as political actors to embrace our (situated, limited, ambiguous, compromised) chance at collective freedom.

To begin this journey I first turn to *The Second Sex* to craft a (re)encounter with Beauvoir's text, but via a detour through "Right-Wing Thought Today." As noted earlier, I make this chapter the first to show how the book unfolds as encounters with enemies, allies, and friends. I identify this organization of the text and parse the formal features of Beauvoir's textual strategy to create friends via affective literary techniques in both "Right-Wing Thought Today" and *The Second Sex*. But for me this discovery (of enemies, allies, and friends) unfolded in the opposite order. It was only after reading Beauvoir in conversation with others that I began to read *The Second Sex* differently. Like "Right-Wing Thought Today," *The Second Sex* has become a completely new text for me.[29] Whereas before I saw in both works a clash between structure and agency, I now see a sophisticated explanation (and use) of how affect works. Beauvoir shows us that ideology is motivated by affects and becomes material and gets located in bodies and practices. What she hopes is that the encounter between text and readers itself might nurture new affects, particularly a desire for freedom. This can happen, however, only if we have friends (or even enemies or allies?) to talk to and struggle with. I hope you will see it this way too and be open to the encounter.

(RE)ENCOUNTERING
THE SECOND SEX

The Second Sex introduces and exemplifies the freedom-enhancing politics of encounter that I foreground throughout this book. Here, in her most famous text, Beauvoir stages a confrontation with enemies of women (authors of male myths about femininity) and makes them speak to each other as well. She seeks out allies (diverse women, real and fictional, who recount their lived experiences). And she nurtures friends by calling out to readers of the book. At the same time she models a conversational literary practice that draws our attention to the movements and feelings of bodies (somatic and affective), the conditions of ontology (time, nature, mortality, nonsovereignty, contingency), and the existence of structures (history, language, material conditions). Just as Beauvoir argues we are never free alone but only in the presence of others, so too she saw that political thinking is generated and enhanced by thinking with and against others in conditions we cannot control (even when we create them as authors, filmmakers, or political actors).

Beauvoir's literary strategy of staging encounters within texts, and between texts and readers, shows us how feelings emerge within material conditions (via bodies encountering other bodies and things in situations) and move in and through ideologies, myths, and systems to produce, reproduce, or challenge inequality and oppression. Affect theorists often distinguish between the terms *emotion*, *feeling*, and *affect*, but following Beauvoir, I see feelings and emotions as themselves political (never solely individual), as arising from material conditions and able to be mobilized into affective political configurations. Affects tend to tether us to the status quo, but might be redirected to better ends. We might say she woos her readers to help us see the mobilization of affect as a site of power and a potential source for resistance.[1] Appealing to her readers not by the usual method of affirming identity but instead by soliciting desires for new forms of freedom, Beauvoir draws us into new affective configurations and opens up new sites of solidarity.[2]

To illustrate how this works in *The Second Sex*, I begin with a reading of Beauvoir's "Right-Wing Thought Today," a text that employs similar literary techniques. This essay is dismissively introduced by Sonia Kruks (2012a, 110) in *Simone de Beauvoir: Political Writings* as "now perhaps mainly of historical interest."[3] But I see much more here. Like *The Second Sex*, "Right-Wing Thought Today" is concerned with how myths and ideologies mobilize feelings to shape and reproduce conditions of inequality and oppression as they leave their mark on bodies, psyches, and desires. As we will see, Beauvoir disputes the idea that emotions spring solely from individual bodies via biological neuropathways or as personal feelings unique to the individual. Her reading of encounters between bodies in situation turns our attention instead to how the feelings we experience are linked to somatic, psychic, physical, and structural conditions. We experience individual emotions as individual and we can sometimes notice them on our individual bodies (blushing, for example, can be both a feeling and a bodily reaction). But feelings that might seem singular or idiosyncratic link us together and situate us in relationship to each other in classes, races, genders, castes, and other hierarchies within political bodies. Emotions flow through us collectively as well as individually. They support but also might potentially undermine systems, structures, and ideologies. In "Right-Wing Thought Today," as I will show, Beauvoir helps us see how affects are mobilized within pernicious political projects; in this case they assist the bourgeoisie in their bid to convince us that it is not only undesirable but likely impossible to challenge the dominance of capitalism. Beauvoir hopes that by staging new encounters between thinkers in her text and between her readers and her texts, she can differently mobilize affects to nurture our desire for freedom and help us find allies and friends to collectively enact this possibility.

"Right-Wing Thought Today" was published in *Les Temps Modernes* in 1955, just a few short years following the appearance of *The Second Sex* in 1949. I switch their historical order to situate my reading of "Right-Wing Thought Today" before my reading of *The Second Sex* so that we are better able to appreciate some of Beauvoir's literary strategies in *The Second Sex* as explicitly political strategies by identifying and naming them first in "Right-Wing Thought Today." *The Second Sex* is, in too many ways, a book we think we already know. Part of that misguided sense of already knowing this book is our inability to recognize it as helping us think politically by engaging with gender questions that are themselves inextricably connected to the ways we think politically. As I claimed in the introduction, Beauvoir is always already "our Beauvoir," a Beauvoir we have identified as taking up a particular place in our narrative of feminism, whatever that narrative may be: how feminism has moved from being centered on white women to (reluctantly) including women of color, how feminist daughters have "abandoned" or "forgotten" feminist mothers, how feminism is narrow and stifling, how gender questions are a subset of political questions rather than themselves shaping the ways we think politically. I want to unsettle these contradictory, but seemingly settled invocations of what *The Second Sex* means for feminism and means for politics. Part of that effort is to show how Beauvoir is a far more complex and nuanced thinker about political processes than we have previously recognized her as being. She begins to think this way when she discovers that the way we create and reproduce the political meanings of sexual difference is a result of particular configurations of feelings in response to complex ontological processes wrongly said to legitimate structures and systems of inequality and oppression.

RIGHT-WING ENEMIES

In *The Mandarins*, Beauvoir ([1954] 1999) fictionalizes the dilemmas of the French Left following World War II and the end of Occupation. This was rich material for a fictional account: not only were there several affairs and political and personal breaks with allies and friends, but there were also real enemies to confront in spite of the fact that the Nazis had been defeated. The cold war was beginning, the Algerian War was heating up, reports of the Soviet Union's gulags and forced loyalty to the Communist Party structure were emerging, and the French were defeated in Vietnam in 1954. Beauvoir and Sartre were fellow travelers with the Communist Party, but even before the Hungarian invasion in 1956, they were seeking an alternative to Soviet-style communism. They and their cohort were trying to find a third option, a political path toward democratic socialism. "Right-Wing Thought Today" was part of this effort, appearing in a special issue of *Les Temps Modernes* devoted to the question "Do the notions of 'Left' and 'Right' still have meaning?"

Beauvoir's essay responds with a diagnosis and evaluation of what unifies and typifies "right-wing thinkers."

My reading of "Right-Wing Thought Today" brings our attention to the way Beauvoir stages encounters with and between her enemies to reveal and also to mobilize configurations of feeling.[4] Her wager is that these conversations might awaken readers to the ideological commitments and material interests that belie any claim to the linguistic, aesthetic, or literary autonomy of writers and motivate us to answer her appeal to political engagement. Beauvoir's immediate goal is to articulate what makes "right-wing thought" cohesive and on the Right. Including a wide range of right-wing thinkers in her essay, Beauvoir gives them space to voice their beliefs, and just as she does in *The Second Sex*, she insists that they speak to each other. In these ways, she is able to make comparisons between kinds and degrees of right-wing ideologies. She even includes some proponents of liberal thought in the category "right-wing" because they buttress the power and self-interest of the bourgeois classes and deny that communism could be a politically and ethically viable alternative. To undermine the claim that right-wing ideas have a legitimacy based in anything beyond self-interest, she shows that their ideas are motivated by fear, worry, and anger and that these emotions emerge from concrete historical material conditions. The Right may not hold power forever and so they should be fearful, she tells us; they should be anxious and may feel angry about challenges to their dominance. Beauvoir diagnoses these feelings and their emergence from material conditions, but she does not justify them. Listening to right-wing thinkers talk to each other, readers suddenly see that right-wing ideologies are chimeras. Their ideas are not universal, their "taste" does not equal elegance. And yet these ideas undergird and create right-wing realities (in this case, capitalism, but also fascism) that have devastating material effects for the majority. Readers may come to see that marketing self-interest as universalism, colonial dominance as the spreading of civilization, and racial superiority as equality are strategies that will not last forever if we can join with allies and friends in opposition.

Beauvoir names several targets in her essay but her main interlocutors are Thierry Maulnier, a fascist journalist; Jules Mormerot, a sociologist and de Gaulle supporter; Pierre Drieu La Rochelle, a Nazi collaborator; Henry de Montherlant, a militarist writer, whom she also attacks for his misogyny in *The Second Sex*; and Raymond Aron, a liberal sociologist. This is a diverse group, to which she quite controversially adds the phenomenologists Karl Jaspers and Maurice Merleau-Ponty. Merleau-Ponty was a friend of Beauvoir's from her youth, and there are several significant resonances between his work and hers, particularly their interest in theorizing the significance of the lived experience of bodies. So it is surprising for her to criticize him, but the explanation may be that he had just published a searing critique of Sartre's pro-communist politics. With Jaspers and Merleau-Ponty included, Beauvoir's essay was a sweeping condemnation of not only right-wing but also liberal thought.

This was intentional on Beauvoir's part. Lumping right-wing and liberal thinkers together brings different, or as she calls them, "pluralist" positions into the same space to show affective and strategic affinities among them. She does this in volume 1 of *The Second Sex* too. Here she lumps all sorts of diverse masculinist thinkers together to show that they often think alike when they are discussing the myth of Woman. Moreover, the myth of Woman is itself rooted in several, often contradictory sources and rumors that are surprisingly plural and wildly contradictory but that all work in their different ways to buttress patriarchy: women are virgins and whores, frigid and too sexual, ideally suited to housework and raising families and yet bad housekeepers and mothers. Fixing multiple and polymorphous women as Woman by denying the variety of their material and somatic experiences is, she says, an attempt to trap women in an all too elastic and yet mythic ideal of femininity. Perpetuating the contradictory and freedom-denying myth of Woman denies what Beauvoir calls the "data" of biology, wherein sexual difference is fluid and contingent. Likewise writing history, psychoanalysis, and theology in ideological and systematic fashion in regard to the question of women ignores and disavows women's bodily experiences, their structural and political material realities, and the emotions, struggles, and actions of their everyday lives.

Just as *The Second Sex* shows that when talking about women men are motivated by their emotions (mostly fear and anxiety), in "Right-Wing Thought Today" Beauvoir says that fear, panic, and worry motivates and situates the thought of right-wing intellectuals: "We know that today's bourgeois is frightened" ([1955] 2012, 113). Because they are frightened (they had erroneously "believed in the harmonious development of capitalism, continual progress, and in [their and capitalism's] own eternity," 114), they engage in forms of "counter-thought" to discount communism as a viable alternative. Having no real core in a positive vision, some right-wing thinkers advance their claims as realist, others as idealist, and still others argue for a form of quietism by, for example, making fatalist claims about the cosmos, fate, and the coming apocalypse. All these positions serve to discourage political engagement by making it seem as if change is not possible or that attempts to challenge privilege are futile or meaningless.

Throughout this essay Beauvoir connects political assemblages of affects as well as individual emotions to material and social reality, always reading bodies in encounter. She worries that the sources of affects are too often wrongly diagnosed as psychological or physiological, a move that reduces the complex production and the political effects of emotions to the quirks of subjectivity or organic forces ([1955] 2012, 130–31). Beauvoir not only says the right wing's precarious grasp on the future motivates *their* fear, she also links the frustrations and emotions of the disenfranchised with their material reality too. She confirms what right-wing thinkers say about the Left: that left-wing intellectuals (and workers too) are driven by "ethical or affective" motivations, for instance, frustration that manifests as a "revolutionary attitude" (123) or as resentment. But rather than see this as a problem, she says frustration, anxiety, and the sense of injustice arises within the lived conditions of people's material lives. These are not individual pathologies. Workers have every right to be frustrated by their material conditions and the stubborn rigidity of their repetitive daily lives, Beauvoir insists. She furthermore claims that right-wing thinkers should indeed be fearful: capitalism is not the only way to organize an economy, and it does not have to, and may not, continue forever.

Material links to feelings, and the mobilization of these feelings, however, do not just move in one direction. Feelings move within and through bodies, arising from bodies in encounter and in turn reshaping those bodies and situations in less than predictable ways. Beauvoir brings the words of right-wing ideologues to the attention of her readers to help us see that their promises and predictions nurture quietism or encourage reactionary action but always with the intention to buttress capitalist self-interest and maintain and deepen inequality. The right wing proclaims the empty promise of individual freedom, the "mission" of the elite, the "ethics" of heroes, and the "beauty" of the aesthetic. "The existence of privilege becomes sacred, its possession a right, and its exercise a duty. The privileged are called the Elite, their privileges are called superiorities, and together they are called Civilization" ([1955] 2012, 134). She uses an example from the U.S. context to make this point: "In America this is the way that Big Business operates cynically. It uses Public Relations to spread among the exploited masses the slogans profitable to the exploiters. It has perfected the art of Human Engineering that is devoted to concealing the material reality of the workers' conditions through moral and affective mystification" (126).

As Beauvoir also shows, once politically launched, certain configurations of feeling take on a life of their own. Much like Marx's commodities, they appear to become untethered from material conditions and move in often unexpected ways. Seeking to understand the contemporary landscape of U.S. politics wherein the most destitute populations are willing supporters of the politicians and ideologues who created, and whose policies reproduce, the harmful conditions of their lives, Arlie Russell Hochschild echoes Beauvoir's lament that we have failed to acknowledge not only how emotions work in politics, but specifically how emotions that arise in diminished material circumstances can be manipulated and moved in multiple ways. Reviewing Hochschild's book, *Strangers in Their Own Land: Anger and Mourning on the American Right*, Nathanial Rich says this:

> The deep story that Hochschild creates for the Tea Party is a parable of the white American Dream. It begins with an image of a long line of people marching across a vast landscape. The Tea Partiers—white, older, Christian, predominantly male, many lacking college degrees—are somewhere in the middle of the line. They trudge wearily, but with resolve, up a hill. Ahead, beyond the ridge, lies wealth, success, dignity. Far behind them the line is composed of people of color, women, immigrants, refugees. As pensions are reduced and layoffs absorbed, the line slows, then stalls.
>
> An even greater indignity follows: people begin cutting them in line. Many are those who had long stood behind them—blacks, women, immigrants, even Syrian refugees, all now aided by the federal government. Next an even more astonishing figure jumps ahead of them: a brown pelican, the Louisiana state bird, "fluttering its long, oil-drenched wings." Thanks to environmental protections, it is granted higher social status than, say, an oil rig worker. (Rich 2016)

The deep story offered here about who gets to cut in line is one that is able to take the feelings that arise from economic and political despair (frustration, anger, anxiety, precarity), and mobilize them in politically pernicious ways. This may be how people who materially have so little, who are "inside the sacrifice zone," as Rich puts it, are drawn into ideological alliance with those right-wing thinkers who will continue to shrink the social net. Not only that: they identify as enemies those who should be allies—blacks, women, immigrants, Syrian refugees, and even brown pelicans. We will see Beauvoir pursuing these questions when she seeks to understand why and how women are drawn to the emotions and behaviors that continue to reproduce patriarchy. Taking seriously the "female complaint," Beauvoir hopes to mobilize it in another direction, away from the re-inscription of femininity and the shoring up of male power. As we will see in chapter 5, Beauvoir always seeks to create space for new solidarities across and within gender, race, and class divisions by describing the objective conditions that make solidarity possible.

Put in staged conversation with each other in "Right-Wing Thought Today" we see many different right-wing thinkers, themselves motivated by anxiety, fear, and anger, creating and promoting ideologies that draw on similar configurations of feelings to buttress their self-interest and reproduce their material dominance. Writing this text Beauvoir seeks not only to diagnose the problem but also to mobilize desire for something else. Her wager is that by reading and witnessing, readers might see things anew. But her strategy may fail, and there are no promises. The only certainty is uncertainty. This fact alone undoes the conceits of right-wing ideologies. History is not decided by "unconscious instincts or dark forces" ([1955] 2012, 147); nor is it determined by absurd, dialectical, mysterious "cosmic fluctuations" (140), the "demands of the Transcendent" (143), or the "caprice and mystery" of nature (148). History is not fated to be won by any preferred class. As Beauvoir insists, the "true history of humanity" is "impossible to foresee" (161).

ENEMIES OF WOMEN

My reading of *The Second Sex* reveals similar textual strategies mobilized toward related goals. Put into conversation with each other, male authorities display their affective preoccupations—fear, disgust, repulsion, hostility, and anxiety—themselves a response to ontological material conditions: their encounter with sexual difference, fear of finitude, lack of control, and unknowingness. These emotions undergird and perpetuate patriarchal ideologies and structures. We might say that patriarchy works as a complex assemblage of affects keeping us emotionally, psychically, materially, and bodily captive to the falsely created hierarchy of sexual difference.

One of my main claims is that *The Second Sex* is written as a series of sometimes dramatic and sometimes mundane encounters to illuminate a complex field of affects that could be configured differently to encourage and create new material conditions. *The Second Sex* has also been caught in its own dramatic encounter with its readers and critics. Responses to it are fraught with ambivalence or excessive emotion, maybe partly because its form itself invites and solicits strong reader response. Note how Beauvoir ([1963] 1992, 197) describes early reception of the book in her 1963 autobiography, *Force of Circumstance*: "Unsatisfied, frigid, priapic, nymphomaniac, lesbian, a hundred times aborted, I was everything, even an unmarried mother. People offered to cure me of my frigidity or to temper my labial appetites; I was promised revelations, in the coarsest terms but in the name of the true, the good and the beautiful, in the name of health and even of poetry, all unworthily trampled underfoot by me." She continues for several pages documenting violent and aggressive reactions to her book.

In an opposing stance, also emotional and deeply ambivalent, Beauvoir was cast as the mother of feminism, a label she disavowed in a 1974 interview, remarking that "mother-daughter relations are generally catastrophic" (Schwarzer 1984, 94) and "people don't tend to listen to what their mothers are telling them" (Patterson 1986, 92). Her text has also been called "the feminist bible," even though Beauvoir herself was an atheist (Thurman 2010, xii). Several decades later *The Second Sex* still solicits powerful reactions. Reviewing the 2010 translation in the *New York Times*, Francine du Plessix Gray writes, "Beauvoir's truly paranoid hostility toward the institutions of marriage and motherhood—another characteristic of early feminism—is so extreme as to be occasionally hilarious." She goes on to say that "pessimism runs through the text like a poisonous river" but reassures us that Beauvoir did not hate men.[5]

Even if Beauvoir did not hate men, the book is centered on women. Unlike Wollstonecraft's *Vindication of the Rights of Woman*, *The Second Sex* is rarely considered a canonical text worthy of being read and studied within the history of political thought. Even specifically within feminist scholarship, though *The Second Sex* is religiously cited (as the feminist bible) and acknowledged, only a few excerpts, mostly the introduction, are regularly read. Some criticisms of the text render it politically noxious. It is said that the claims of *The Second Sex* are limited to midcentury French women or that despite a half-hearted nod to inclusivity and diversity, Beauvoir's text reproduces a white intellectual perspective (Markowitz 2009; Spelman 1988). We are also told that were we sensitive to Beauvoir's own criticisms of claims to universality proffered by traditional philosophy, we would regard *The Second Sex* as historically situated and limited by a particular perspective produced in a unique moment.

Overall, appreciating the political and philosophical significance of *The Second Sex* has been marred by intense emotional rejection or veneration, by excessive historicizing, and by the translation debates that ensued when the text was translated into English by H. M. Parshley in the 1951 edition and by Constance Borde and Sheila Malovany-Chevallier in the 2010 edition.[6] Given these caveats and criticisms, why and, more important, how should we read *The Second Sex* as political theory? In her witty first lines Beauvoir introduces her topic of conversation, "a book on woman," in a seemingly dismissive way.

She says that the "subject is irritating, especially for women; and it is not new"; indeed "enough ink has flowed over the quarrel about feminism; it is now almost over: let's not talk about it anymore. Yet it is still being talked about" ([1949] 2011, 3). There is no doubt that we have stumbled upon a creative (often baffling, sometimes enigmatic) textual beast, one that has inspired but also has confused and angered many. Introducing woman as a subject that is suitable, although irritating, to talk about, the text unfolds as two sequential parts of an extended conversation, or we might think of it as like attending two dinner parties, with different guests talking about the same topic on sequential evenings. Volume 1 features male authority figures—scientists, historians, psychoanalysts, philosophers, playwrights, theologians, and novelists—declaiming on the roots, legitimacy, and meanings of sexual difference. As diverse women are introduced in volume 2, the conversation gets even more heated. The women argue much *more* than the men! They have profoundly different experiences on everything from sex and pleasure and joy to motherhood, love, work, and fulfillment. With these women, we see the world from many new perspectives. We meet famous and minor characters from fiction, authors of autobiographies, Beauvoir's friends and acquaintances, actresses, prostitutes, wives, mothers, girlfriends, girls and friends, and we hear lots of stories. These are the lived experiences (bodily, emotional, material, structural) of becoming women.

One of the literary techniques Beauvoir employs throughout volume 1 of *The Second Sex* that mimics her strategy in "Right-Wing Thought Today" is to give male authority figures space to speak for themselves and in conversation with other authority figures, while at the same time allowing them to undermine, sometimes explicitly and sometimes in more subtle ways, their assumed right to shape, determine, and dominate conversation. Beauvoir admits early on that she "used to get annoyed in abstract discussions to hear men tell [her]: 'You think such and such because you're a woman'" ([1949] 2011, 5). In response to this conversation stopper, Beauvoir says a woman is forced to answer, "I think it because it is true" rather than "You think the contrary because you are a man." "It is understood a man is in his right by virtue of being a man; it is the woman who is in the wrong" (5). Today in most instances a woman can hold her own, if not carry the day, by responding, "You think the contrary because you are a man." Yet this assertion of equal particularity, or equally shared and competing claims to authority via subjectivity, does not ultimately serve to undermine masculine authority and norms of bourgeois ideology. Just as in "Right-Wing Thought Today," Beauvoir is doing something far more radical and potentially transformative than simply adding more voices to the mix when she stages conversations in *The Second Sex*.

Another textual technique at play is Beauvoir's mimicking of male voices.[7] She warns us about her strategy: "It is noteworthy that physiologists and biologists all use a more or less finalistic language merely because they ascribe meaning [in this case, gendered hierarchical meaning] to vital phenomena; *we will use their language*" ([1949] 2011, 26, emphasis added). Sometimes readers fail to discern who or what position Beauvoir is endorsing, in spite of the fact that she steps in at key moments, aggressively inserting herself into the conversation to make a pointed and often damning observation. Commenting on the conclusion that the ovum is likened to immanence and the sperm to transcendence, for example, Beauvoir says, "In truth, these are merely ramblings" (28).[8] As readers, though, we have to be attentive or we might lose track of who is speaking when, as in several instances Beauvoir cedes the floor to a misogynistic male scientist or historian who chimes in to conjure images of "devouring femininity" and "woman's dream of castration" (33).

Always noting the assemblages of affects that captivate male authorities and cloud their ability to see complex factual realities, Beauvoir notes repeatedly in the chapters on "facts" that male emotion clouds judgment. Anxiety, fear, and disgust are common male responses to biological realities and historical contingencies. The chapter "Biological Data" begins by noting that the term *woman*, when uttered by "those who like simple answers," such as "womb," "ovary," or simply "female," is hurled as an insult; "female" is "pejorative not because it roots woman in nature" but due to the "disquieting hostility" "woman triggers in man" ([1949] 2011, 21). "He" (speaker of ideology made material, and hence made truth, by scientific male authority) abandons scientific method to "find a justification in biology for this *feeling*" (21, emphasis added). In chapter 3 we will meet another HE in von Trier's *Antichrist*. Von Trier's HE is trained in cognitive-behavioral therapy, which he uses on his wife (SHE) to try to cure her of her (to his mind, excessive and misguided) feelings. (Spoiler alert: this turns out badly, and as Beauvoir would anticipate.) Not surprisingly the conversation that Beauvoir constructs among male scientists shows that "scientific" findings on biological reproduction, the demands of the species, and the significance of sexual difference are all motivated by the search to find justification for a "feeling," in this case hostility (in von Trier's example, a toxic mix of fear and arrogance).

Male myths about women are likewise a response to unsettling and uncomfortable facts of existence that trigger male anxieties. Myths rescue men from the existential dilemma of longing for both "life and rest, existence and being"; they cast woman as an "embodied dream," "the perfect intermediary between nature that is too foreign to man and the peer who is too identical to him"; "she pits neither the hostile silence of nature nor the hard demand of a reciprocal recognition against him; by unique privilege she is a consciousness, yet it seems possible to possess her in the flesh" ([1949] 2011, 160). Male myths, many and variable, depict woman as "privileged prey" as well as "Mother," "Spouse," "Idea" (161–63); they coexist in "opposition, and each has a double face" (160). Like science, myths are not the products of rational thought; instead they spring from men's "hearts," inspired by disgust, horror, embarrassment, fear, loathing, and repulsion (164–65, all Beauvoir's terms). Myths arise in response to the grotesque truth of women's flesh: the "chaotic obscurity" of women's genitals; the "quivering gelatin that forms in the womb"; the "living magma" of the "pregnant woman's stomach"; the "swollen breasts of the wet nurse"; the "regions of immanence" he "wants to escape"; the "roots he wants to pull himself away from" (163–65). Even the incest taboo, typically explained in structural anthropological terms as enforcing exogamy (Claude Lévi-Strauss) and initiating the exchange of women (Gayle Rubin), is explained by Beauvoir as arising from the *fear* of finding the mother's dreaded "essence in the woman" (170) in her role as sexual partner or wife.

What we learn in volume 2, when Beauvoir includes women in the conversation to talk about their own bodies and experiences, is no surprise: women are drawn into the web of these affective states by the demand to "*be* women, *stay* women, *become* women" ([1949] 2011, 3, emphasis added). There are good feelings generated by the comfort one receives from belonging to the community of women who embrace and manage femininity, and bad or uncomfortable feelings experienced by belonging inexpertly or not at all. And yet, via the formal and affective literary techniques Beauvoir utilizes to create new conversations (the staging and the appeal), new ways of seeing and feeling patriarchal structures and their emotional hold on us are allowed and encouraged. These methods, she contends, will help us see our shared world anew and solicit our investment in changing it.

CREATING ALLIES, REMAKING FEMININITY

Witnessing the conversations that Beauvoir sets into motion among male authorities in volume 1 of *The Second Sex* and "Right-Wing Thought Today" discloses not only the way ideologies and affects are tied to material interests but also how feelings motivate oppression and work with and through oppressive structures and ideologies to hold us captive and limit our agency. Reading volume 2 of *The Second Sex* as tracking what Lauren Berlant has called "bargaining with power and desire in which members of intimate publics always seem to be engaging," I show that Beauvoir is exceedingly attentive to and tracks in detail the attractive feelings that femininity motivates, and the ways these feelings bond us with each other and with repressive power.[9] Just as in "Right-Wing Thought Today," in volume 2 of *The Second Sex* Beauvoir tracks how affects circulate via complex mechanisms of social, political, material, and somatic relationships to make it seem as if the individual is the source of feeling when in fact the individual psyche is in large part the product of these circulations. Having recognized this, Beauvoir takes a huge risk in the second volume by drawing on the feelings and fantasies patriarchy solicits in order to mobilize women to desire freedom instead.

Put as an explicitly political question, Beauvoir asks: Does femininity ever become a site of resistance whereby affects produced and nurtured via oppression can lead elsewhere? While she is expressly attentive to both the attractive allure of femininity and the pathological characteristics its demands engender,[10] her appeal to her readers via the conversational form invites us to embrace the risks of freedom and collective action that a dissociation with identity and its affects makes possible. It is here we see Beauvoir as a precursor to today's feminist affect theorists (such as Berlant, Ahmed, and Ngai) and as doing something far more political. She links affects to material realities and to collective conditions, and, using conversation as a political technique, she appeals to her readers to form collectivities to feel differently and to transform oppressive material and structural conditions.

Volume 2 begins with a famous phrase: "One is not born, but rather becomes a woman."[11] Many scholars have interpreted Beauvoir as introducing a sex/gender distinction to claim that sex is natural and gender is cultural.[12] But as we saw earlier, she says instead that while biology is indeed a concrete reality (we have a body, we reproduce, we die; we are slaves to the species; we are configurations of cells, blood, tissues, bones, and muscle), the meanings ascribed to sexual difference, as one of these realities, are politically motivated and stem from an actively emotive fear of bodies, biology, and the complexity and vitality of life processes.[13] Rather than claim anything essential about gender, sex, and the relationship between the two, Beauvoir seeks to question and undo any and all assumptions about women by posing the topic for conversation in the form of the question "What is a woman?" ([1949] 2011, 5).

Circumventing what has been called the "category of women" debates or the "subject question" in feminist discourse, Beauvoir acts as if women exist, since for all practical purposes they do, in order to question the way the idea of Woman and the meanings of femininity take hold—structurally, ideologically, and emotionally—in women's lives.[14] Dismantling all claims about the "eternal feminine" while at the same time rejecting nominalism ("women *are* not men" [(1949) 2011, 4]), Beauvoir says that nevertheless we can and should in fact speak in everyday language about and to women even though, or maybe precisely because, we do not know the answer to the question of what it *is* or what it *means* to be a woman. Indeed we must speak with and to those identified *as* women, and even speak emotively *as if* the category were meaningful, in order to begin to dismantle the many mechanisms that undergird the hierarchy of sexual difference.

Thus recognizing the draws and dangers of affectively lived identity and community, Beauvoir willingly calls to women as female-identified selves, with their habits and experiences drawn and lived through femininity, but the conversation unfolds to question the very ground on which such experience is located. In so doing she creates a conversation among female strangers that feels intimate and revelatory in order to challenge the emotional basis (our ties to femininity) of this same intimacy and shared feeling.

Rather than track the way affective bonds and women's emotional life are presented in *The Second Sex*, scholarship on the text has tended to focus on Beauvoir's theorization of situation to explain her unique contribution to understanding women's oppression under patriarchy. This is an important contribution; my own previously published work on Beauvoir has been mostly in this vein. Indeed Beauvoir argues that all humans are situated, located as we are within constraints of biology, history, social and political conditions, ideology, the existence of others, and webs of discourse. She recognizes these constraints and furthermore argues that some of them—the ontological aspects of conditions within biology, for example, such as time and death—should be embraced. Moreover to avow and embrace ambiguity is to accept that we are each simultaneously self and other, transcendence and immanence. Throughout her oeuvre, especially in *The Ethics of Ambiguity*, Beauvoir seeks to understand how some subjects (race, class, gender, and power are interlinked here) have been able to exploit the denial of ambiguity, systematically and structurally, by assuming the role of transcendence for themselves and confining others to immanence.

Other readers of *The Second Sex* focus, in contrast, not on structure and situation but on individual agency. These readings too can be supported by the text, as individual agency and free choice are an important emphasis for Beauvoir and an important goal to achieve. Choosing freedom, however, has slightly different connotations for Beauvoir: this is a path that entails risk and responsibility, a path that is made possible only by the ability and willingness to move beyond socially mandated roles and demands to risk freedom in encounter. As central as individual agency is in the pages of *The Second Sex*, we should not miss that freedom can be experienced only in encounter. We can better see this key dimension of Beauvoir's thought when we read the text as a series of encounters.

Thus my focus here—on Beauvoir's conversational form, literary technique, and the affects and intensities of emotion that she draws out—redirects attention from structure, on the one hand, and individual agency, on the other, to think instead about how socially and politically produced mechanisms such as desire and fantasy work with and through structures but cannot be reduced to them. Moreover, although Beauvoir acknowledges and avows psychoanalytic perspectives to understand individual pathologies and symptoms, she consistently moves away from the focus on individual psyche to think instead about individuals as produced by and through complex networks of power. As one key example, she says women often desire to simply accept their oppression. She recognizes that it is not so easy to claim your freedom in the encounter. Just thinking of it triggers the (psychological, emotional, material) burdens that always accompany making a choice and especially accompany agonistic interaction. "The temptation to flee freedom" and make yourself "into a thing" ([1949] 2011, 10) always lurks. This is what Beauvoir calls "an easy path," where "the anguish and stress of authentically assumed existence is avoided" (10). Along with avoiding existential anguish, women also have a vested material interest in assuming their inferior position: "Refusing to be the Other, refusing all complicity with man, would mean renouncing all the advantages an alliance with the superior caste confers on them" (10). She concludes this part by noting, "The man who sets the woman up as an *Other* will thus find in her a deep complicity. Hence woman makes no claim for herself as subject because she lacks the concrete means, because she senses the necessary link connecting her to man without positing its reciprocity, and because she often derives satisfaction from her role as *Other*" (10). The claim that women get emotional sustenance from their role as other has been mostly neglected in Beauvoir scholarship. But to explain women's unfreedom and their relative lack of collective protest, Beauvoir returns to the emotional and affective register again and again in volume 2. She points to why and how bad faith can be such an attractive option, why and how the bonds that hold us captive look, and even sometimes can feel, so good.

Part of the attraction of belonging to an "intimate public," in this case an affectively felt "women's culture" built around norms of femininity, is that "aloneness is one of the affective experiences of being collectively, structurally unprivileged" (Berlant 2008, viii). When you are part of a woman's culture, when you conform to the demands of femininity, you can feel good. Not only do you get positive reinforcement from patriarchal structures and from the individual men to whom you are attached; you also get the feeling of belonging to a culture that points beyond the self. "Women's culture" enacts a "fantasy that my life is not just mine, but an experience understood by other women, even when it is not shared by many or any" (x).

Women repeatedly consume the message that good feelings arise from belonging to "the second sex" as men have shaped it, and indeed women are often able to take pleasure in relinquishing agency, as Beauvoir shows us in the chapters titled "The Narcissist," "The Woman in Love," and "The Mystic." At the same time, however, she shows us that feelings of anxiety, melancholy, envy, and the ongoing feeling that one does not belong are possible and acceptable. But here is a key point for Beauvoir: they also are fodder for networks of political affects. One thing, of several, Beauvoir accomplishes in the conversation she creates in volume 2 of *The Second Sex* is to show that the "good" feelings women are supposed to get through their identity as wife, mother, girlfriend, and sexual partner are, after all, often not the feelings that women actually end up having. Both positive and negative feelings are thus exposed, and explored, by drawing us into conversation through our identity as women, as beings who are *supposed to* feel good by fulfilling patriarchal roles.

Beauvoir's ([1949] 2011, 439) chapter "The Married Woman," as just one example, asks whether being a wife, the "destiny that society traditionally offers women," is all it promises. Even the single woman is defined by marriage, though she might be "frustrated by, disgusted at, or even indifferent to this institution" (439). Many women end up feeling melancholic as a result of being "locked into the conjugal community" (470). We can read this, however, not just as a case of individual unhappiness but as the mark of a collective condition.

Beauvoir attends to the situation of the melancholic woman by diagnosing the condition as a *response to situation*, expressed on the body and its comportment as one of many possible kinds of responses. Take the following passage, where Beauvoir ([1949] 2011, 488) quotes from a diary, one example of many where she discusses the experiences of wives: "I am terribly, terribly sad, and withdrawing further and further into myself. My husband is ill and out of sorts and doesn't love me. I expected this, yet I could never have imagined it would be so terrible. Why do people always think I am so happy? What no one seems to realize is that I cannot create happiness, either for him or for myself." Beauvoir reads this young woman's unhappiness as a social condition: "This distress is what often causes long depressions and various psychoses in the young woman. . . . In particular, in the guise of different psychoasthenic obsessions, she feels the giddiness of her empty freedom" (491). In a similar vein Sara Ahmed (2004, 131) suggests that unhappiness gets attached to particular individuals, or "sticks to some bodies," as a psychic condition but is generated by past histories of political, material, and social significance. As Ahmed shows in *The Promise of Happiness* (2010), emotions coalesce in social and material form to falsely appear to individuals as specific orientations that are the result of conscious choice. It seems that as individuals, we are oriented on the right path or the wrong path, that our "unhappiness" or "melancholy" is the result of the wrong choice or a wrong relationship to our world. Like Beauvoir, Ahmed helps us to see affects and emotions such as unhappiness, melancholy, worry, anxiety, grief, obsessions, and so on as produced within a social system, in this case under patriarchy. We see the circulation of affects between and across bodies and histories as registering a potential critique. Beauvoir brings this critique to the forefront of the analysis.

For example, Beauvoir ([1949] 2011, 646) names "the female complaint": "Together, women friends groan individually about their own ills and all together about the injustice of their lot, the world, and men in general." What Berlant (2008, 1) identifies as "the bitter vigilance of the intimately disappointed," Beauvoir ([1949] 2011, 646) calls an expression of "impotent anger." Beauvoir cites and interprets the diary of Sophia Tolstoy:

> January 11, 1863: My jealousy is a congenital illness, or it may be because in loving him I haven nothing else to love; I have given myself so completely to him that my only happiness is with him and from him.

> January 15, 1863: I have been feeling [out of sorts and] angry that he should love everything and everyone, when I want him to love only me. ([1949] 2011, 496)

Although these behaviors and symptoms cannot be categorized as collective agency or anything approaching a conscious rebellion, Beauvoir ([1949] 2011, 649) says that we can interpret them, as well as symptoms and forms of melancholy, "as protest." Denied the possibility of acting and living in conditions of freedom—wherein all are acknowledged as both subject and object, transcendence and immanence—and reduced solely to immanence, women unconsciously register resistance in affects, behaviors, and symptoms that we can certainly read as critique and potentially mobilize to create more freedom-affirming alternatives. Because women live "life's becoming" they are "suspicious of the principle of identity" and the "notion of causality." Due to their situation, and how this situation expresses itself on bodies, women are poised to grasp something men cannot: "the ambiguity of all principles, of all values, of all that exists" (651). Beauvoir names ambiguity, lived both structurally (within situation) and somatically (on or in the body), as *itself* as a protest against patriarchy's taxonomies and structural dualities.[15] In subsequent chapters I further explore the relationships among ambiguity, violence, pathologies, resistance, and the need for collective action to enhance freedom within encounters.

HOW TO FIND FRIENDS

By staging a conversation between "Right-Wing Thought Today" and *The Second Sex* I have tried to make room for *The Second Sex* within the conversation of political theory. But I want much more: to convert the conditions, topics, and rules of conversation, and in doing so, find friends with whom we can together change the world. In the chapters that follow I demonstrate that formally and substantively, and particularly when read in encounter with other texts and thinkers in and out of context, *The Second Sex* helps us see the conditions of unfreedom, and how to move with others to create conditions for collective freedom.

Why haven't we recognized this potential in *The Second Sex* previously? Our inability to see *The Second Sex*'s significant contribution to political thinking stems in part from the ways feminists have claimed "our" Beauvoir, but also in part from its trivialization, historicization, and because it is indelibly marked by sexual difference. Must we de-sex *The Second Sex* to take it seriously? Beauvoir draws attention to the way male-dominated conversation forces women to remove their subjective selves from the argument when trying to enter a conversation. Linda Zerilli (1991, 268) suggests that Beauvoir's "defense," "I think thus and so because it's true," to the man's claim, "You think thus and so because you are a woman" "articulates the paradoxical relationship in which feminists stand to discourse: being and not being a 'woman.'" As Zerilli parses Beauvoir, "if the woman who would speak is effectively silenced by being shut up in her femininity, the defensive claim to 'truth' merely repeats the effacement of self by affirming the masculine claim to the universal" (268).

Caught in this paradox, within the rules of (the same old, extremely tiring) conversation, *The Second Sex* has to be de-sexed in order to be included.

But *The Second Sex* can never, and should never, be de-sexed. If we recognize its focus on encounters wherein the acknowledgment of the political meanings of sexual difference is at its center, our (re)encounter with *The Second Sex* transforms not only the way we enter into conversations, but also whether we are recognized as able to do so, as able to be heard, as speaking a language that is discernible. It also transforms the way we think and do political theory. As we have seen so far, and as I will explore in even more depth in the coming pages, this text does not traffic in acceptable idioms or follow any of the unwritten rules for how to do political theory, either in terms of form or in terms of content. Its subject matter is sexual difference and its form is conversational. The topic, the talk about it, and the way it is talked about reveal the affects that motivate and undergird the structures of power and violence within conversations, at the same time appealing to us, its readers (potential friends), to change how we talk, what we talk about, the languages we use to describe things: in short, what we can see, say, and imagine.

The formal conditions of conversation, that "there must be men ready to hear me close by, and that these men must be my peers," was both met and not met when Beauvoir ([1944] 2004, 137) wrote her famous text. There were men close by, but they were clearly not ready to hear Beauvoir's voice. As witnessed by reactions to the book when it was published, and the repeated need for reassurance that Beauvoir did not hate men (even in 2010 with the reception of the new translation), we can conclude that those who set the terms for conversation are still unwilling to hear her voice. Nevertheless, there were some who heard and responded. To put it another way, the text found friends (and over the years, it has found many). Beauvoir ([1963] 1992, 203) took heart when she was told the book "helped women" because "it expressed them, and they in turn gave it its truth."

What possibilities does *The Second Sex* create for finding friends and mobilizing new collectivities? If we read it as an appeal to realign our senses, recognize new languages and topics, and open up new spaces for politics, we can see the text as a political conversation that is perpetually new rather than being "now almost over" ([1949] 2011, 3). Beauvoir's focus on encounter utilizes literary strategies to solicit (female, worker, black, colonized, queer) complaints, acknowledge their material conditions, and open up spaces where we might forge new solidarities. These are agonistic encounters wherein affects are revealed and mobilized. Where do we go from here? There is never a guaranteed good outcome, nor a place of rest, nor an end to struggle. We are each and collectively responsible for talking to enemies, creating allies, and finding friends to create possibilities for bringing new meanings to what could be a happy ending.

As Beauvoir insists repeatedly in both *The Second Sex* and "Right-Wing Thought Today," to seek meaning through identification with god, history, the transcendent, myths, humanity, any universal or indeed any identity category (femininity, negritude, Jewishness) destroys the space between us and thus destroys politics. Politics with Beauvoir entails making an appeal to an "other," or to others. Politics done this way promises no guarantee of response, understanding, or closure. Theorized as an "endless becoming," each person's point of departure creates "requirements and appeals to which only the creation of new requirements will respond" ([1944] 2004, 110). This open, never-ending appeal and potential response of individual subjectivities, each themselves continually breaking the bonds of preset identities, happens within a context where "our judgment alone" (120) allows us to examine the conditions of our lives. Because "there exists no heaven where the reconciliation of human judgments is accomplished" (131) and because we are each singularly situated but necessary in our freedom as a "foundation" for the existence of others, it is only through encountering others in their freedom that we can create a new and potentially liberating future.

The conversations of *The Second Sex* and "Right-Wing Thought Today" demonstrate the roles formal literary practices play in producing and reproducing (and potentially changing) affective, social, and material situations. Key to Beauvoir's method and message is her choice of form: the conversation, its literary techniques, and the affective encounters it reveals and solicits. Like the ending of most conversations, *The Second Sex* reveals some features of our world and relationships but promises nothing. It portends no certain future. Beauvoir leaves it up to us to find our way: to talk back to those situated as enemies, to create allies, and to find friends via a politics that is located in encounters and is affective and agonistic. We begin by encountering more enemies.

PART I. ENEMIES
MONSTERS, MEN, AND MISOGYNIST ART

The textual encounters in "Right-Wing Thought Today" and *The Second Sex* show how affects are tied to material worlds and political interests; and they make an appeal to readers to woo their participation and risk their judgment. Hearing from workers and women (and women workers), readers might see how lived experiences belie myths about capitalism and Woman, themselves revealed to be ideologies motivated by uncomfortable feelings and made material by bourgeois and male power. Beauvoir's textual strategies demonstrate that encounters might create new coalitions to enhance freedom and imagine the world differently. In these texts Beauvoir named enemies, developed allies, and, in encounter with readers, sought to solicit new friendships. My book follows this pattern too.

Reading Beauvoir and Arendt on judgment reminds us that following the events of the Second World War, we faced new kinds of enemies, new kinds of criminals, and new crimes. These enemies, men who appeared to be ordinary but had acted like monsters, could not be adequately judged, nor justice served, by trying to fit what they had done, or what they had failed to do, under determinate rules. The crimes simply were like no others; the criminals too defied imagination. Robert Brasillach, for example, was an intellectual. He was the author in 1935 of an influential book on the history of cinema; he also wrote fiction, and he became a journalist. A committed fascist and anti-

Semite, he was the editor of *Je suis partout*, a fascist newspaper, from 1935 to 1943, using his wits, his pen, his elite education, and his standing as an intellectual to incite hatred and cause the loss of citizenship and the deportation of Jews in hiding. Adolf Eichmann, a character lacking Brasillach's advantages (he had no elite education or special talents), took a job in 1934 in the intelligence agency of what became the Gestapo. At first he was in charge of simply filing all "information concerning Freemasonry," which Arendt (1963a, 37) tells us was "lumped with Judaism, Catholicism, and Communism," but he later became the head of "forced emigration." In other words, he was in charge of efficiently sending millions to their deaths. Facing Brasillach and Eichmann in the courtroom, Beauvoir and Arendt make a case for reflective judgments and defend (each differently) collective freedom.

Arendt's argument that Eichmann's failure was his inability to think from the place of others is well known. She famously reported on Eichmann's 1961 trial in Jerusalem for the *New Yorker* magazine, controversially coining the phrase *the banality of evil* to capture Eichmann's baffling (to her) appearance as an ordinary man rather than a monster. Sixteen years earlier Beauvoir had faced her enemy Brasillach in the French court, where he was on trial for treason. While both women make careful arguments to criticize the ways the Israeli and French courts used these cases to buttress nation-building narratives, they still each argued for the execution of the criminals. Both launched passionate defenses of collective freedom—why and how Brasillach's and Eichmann's actions are enemies to plurality, as Arendt puts it, and our collective future, in Beauvoir's language. But Beauvoir's willingness to acknowledge how freedom is lost or gained in concrete encounters between bodies is, to my mind, a more persuasive way of capturing what is at stake in these crimes.

In chapter 3 we see bodies in encounter in a more intimate way. In Lars von Trier's 2009 film, *Antichrist*, we witness the (maybe too) vivid encounter between HE and SHE as they turn away from freedom and on each other in unexpected, and unexpectedly violent, ways. Inspired by Beauvoir's eagerness to capaciously engage the Marquis de Sade, our feminist encounter with von Trier is not predetermined or wedded to an ideological nexus that would keep us from being open to discovery and transformation. A key thing we will learn from Beauvoir and Arendt's conversation is something on which they fully agree: the importance of reflective rather than determinative judgment for politics. Judgment is not, for either of them, a rule-governed activity; instead it is a risk-taking venture that prizes the surprise and discomfort of encounter. We can *never already know* how to judge an enemy or object prior to an encounter. So it goes, also, for our encounter with aesthetic objects, and on this topic too Arendt and Beauvoir agree. Writing on Arendt's 1961 essay, "The Crisis in Culture," Patchen Markell (2014, 63) shows that Arendt's idiosyncratic encounter with Kant's *Critique of Judgment* preserves the power of reflective judgment against the "currencies of social status and markers of aesthetic and political righteousness." Although I know of no evidence to make this case, I like thinking of Arendt's "The Crisis in Culture" as inspired by "Must We Burn Sade?," published by Beauvoir in 1952, the essay that inspires chapter 3. Here we will see Beauvoir independently judging an aesthetic object (Sade's writings) widely thought to be certainly in "bad taste," if not outright misogynist and despicable. But Beauvoir, ever open to the encounter, sees other things here.

Schooled by Beauvoir's reading of Sade's literature, we can see that his enemy target was not necessarily women but rather the bourgeois taxonomies that themselves leave their violent marks on women's bodies. I argue that von Trier's film is not an enemy of women but names other enemies—abstract categories, liberal pieties, and clichés of marriage and motherhood. Is it possible that von Trier's target is compulsory and normative sexuality rather than bad mothers who conspire with the devil?

"AN EYE FOR AN EYE" WITH HANNAH ARENDT'S *EICHMANN IN JERUSALEM*

In the preface to *Men in Dark Times*, Hannah Arendt (1955, vii) explains that her collection of essays is primarily about "persons—how they lived their lives, how they moved in the world, and how they were affected by historical time." She concedes that these persons might object to being "gathered into a common room" since what they share is only "the age in which their life span fell" (vii). Some might argue that Arendt and Beauvoir might also object to encountering each other in a common room, but to heed their wishes would be to miss out on their conversation about violence, freedom, and judgment.[1]

In this chapter Arendt and Beauvoir encounter each other—we might say they are unrecognized allies—and they encounter enemies. As witnesses to the political crimes of the twentieth century, they couldn't avoid encounters with enemies, and in fact each was drawn to them. As I noted in the introduction, wanting to see a "conscious author of genuine evil," as Beauvoir ([1949] 2004, 248) put it, or to "expose" herself to an "evildoer" (Berkowitz 2016), in Arendt's case, each ends up in company they did not want to keep. But keep it they did, as they desperately wanted to understand how such catastrophic events had occurred. Who put them in motion? Who was to blame? How could we stop this from happening again? In their subsequent writings on the two trials, neither thinker returns the crimes or the enemies to familiar categories. Making reflective judgments about the particular wrongs committed, each of them rejects explanations that would see these crimes as part of larger forces of history or as able to be easily subsumed under universal, metaphysical, or moral laws.[2] They also reject our usual thinking about enemies: they are neither complete monsters, nor are they just like one of us choosing badly in tense or difficult, even catastrophic circumstances. And as we will see, both writers desired the death of these two enemies, arguing that execution was a justified form of punishment.

Although Beauvoir and Arendt share a commitment to political judgment and especially its role in affirming freedom, the disagreements that arise between them are especially instructive to consider. Probing their views on when and why individuals are culpable for relinquishing their ethical responsibility to make judgments, we can see how Beauvoir's and Arendt's articulations of how and when judgment fails are linked to their very different conceptions of the conditions necessary for experiencing freedom. Capturing a dimension of politics that Arendt regards as social, Beauvoir directs our attention to a political sphere structured by embodied oppression and inequality. What I parse as Beauvoir's thinking about "freedom in the encounter" helps us to see that encounters occur between actors making choices with and as *embodied* individuals. Beauvoir's work forces us to acknowledge that bodies have political meaning that can restrict or enable imagination, movement, and action. She also says that freedom is not possible unless and until we throw in our lot with society's most vulnerable members.

To get at these questions I focus on two trial reports, Arendt's account of the Eichmann trial in Jerusalem in 1961, first published in the *New Yorker*, and Beauvoir's reflections on the trial of Brasillach in France in 1945, first published in *Les Temps Modernes*. For each of these women, encountering a fascist enemy was not only dramatic but also life changing. Margarethe von Trotta's film *Hannah Arendt*, discussed in the final chapter of this book, emphasizes the personal impact on Arendt of confronting Eichmann. Likewise Beauvoir's encounter with Brasillach was equally, although differently, impactful; the fact that Brasillach was an intellectual, a journalist, a fellow traveler in the life of the mind made his horrific actions all the more baffling and despicable to her. Bringing Arendt into conversation with Beauvoir via this chapter's encounter, and revisiting their conversation along new dimensions in the final chapter on feminist friendship, illuminates the comparison and ignites fresh thinking on how to protect and nourish collective conditions for freedom.

THEORIZING FREEDOM

What initially comes into focus by staging this particular conversation between these two thinkers is the question of how to reckon with the violence (judging it after the fact and to prevent it in the future) that threatens conditions of freedom in the space of politics. Beauvoir and Arendt share a commitment to the priority of freedom, as well as to the idea that freedom can exist only with others and never alone. While Arendt's theorizing of freedom as acting in a plural world with others is widely known, Beauvoir is often mistakenly thought of as deriving her theory of freedom from Sartre's early (and later revised) commitment to the radical (ontological) freedom of the individual.[3] But as I (and several others) have argued, Beauvoir consistently theorizes freedom as constrained and enabled by situation, able to flourish only when others are also free. For Beauvoir, situated freedom describes self-chosen action that is always already constrained. The constraints refer to history, social conditions, ideology, and the webs of discourse (including the meanings given to forms of embodiment) that produce and position subjects and their experiences. My emphasis on freedom in encounter recognizes situated freedom but shows that others are not a limit to our freedom, but rather the only way to experience freedom is within encounter. While others can oppose us and even limit our movement, it is in encounter that we can diminish or enhance the possibilities for freedom to flourish. Arendt also recognizes constraints on freedom, but she dismisses oppression based on race or gender (and other political interpretations of bodies) as matters of social rather than political concern. She wants to secure political space as untouched by social concerns precisely so that freedom can be enabled and our fundamental plurality as unique individuals can emerge. Thus one important difference between Beauvoir's and Arendt's political thought concerns how to best enable freedom to flourish. Beauvoir worries about social identities and the political meanings given to embodiment that diminish the potential for agency of certain individuals, while Arendt seeks to protect political spaces from these identities in order that our singular personalities and perspectives can be disclosed in freely chosen actions with others. I argue that Beauvoir's attention to how political meanings of embodiment shut certain individuals out of the space of encounter is a Beauvoirian remedy to Arendt's too idealized conception of freedom.

To get to this conclusion we first have to consider what happens in the encounter between evildoer and potential victim that forecloses the possibility for freedom to emerge. Recall that Beauvoir says, "The category of *Other* is as original as consciousness itself" ([1949] 2011, 6). Using an everyday example, she goes on to say, "It only takes three travelers brought together by chance in the same train compartment for the rest of the travelers to become vaguely hostile 'others'" (6). What interests her, and what I bring out in my reading of the politics of encounter, is how and why it is that some are able to look back, to challenge their status as "others," and some are not. There can be no freedom without this struggle.

What happens in this space attracts the attention of both Arendt and Beauvoir. Arendt's focus on representative thinking values the priority she accords an individual's ethical ability to imagine how to think or feel in someone else's place or make present the standpoint of someone else. Beauvoir's emphasis on ambiguity, in contrast, makes visible our embodiment and our mutual vulnerability in relationship and encounter with others: we are always both the self we imagine and the body others see. What Beauvoir notices and Arendt does not is that derogatory public discourse (not to mention physical violence or restrictive policies such as denial of citizenship, closing businesses, forcing Jews to wear a yellow star, etc.) about political meanings of embodiment sometimes saturates consciousness so thoroughly that the body others see engulfs the self we can imagine. In spite of their common commitment to freedom as the disclosure of the self in concert with others, Arendt and Beauvoir think differently about how freedom might be preserved, the terms by which we judge when and how freedom is threatened, and the centrality of embodiment to imagining freedom, and then engaging (or looking, speaking, or fighting back) in encounters with others.

Writing about Eichmann, Arendt elucidates how an ordinary but thoughtless individual can undertake actions that result in the destruction of conditions of worldly plurality. According to Arendt, plurality should be present both in the individual's mind (as the two-in-one, which I discuss in more detail in chapter 7 and in my conclusion) as well as in worldly conditions. Arendt characterizes thinking's link to plurality within the mind in claiming "conscience is the anticipation of the fellow who awaits you if and when you come home" (1981, 191). Noting in *The Life of the Mind* that "a life without thinking is quite possible" (191), she states that in Eichmann's case this failure to think contributed to genocide. Throughout her report of the trial Arendt laments Eichmann's inability to think, and more specifically his inability to use representational thinking or enlarged thought whereby he would "think from the standpoint of somebody else" (1963a, 49). Eichmann's unique crimes result in a violation of the "nature of mankind" in making "Jewish people disappear from the face of the earth" (268).

In contrast Beauvoir emphasizes that Brasillach's crimes resulted not from an inability to think with and against himself or from the standpoints of others (all in his head) but rather due to his refusal to avow ambiguity in his encounter with others. As Beauvoir defines it, to accept and affirm rather than mask human ambiguity is a daunting responsibility: we must reject philosophical, moral, and ideological systems that impose a predetermined meaning on the world; we must recognize our fundamental human failure to control others or to determine the future; we must accept that each individual is, like ourselves, both subject and other; and we must act in ways that not only affirm our own freedom but also enhance the freedom of others. Detailing a range of ways people exercise bad faith in refusing to recognize ambiguity and shoulder the responsibility of freedom, she describes the actions of those she calls "sub-men," men such as Eichmann, who "have eyes and ears but make themselves blind and deaf" (1948, 42) as well as those such as Brasillach, who subjugate their freedom to a "fanaticism." In Brasillach's case, this fanaticism further violated ambiguity in treating embodied, unique, and free human beings as things able to be manipulated and destroyed, thus completely denying their "existence as men" ([1949] 2004, 248).

In what follows I first explore Arendt's and Beauvoir's willingness to make reflective judgments in these cases and hold the criminals responsible, but for reasons different from those articulated by the national courts. Interpreting their trial reports, I then put Beauvoir and Arendt into conversation on the question of how to preserve conditions of freedom in politics by holding individuals responsible for egregious violations of the human condition. Reading them in a conversational encounter sharpens our comprehension of the deep burdens of judgment and helps us to evaluate when and how embodiment situates freedom.

JUDGING BRASILLACH AND EICHMANN

In her essay "An Eye for an Eye," first published in 1946 in *Les Temps Modernes*, Beauvoir reported on the Brasillach trial, which she attended on January 19, 1945. It was a six-hour trial and the jury took only twenty minutes to reach their decision. Brasillach was accused of treason by the French government, found guilty, and executed. He had been the editor of a fascist newspaper from 1935 to 1943 in which he published a column during the German

Occupation revealing the location of many Jews in hiding. This information led to loss of jobs, loss of citizenship, deportation, and death for many Jews.

According to Beauvoir's ([1963] 1992, 28) account of the trial in *Force of Circumstance*, Brasillach had "claimed the right 'to point out those who betray us' and had used it freely; under his editorship, the staff of *Je suis partout* denounced people, specified victims, and urged the Vichy Government to enforce the wearing of the yellow star in the Free Zone." In journal entries recorded in *The Prime of Life*, Beauvoir ([1960] 1992, 502) recalls her anger with French colleagues who collaborated with the occupiers, particularly intellectuals: "Pétain's speeches had a more inflammatory effect on me than Hitler's; and while I condemned all collaborators, I felt a sharply defined and quite excruciating personal loathing for those of my own kind who joined their ranks—intellectuals, journalists, writers." When a petition urging a pardon for Brasillach was authored by Beauvoir's usual allies, she refused to sign. Though forty-nine of her compatriot intellectuals, Camus among them, did so, Beauvoir's dissent registered her judgment that Brasillach should be executed.[4] However, she wrote her essay to clarify that Brasillach should not be executed for the reasons given by the French court. In her eyes, he was guilty of reducing human beings to things—regarding people as body-objects and denying their subjectivity and future—rather than the crime of treason to the French state. Beauvoir contends that although all forms of punishment, including vengeance and abstract justice, fail to restore the reciprocity originally violated by the crime, we must still judge and punish Brasillach.

Tony Judt's (1994) argument in *Past Imperfect: French Intellectuals 1944–56* inadvertently reveals how dissimilar Beauvoir's judgments were from those of her compatriot intellectuals. Judt includes Beauvoir in the group of postwar French intellectuals he criticizes as unwilling to name Stalin's crimes (and therefore ethically culpable). The trend he identifies (and condemns) among the French intellectuals was the absolving of crimes as part of the progress of history (as long as history was seen moving toward freedom). Naming disdain for liberalism as part of the general mood of French intellectuals at this time, Judt writes:

> At the heart of the engagement of the 1940s and 1950s there lay an unwillingness to think seriously about public ethics, an unwillingness amounting to an incapacity. An important source of this shortcoming in the French intelligentsia was the widely held belief that morally binding judgments of a normative sort were undermined by their historical and logical association with the politics and economics of liberalism. It

was a widely held view that liberalism, with its political language based on individuals and their rights and liberties, had utterly failed to protect people against fascism and its consequences, in large measure because it provided them with no alternative account of humanity and its purposes—or at any rate, no alternative account sufficiently consistent and attractive to fight off the charms and dangers of the radical Right. (230)

But Judt's desire to put Beauvoir into this category is entirely unconvincing. He sees Beauvoir as always echoing and supporting Sartre's positions rather than carving out a political and theoretical ground of her own. While we saw in "Right-Wing Thought Today" that Beauvoir included some liberal thinkers among those she names as right-wing enemies, she also distinguishes their positions from others, and identifies the specific ways liberals justify capitalism but fear it may not continue forever. "An Eye for an Eye" and parts of Beauvoir's autobiography are quoted out of context by Judt to support Sartre's ideas rather than to understand Beauvoir's argument as part of a larger distinct political thinking on freedom that she was developing in *The Ethics of Ambiguity*, "Right-Wing Thought Today," *The Second Sex*, and here in "An Eye for an Eye." I mention Judt's book not to substantively engage with his interpretation of Beauvoir's work but rather to demonstrate that if we take his argument seriously, we see the novelty of what Beauvoir was doing in making judgments outside the philosophical universe of either liberalism or communism.

In 1961 Arendt was sent by the *New Yorker* magazine to cover Eichmann's trial in Jerusalem. Her report, first published as essays in the *New Yorker* and later as the book *Eichmann in Jerusalem*, elicited tremendous controversy.[5] Like Beauvoir but under vastly different circumstances, Arendt fell out of favor with her compatriot intellectual cohort for the judgments she made in her interpretation of the meaning and significance of the trial and the role of ordinary citizens, even Jewish Council leaders, under Hitler's regime. Specifically by objecting to Israeli prime minister David Ben-Gurion's way of "teaching" moral principles through the trial, and in exploring the compromised actions of the Jewish Council leaders, Arendt angered many. Although in *The Origins of Totalitarianism* she had talked about the extermination camps as the appearance of "radical evil" on earth, in *Eichmann in Jerusalem* she introduced the controversial term *banality of evil* to discuss how a minor bureaucrat efficiently arranged the murder of millions. Unlike Brasillach, who, as an intellectual, journalist, and newspaper editor, identified Jews for extermination and demonstrated his anti-Semitism early and often,[6] Eichmann was employed by the Nazi state and claimed to merely be following orders. He claimed to have a conscience, to be able to distinguish right from wrong, and that anti-Semitism did not motivate his actions. In bringing to light the failure of all moral principles and yet judging Eichmann the individual as guilty of a crime against humanity, Arendt's report was troubling to those who instead wanted to condemn the movement of history that would make Eichmann into a cog in a killing machine and interpret all Jews as unique victims subject everywhere and always to the forces of anti-Semitism.[7]

In addition to the differences in the actions and motivations of the defendants, as well as the different national contexts for the trials, Arendt and Beauvoir are of course differently situated in relation to the nations where Eichmann and Brasillach face prosecution. Arendt is a German Jewish refugee and (as of 1951) a U.S. citizen critical of an Israeli court intent on legitimating the Zionist state by insisting on the constancy of anti-Semitism throughout history and the unique nature of the crimes against Jews. Beauvoir is situated as a French citizen, a French Gentile in fact, who insists on the necessity of recognizing Jewish vulnerability to Nazi persecution as a critical counterpoint to the French state's narrative that seeks to prosecute collaboration as a more general offense against the nation. These differences in the situation of the two thinkers, as well as the national contexts and the particular actions of the defendants, will be explored more thoroughly later in this chapter. For now I want to focus on some striking similarities in how Beauvoir and Arendt analyze the meaning and significance of the trials.

THE POLITICAL CONTEXTS

One of the important points Beauvoir and Arendt have in common is that both discuss the political context of the trials themselves as significant to the judgments of the courts. Arendt and Beauvoir each see the trials as nation-building exercises, for a defeated and formerly occupied France (in the case of Brasillach) and for a newly formed and legitimacy-seeking Israel (in the case of Eichmann). For France to condemn its traitors and collaborators was to flex its muscles following deep humiliation and impotency; for Israel to show its legitimacy by claiming Eichmann's acts were rooted in deep-seated, forever existing, and widespread anti-Semitism was to validate Israel as an essentially needed homeland and a Zionist nation-state for Jews. As such, Beauvoir and Arendt were sensitive to the new political formations being advanced through these high-profile trials, and to some extent, for both authors, these political motivations served to impair the nature of the justice delivered.

Both thinkers particularly object to how the trials turned into nation-building exercises that obscured the actions of the individual defendants (seen as scapegoats or as emblematic of the role played by all bureaucrats, all Germans, all French collaborators and traitors), resulting in a failure to enact the requirements for justice: the assignment of responsibility for particular deeds. Arendt (1963a, 5) says of Eichmann, "On trial are his deeds, not the suffering of Jews, not the German people or mankind, not even anti-Semitism and racism." Beauvoir ([1949] 2004, 258) argues that punishment must "be attached to the wrong by a concrete bond," one that can be established only by the "accused in his singularity." In these two cases the thinkers affirm that it is the individual, Eichmann or Brasillach, who is on trial, not the German or the French people, not Nazism or collaborators in general, and they argue that the trials must hold the defendant responsible for his acts.

They also each acknowledge the obstacles that stand in the way of holding individuals responsible, given the political orders in which the defendants were situated. These were political orders systematically designed and legally authorized to eliminate certain forms of difference and tempting, sometimes even ordering individuals to take part. As Beauvoir ([1954] 1999) demonstrates in *The Mandarins*, her fictional account of the lives of French intellectuals during and after the war, the postwar moral terrain was quite confusing. It was certainly not so clear who had collaborated with the German occupiers and why, nor what punishment should be meted out and by whom. One of the difficulties in situating Brasillach's guilt, particularly for French intellectuals, was his identity as one of them: a French writer who used his pen to make his living. Some intellectuals felt that as a writer Brasillach should bear even more responsibility; others were disturbed by the fact that he was singled out for prosecution. Though Beauvoir did not sign the petition for clemency and wrote "An Eye for an Eye" to justify Brasillach's execution, she also condemns the French state's desire to make him into a scapegoat while allowing some real killers, as well as Vichy officials and businessmen, to go free.[8] By holding Brasillach responsible for particular crimes, Beauvoir sought to disentangle his responsibility from the narrative the state was promoting, that most French citizens had been resistors and that collaborators and traitors should be punished.

Eichmann's case was equally yet differently situated within a unique political landscape. Fifteen years after the conclusion of the Nuremberg trials, Eichmann was apprehended by Israeli officials in Argentina and brought to Jerusalem to be tried in an Israeli court. Arendt (1963a, 9–10) states that Ben-Gurion's motivation for Eichmann's kidnapping included a lesson to the non-Jewish world about how and why Jews, in particular, suffered from Nazi crimes, and a lesson to the Jewish world about how Jews always and forever have faced hostility. While Ben-Gurion hoped to promote the narrative that Eichmann was both an ordinary German and a vicious anti-Semite, such that he could be both an "innocent executor of some mysteriously foreordained destiny" (19) and evil incarnate, Arendt clarified exactly what Eichmann had done in order to specify how and why this person (and many more like him) acted in such a way that millions of Jews were dead by the end of the war. In other words, Arendt sought to take the focus off legitimating the Israeli state and widen the scope to understand the ethical and political complicity of Eichmann himself, as an individual. In Arendt's estimation, Eichmann was neither a cipher of anti-Semitism nor the devil in disguise. And to judge him Arendt restores his humanity: "medium sized, slender, middle-aged, with receding hair, ill-fitting teeth, and nearsighted eyes, who throughout the trial keeps craning his scraggy neck toward the bench" (5).

ARGUMENTS AGAINST AND FOR JUDGMENT

Many classified crimes like Eichmann's and Brasillach's, as different as they were, as impossible to judge for many contradictory reasons: some argued that such deeds defied the possibility of human punishment; some said they were acts that we too, under similar circumstances, might have committed; some claimed that their acts defied individual responsibility because they were part of larger forces of history; and some, in sympathy, said that criminal acts never define the whole person.[9] Arendt (2003b, 19) thinks these explanations and arguments signal a fear of judging, stemming not from the biblical "Judge not, that ye be not judged" but rather from the suspicion that "no one is a free agent." Beauvoir ([1949] 2004, 245) seems to confirm this view in remembering that before the war she and her compatriot intellectuals "lived without wishing any of our fellow humans any harm." She elaborates: "As for individuals like assassins and thieves, whom society denounced as dangerous, they did not seem to be our enemies. To our eyes their crimes were only accidents provoked by a regime that did not give everyone a fair chance.... Conscious of our privilege, we forbade ourselves to judge them" (246).

Both Beauvoir and Arendt argue, however, that these unprecedented circumstances introduced an especially urgent need for judgment. The crimes of Eichmann and Brasillach were definitely not "ordinary" (Arendt 1963a, 246). Were it not that Brasillach's identification of Jews led to their deportation and death, we might justify his vehement anti-Semitic writing under the category of free speech. Beauvoir ([1949] 2004, 252) admits of Brasillach that neither he "nor Pétain, nor Laval directly killed anyone." Likewise Arendt (1963a, 246) stipulates that Eichmann was guilty only of "aiding and abetting" in the commission of crimes with which he was charged, and he "himself had never committed an overt act." Nor did Eichmann give orders or make policy; instead he efficiently carried out Nazi policies. Because there were no clear definitions of these crimes, because they were unprecedented and there existed no general rules under which these crimes could neatly "fit," Arendt and Beauvoir felt the urgency to understand them, to name specifically what was "new" in these unforeseen circumstances and uncharted territory. What was most directly at stake for both Arendt and Beauvoir was not only that history plays out against a backdrop of accidents not of our making but that in light of these particular political configurations and accidents there is an even greater urgency to figure out what role the individual plays. The crimes committed may not be acts of will strictly speaking, yet they are tangible acts that have concrete effects on the world and the lives of others. Arendt repeatedly reiterates that though Eichmann's crimes were part of a systematic attempt to wipe a people from the earth, he nonetheless bears responsibility for his participation within this system. In holding Brasillach responsible, Beauvoir ([1963] 1992, 30) argues that "there are words as murderous as gas chambers."

Rejecting the view of charity that she had laid out as a potential argument against judgment, Beauvoir argues that we enact our freedom by choosing good over evil. This choice itself, and maintaining the value of that choice in our willingness to judge, creates meaning and affirms our freedom.[10] Arendt signals her agreement in distinguishing between temptation and force, arguing against those who say we cannot be trusted when the chips are down.[11] To fail to judge, for Arendt as well as for Beauvoir, is to abdicate the responsibilities of freedom, both to ourselves and to others.

Thus, against prevailing voices, Arendt and Beauvoir argue that judgment is not only possible but absolutely necessary. Brasillach the writer and Eichmann the bureaucrat are each responsible in a real way for their crimes.[12] Thus Arendt and Beauvoir stress (with the courts) that we must hold the individual defendant responsible for his deeds. In justifying the death penalty as a legitimate punishment for each man, however, Arendt and Beauvoir display some important differences in what they think is at stake in how to best preserve conditions of freedom. Near the end of the epilogue to *Eichmann in Jerusalem*, Arendt (1963a, 277, 279) argues that the justice done in Jerusalem would have "emerged to be seen by all if the judges had dared to address their defendant in something like the following terms": "Just as you supported and carried out a policy of not wanting to share the earth with the Jewish people and the people of a number of other nations—as though you and your superiors had any right to determine who should and who should not inhabit the world—we find that no one, that is, no member of the human race, can be expected to want to share the earth with you. This is the reason, and the only reason, you must hang." Accusing Eichmann of not being willing to "share the earth" with others, Arendt stakes out her defense of the death penalty by condemning Eichmann on behalf of the "we" of worldly plurality. Calling Arendt's defense of the death penalty for Eichmann an act of "nonreconciliation with the world," Roger Berkowitz (2011) distinguishes this type of judgment from notions of revenge and forgiveness. Berkowitz argues that Arendt neither calls for vengeance on behalf of the wronged, nor does she forgive Eichmann's crimes, which would serve to reconcile us to a world with persons such as Eichmann in it. Instead the judgment of nonreconciliation with the world suggests "a break, a crisis, a new beginning, one that makes a claim either to reaffirm a common world (reconciliation) or to re-imagine and re-form our common world (non-reconciliation)." Reading the death sentence differently from Berkowitz, Ariella Azoulay and Bonnie Honig (2016, 73–74) argue that Arendt calls for a reconciliation with the world in calling for Eichmann's death:

> Butler calls it [the death sentence] an "archaic formulation," one that positions Arendt "rhetorically as a sovereign delivering a fatal sentence and one that some might consider barbaric indeed." Butler cites Rogat, who cited the vengeful Furies of Aeschylus's *Eumenides* in his own account. The formulation may be archaic in this way, but it is not only archaic; it is also historically recent, pronounced a decade and half earlier twelve times at Nuremberg: "[O]n the counts of the Indictment on which you have been convicted, the Tribunal sentences you to death by hanging" ("Nuremberg Trial Proceedings Vol. 1"). Thus, Arendt's death sentences are an act of citation. As such they are carriers of the archaic and the recent, both. Of particular importance here, though, is that her sentencing, which puzzles Butler in its multivocality ("the verdict-voice is and is not her own") repeats the Nuremberg formula. Addressing Eichmann directly, Arendt cites the Nuremberg court, joins its judges, and thus ties the deeds judged in Jerusalem to the ones earlier judged at Nuremberg as crimes against humanity.

While Arendt's call for Eichmann's death presumes a solidarity (or not) with the world as it is, Beauvoir's emphasis on the victims of Brasillach's crimes presumes a solidarity with the oppressed: a solidarity with the *new and transformed world* Beauvoir calls for. Evoking a different "we" than Arendt, Beauvoir ([1963] 1992, 29) writes, "Certain men have no place in this world we're trying to build." Affirming that it is with Brasillach's victims, dead or alive, that she feels solidarity, Beauvoir writes, "They [Brasillach and others at *Je suis partout*] had demanded the death of Feldman, Cavaillès, Politzer, Bourla, the deportation of Yvonne Picard, Pèron, Kaan, Desnos. . . . If I lifted a finger to help Brasillach [by signing the clemency petition], then it would have been their right to spit in my face" (28–29). Not a victim of injustice herself, Beauvoir helps us to see how we can actively affirm justice via solidarity, even as observers from afar. Moving from the "we" of plurality for Arendt to the "we" of solidarity for Beauvoir also foreshadows the emphasis Beauvoir will place on embodied struggles for acknowledgment and recognition as political struggles for which we, as a collectivity, are responsible.

In sum, Arendt and Beauvoir each judge these individuals against dominant national narratives and in spite of voices cautioning against judgment. Each rejects the enlistment of moral precepts, historical movements, or even prior rules and definitions as a way to make sense of these political systems and the roles of individuals within them. Both hold the individual defendant responsible for his deeds, knowing full well that he acted in light of political circumstances that arguably might serve to mitigate individual responsibility. Arendt and Beauvoir acknowledge that although these individuals alone do not bear responsibility for these structures or this moment in history, they do indeed bear responsibility for the particular deeds they committed within these systems. Thus, in holding the defendants individually responsible for their acts, Arendt and Beauvoir also affirm the capacity for individuals to do evil without endorsing the idea that the individual is best conceived as a self-possessing subject acting outside of structural constraints. Finally, Arendt and Beauvoir each affirm the death penalty for the defendants, but not, as explained earlier, for the reasons given by the courts. Opposing the argument of the Israeli court that Eichmann was an agent of larger and inevitable anti-Semitic forces, and opposing the argument of the French court that Brasillach's main crime was to collaborate against France with the German occupiers, Arendt and Beauvoir resist these moves toward easy moral closure. Instead these thinkers make judgments that, in their eyes, affirm freedom and the role of judgment in sustaining it. They each seek to articulate the responsibility of ordinary citizens to our shared world and the dangers that arise from a refusal of these responsibilities.

TWO KINDS OF FAILURES

Although Arendt and Beauvoir agree that Eichmann and Brasillach should be held individually responsible for their respective acts, they differ in naming their particular failures as well as in detailing the conditions that must exist in order for freedom to prosper. Different explanations for Brasillach's and Eichmann's specific failures and crimes arise from the undeniable fact that the two were indeed very different kinds of criminals; totalitarian and other police-state regimes provide numerous and various kinds of opportunities for people to betray their responsibilities toward others. As noted earlier, Brasillach was a journalist, an elite alumnus of the Ecole Normale Supérieure, and a recognized intellectual and fervent anti-Semite who, in addition to serving as editor of *Je suis partout*, during which time he condemned individual Jews by fingering them to state officials, also published highly regarded fiction, literary criticism, plays, and poetry. In contrast Eichmann was a state employee with bureaucratic duties who claimed to hold no grudge against Jews specifically. As Arendt (1963a, 31–35) puts it, Eichmann was a "joiner"; he wanted to act in accordance with directives, orders, and commands; he had failed as a traveling salesman and saw the possibility for advancement of his career with the Nazis.

Specifically rejecting *mens rea*, Arendt describes Eichmann's crimes as a result of thoughtlessness. She parses thoughtlessness both as an inability to think for oneself (Eichmann almost blindly did his "duty," or did what others around him were doing) and as an inability to think from the position of others. In regard to the first aspect, she remarks, for example, that Eichmann "could see no one, no one at all, who actually was against the Final Solution"; that "his conscience was indeed set at rest when he saw the zeal and eagerness with which 'good society' everywhere reacted as he did"; and that his "conscience spoke with a 'respectable voice,' with the voice of respectable society around him" (1963a, 116. 126). Regarding these observations, Arendt emphasizes that we cannot count on the dictates of conscience, moral law, legal standards, or Christianity (or any religion) to guide individuals in dark times. And yet there were people who did demonstrate an ability to think: Arendt references Anton Schmidt, for example, a German sergeant whom Abba Kovner credited with helping Jewish partisans (230) as well as the resistance of the Danish people and their government (171) as evidence that not everyone was unable to think from the standpoint of others, nor was everyone following Nazi orders. Eichmann, in contrast, exhibited what Arendt calls "sheer thoughtlessness": he "never realized what he was doing" and maintained a distinct "remoteness from reality." Tragically this inability to think had the effect of "wreak[ing] more havoc than all the evil instincts taken together" (287–88).

Would Beauvoir concur in Arendt's diagnosis of Eichmann's thoughtlessness? We can look to the way Beauvoir describes the "sub-man" in *The Ethics of Ambiguity* to understand how she might see things a little differently. Explaining the attitudes and actions of "sub-men," Beauvoir (1948, 44) notes that they are "led to take refuge in the ready-made values of the serious world." More dangerously, they gladly offer themselves up for movements and ideologies that help them escape the "agonizing evidence" of freedom (45). "One day, a monarchist, the next day, an anarchist, he is more readily anti-semitic, anti-clerical, or anti-republican"; the sub-man is willing to "proclaim certain opinions" and "take shelter behind a label"; "to hide his indifference he will readily abandon himself to verbal outbursts or even physical violence" (44). When the sub-man subordinates his freedom to a movement or ideology, he turns away from encounter in denying the space of difference, and he violates ambiguity in refusing his responsibility to make judgments and choices that affirm his freedom with others.

By reading Beauvoir's work on the sub-man as a way to understand how she might judge Eichmann, we can see that in contrast to Arendt's focus on Eichmann's inability to think for himself, particularly his inability to engage in a Kantian exercise of enlarged thought, Beauvoir (1948, 7) would frame his crime as resulting from a cowardly refusal of an encounter with others: a denial not only of what she names the "tragic ambiguity" of the human condition but also of freedom itself. Like Arendt, Beauvoir emphasizes the ordinariness of the sub-man's attitude toward the world, but in contrast to Arendt she explicitly describes this attitude as a refusal of the anguish and responsibility that human freedom demands of each individual in encounter with others. To embrace freedom would demand taking responsibility for one's actions in light of the fact that one's existence and actions are always and inevitably linked to others.

Maybe Arendt's and Beauvoir's different terms are just two roads for getting to the same destination. Beauvoir would likely agree with Arendt's (1958, 5) judgment of Eichmann's thoughtlessness when understood as a "hopeless confusion or complacent repetition of 'truths.'" She might also approve of Arendt's (1992) interpretation of Kant's notions of representative thinking (or enlarged thought) in her *Lectures on Kant's Political Philosophy*, where Arendt argues that enlarged thought entails "comparing our judgment with the *possible* rather than the actual judgments of others, and by putting ourselves in the place of every other man" (43, emphasis added). This does not imply a need to actually know the thoughts or feelings of the other but just to know something about her situation. But what is it we need to know? Unlike Beauvoir, Arendt ignores the fact that bodily attributes and their political interpretations bear on the conditions of political (collective) freedom.

Beauvoir too says we might and should imagine the situation of others, even though we cannot know their true state of mind, intentions, or emotions, but by "situation" she includes much more than does Arendt. Beauvoir insists that the way an "other" sees the world is always opaque to us, but to find a justification for our own existence and to care for our shared world by enhancing freedom, we have to avow the existence of others who strive for freedom but are systematically, psychically, and socially (thus politically) blocked from achieving it. What Beauvoir sees and Arendt does not is that when people are diminished by derogatory language, restrictive policies, and structural and physical violence, they sometimes adapt to the new material circumstances these conditions create by themselves thinking of their freedom and potential as limited. I develop these ideas more extensively in the next section.

Beauvoir articulates the nature of Brasillach's failure (although very different from Eichmann's or what she would name as the sub-man's) by focusing on the demands that freedom makes on each of us in encounter. Acting in the role of the tyrant, as pure transcendence and sovereign agent, Brasillach sought to control and manipulate events and people, thinking he could determine the outcome of the future and impose his meaning, in this case Nazi meaning, on the world. In chapter 1 I pointed to a similar dynamic in my reading of "Right-Wing Thought Today." Part of what was scandalous about that essay in the mid-1950s, and part of what bothers Sonia Kruks in her reading of the text, is the way Beauvoir cavalierly lumps liberal thinkers such as Karl Jaspers and Maurice Merleau-Ponty into the same category as right-wing fascists and antiliberal thinkers. But as I argued in chapter 1, with this move Beauvoir is encouraging readers to see that the kinds of strategies all too obvious in fascist and reactionary thought (shutting down the future, trying to control the other) are key for liberal thinkers too. Judt's criticism of French intellectuals on the Left, that they justified any and all tactics as long as they aimed at a better future, is precisely the same thing that Beauvoir here accuses liberals (and right-wing thinkers) of doing.

In subsequent chapters I will point out that besides Nazis and some liberals, the seemingly well-intentioned (and appropriately sensitive) male characters in Lars von Trier's films engage in similar violations of freedom. HE in *Antichrist*, John in *Melancholia*, and Seligman in *Nymphomaniac* each impose their worldview on female characters, failing to even try to imagine what the world looks like from inside a female body, but also asserting their arrogance by trying to control the future via rationalism, science, tired liberal precepts and clichés. Arguing that von Trier urges us, as spectators, to "feel" the suffering of these women and see the world from within this embodied perspective, I claim that if we are inclined to see the films from a feminist perspective, we might feel women's desire for freedom.

In contrast to these ways of shutting down embodied encounters and closing off potential and as yet unimagined futures, Beauvoir (1948, 71) stresses repeatedly that freedom aims at "an open future" and that only "the freedom of other men can extend [the ends toward which we project our freedom] beyond our life." As she puts it, "every man needs the freedom of other men" since only "the freedom of others keeps each one of us from hardening in the absurdity of facticity" (71). Brasillach denied his own ambiguity by acting as pure transcendence; he denied the ambiguity of his victims in treating them merely as things, or as body-objects with no legitimate access to the future; he denied the ambiguity in existence by acting as if Nazi control over the future was certain; and his actions denied his victims the opportunity to think and act freely in the world.

Important for Beauvoir is the fact that we are responsible to ourselves *and to others* to expand the scope of freedom for all by collectively altering the political conditions in which our acts play out. To capture the urgency of this call, we remind ourselves of our radical freedom to act and (re)create the world outside of any moral standards. Living through the events of the mid-twentieth century, Beauvoir and Arendt are well aware of how suddenly things can change, how precarious our world really is. They both emphasize our daunting responsibility to and for the lives and freedom of others. Beauvoir insists that when confronting others, we cannot seek to control them, nor should we see our freedom as a zero-sum game in competition with the freedom of others. The meaningful exercise of our own freedom depends on the willingness of others to respond to and take up the call of our appeals in a world where oppression is minimized.

The situation in which Brasillach's actions played out, in which oppression was so prevalent, serves to magnify rather than mitigate his responsibility. While Brasillach's anti-Semitism was despicable and his refusal of freedom was clearly an ethical violation, that his anti-Semitic actions would result in the deaths of particular Jews was possible only under political conditions whereby Jews were already isolated and targeted. His naming of the location of Jews in this particular political environment made it possible for them to be rounded up by authorities, deported, or killed.

Thus when Beauvoir posits ambiguity as constitutive of the human condition, she complicates the conditions of judgment by making them explicitly and always political. Unique individuals do not and cannot "know" the situation of others beyond the recognition that they too desire and deserve freedom, that they too have bodies and desires, and that encounters occur between politically unequal parties. This reflection on the existence of others, as Arendt too contends, is the function of imagination, and it makes reflective judgments possible. There is no autonomous, rational, or dispassionate judge, nor a principle or rule, to guide us.[13] Instead judgment is always politically situated and occurs within political conditions and within encounters outside our control. While each individual has a responsibility to alter these political conditions to reduce oppression, it is also the case that individuals are usually acting under conditions where oppression and inequality are present and must be acknowledged. Facing up to the fact of encounter and the avowal of ambiguity thus also entails looking carefully at larger structural and political contexts that foreclose the possibilities for individuals and the collectivity to embrace and enhance freedom. Expanding the concept of the political in this way, Beauvoir asks us to think about the ethical realm of the responsibility of individuals and also, more explicitly, about the political conditions in which people act.

Arendt's articulation of the importance of thinking—her claim to plurality enacted in thinking (needing to live with oneself), to representative or enlarged thought (thinking from the perspective of others and considering their situation), and her theorization of the role of thoughtlessness in destroying plurality—helps us see the ethical responsibility of individuals in making or failing to make judgments, even against positive law and under conditions of coercion. In her focus on ambiguity Beauvoir also helps us to see the ethical responsibility of individuals and their role in judgment, but takes us even further. Beauvoir directs our attention to how pernicious meanings attached to embodiment, such as racism, introduce inequality and oppression into the political realm.

Beauvoir makes her claims more tangible through her focus on how the political meaning of certain bodies in public spaces threatens the freedom, and sometimes the lives, of distinct individuals and erodes the conditions of collective freedom. It is under these demeaned conditions for freedom and action, or as Beauvoir puts it, when oppression takes root, that it becomes especially difficult for the Eichmanns and Brasillachs of the world to resist temptation. And as both Beauvoir and Arendt warn, when such individuals fail to resist temptation, as many inevitably will, the results are calamitous.

THE DEMANDS AND CONDITIONS OF FREEDOM

Recall that while Arendt and Beauvoir are both eager to explain each state's motivation for prosecuting these individuals, the contexts are markedly dissimilar. Beauvoir observed that within the French state's narrative of Brasillach as collaborator and traitor, his acts against individual Jewish victims were obscured. Hence she hoped to bring embodiment and the suffering of the victims to the fore by illuminating Brasillach's specific actions against particular, named Jews. In contrast Arendt argued that the Israeli state was overinvested in the narrative (as well as the testimony) of individual victims in its emphasis on the role of anti-Semitism. In countering the "Jews are unique victims" narrative, both through her "banality of evil" interpretation as well as by noting "Jewish help in administrative and police work," Arendt (1963a, 117) hoped to redirect the focus to more general questions of political accountability.

These differences certainly move us a good distance toward explaining why Arendt seeks to direct attention away from the embodiment of the victims and Beauvoir seeks to direct attention toward it. Throughout her account of the Eichmann trial Arendt repeatedly insists on the fact that this was not a case of anti-Semitism per se but rather an attempt to destroy an entire people. She shows her frustration with Ben-Gurion and the Israeli court in her claim that theirs was a show trial meant to expose the "complicity of all German offices and authorities in the Final Solution," to demonstrate "what the Jews had suffered" rather than "what Eichmann had done," and to hold responsible not only the Nazi regime but "anti-Semitism throughout history" (1963a, 18, 6, 19). Arendt thus argues that the charge of anti-Semitism misses the mark because it implies that only a single people, the Jews, were harmed, when in fact it was the "order of mankind" that was at stake (272).[14] In contrast, throughout "An Eye for an Eye" Beauvoir links the personal, the intimate, and the concrete to the political, the public, and the general. Specifically she seeks to bring personal embodiment and suffering into view and think concretely about whether any form of justice (personal vengeance or the impersonal justice of the state) can restore or even account for the wrongs that have been committed as violations of ambiguity, freedom, and human solidarity.[15]

The different national and embodied situations of the two thinkers in relation to these two trials partially account for the contrast between Beauvoir's desire to illuminate and Arendt's desire to deemphasize the suffering of individuals and the embodiment of the victims. Yet it is Beauvoir's articulation of the relationship between embodiment, oppression, and political freedom that better explains the difference in emphases between the two in regard to the suffering of victims. Arendt argues that we must draw a bright line between the social and the political in order to preserve the possibility of disclosing our unique selves in the political realm and preserve plurality.[16] My interpretation of Beauvoir reveals that this focus obscures the dynamics of power at the level of bodily existence and the specific vulnerabilities of the body as relevant to creating and maintaining conditions of political freedom. To understand why, for Beauvoir, embodiment is so relevant as a distinctly political question, it is important to revisit the different ways Arendt and Beauvoir theorize how freedom is made possible in the political sphere.

In works such as *On Revolution* and *The Human Condition*, Arendt demonstrates that she is acutely aware of the way social conditions automatically exclude some from active participation in the political process. Being enslaved, being in charge of taking care of household activities and the realm of reproduction, being poor and hungry, all put one under the sway of necessity. And for Arendt liberation from necessity is an important precondition for the possibility of political freedom. These concerns, all of which Arendt (1963b, 59–114) deems prepolitical or antipolitical, are classified under the umbrella of "the social question," and thus she does not believe their oppressive effects, ever-present and ongoing, have direct or urgent political implications. Of the distinctly political realm Arendt (1958, 179–80) remarks in *The Human Condition*, "In acting and speaking men show who they are, reveal actively their unique personal identities and thus make their appearance in the human world. . . . Without the disclosure of the agent in the act, action loses its specific character."[17] Defining human plurality as the "paradoxical plurality of unique beings," she designates the political sphere as the space in which we "appear to each other, not indeed as physical objects, but qua men" (176). Motivating Arendt is her desire to preserve the "equalizing of differences" promised by the conferral of citizenship. And while she acknowledges that the line between public and private is continually and constantly eroded by the meanings that our "single, unique, and unchangeable" private existences (1966, 382) take on in public, she fails to theorize this as having implications for our understanding of what she says is the strictly "political" realm of speech and action. As is well known, Arendt seeks to make the political sphere, or the *vita activa*, as distinct and contained as possible. Here our appearance is more than an exposure of "mere bodily existence"; here we can express ourselves as "subjects, as distinct and unique persons" (1958, 176, 183) beyond the "merely given" (1966, 382) and in the context of our "human togetherness" (1958, 180).

Arendt's account of the political realm can be contrasted to Beauvoir's theorization of how freedom is always situated and can be experienced only by acknowledging ambiguity with others in encounters. In writings after *The Ethics of Ambiguity*, Beauvoir fully develops her concept of freedom, the idea that the extent of one's freedom is linked with the freedom of all and that the experience of freedom (especially the desire to experience freedom) is conditioned by political understandings of embodiment and emerges only with others in the world, in encounter. It is not the case for Beauvoir that freedom is absolutely circumscribed by the meanings attached to embodiment, but freedom is always situated within encounters. She insists that even oppressed individuals exercise agency and respond to their situations in a variety of ways. For example, we can think about how racism as a persistent, single, and pernicious account of embodiment adversely affects the scope of freedom for nonwhites, and yet agency and resistance are still often possible, even though it is sometimes not easily recognizable as such. Chapter 4's conversation with Fanon alerts us to pathologized behavior that is a kind of agency turned inward on the body. In chapter 6 I introduce isolated women in individual households, each of whom defies patriarchal authority and acts, or acts out, albeit in violent ways.

What Beauvoir particularly helps us to see is that it was the political meanings that adhered to certain forms of embodiment that put specific individuals at greater risk. Extending the work she began in "An Eye for an Eye" in *The Second Sex* and *Old Age*, Beauvoir explains at length how the body's vulnerability and political meanings, both ontologically and socially situated, are the very conditions that structure the possibility for political freedom. Here she emphasizes that the political meaning of certain bodies makes some populations, indeed some individuals, far more vulnerable to oppression, abuse, and dehumanization than others, and we all have a responsibility to work against such political conditions. To affirm the political community and the demands of freedom within relations marked by ambiguity, Beauvoir brings into view the fate, as well as the structural position, of individual victims. She demonstrates that in targeting individual Jews, Brasillach identified people who were already structurally disadvantaged and politically at risk because of anti-Semitic ideologies and policies.[18] Brasillach took advantage of these conditions, jumping on the bandwagon to isolate and condemn these vulnerable individuals, but it was the situation in which these acts played out that is most important to emphasize. In "An Eye for an Eye," Beauvoir says there are many offenses, even crimes, that we might want to excuse; it is certainly the case that, as individuals, we fail to acknowledge ambiguity on a daily basis. But it is when political conditions are such that Brasillach's deliberate degradation of individuals reduced them to things, paving the way to physical violence and mass murder, that there is no compensation "for the abomination he causes to erupt on the earth" ([1949] 2004, 257).

Beauvoir thus emphasizes that particular conditions of oppression are what make crimes such as Brasillach's or Eichmann's possible. When groups of people, through a variety of mechanisms or institutional processes (substantive economic inequality, racial and sexual discrimination, blocked access to citizenship, etc.), are systematically rendered body-objects, they are open to dehumanization, their bodies are especially vulnerable, and the possibility of enhancing collective freedom is denied. Beauvoir repeatedly emphasizes how difficult it is to affirm the freedom of those who have been dehumanized by political meanings that have been given to their body. In *The Ethics of Ambiguity* she says the victims themselves began to justify their own humiliation and abuse due to conditions that made them feel their abjection so acutely: "That is why the Nazis were so systematically relentless in casting into abjection the men they wanted to destroy: the disgust which the victims felt in regard to themselves stifled the voice of revolt and justified the executioners in their own eyes" (1948, 101).

If oppressed subjects themselves must struggle to even desire their freedom because others see them as dehumanized things, not only will ambiguity be denied, but there will be no possibility for plurality and the kind of freedom that both Arendt and Beauvoir hope to see flourish. As Beauvoir often states, within the space of appearances lauded by Arendt in *The Human Condition*, we might make an "appeal" to an Other, but she may fail to heed that appeal or be unable to act upon it. Whole classes of people, made up of unique individuals, are cast into the position of the other and thus systematically unable to make any appearance in public space and disclose themselves as human beings. Beauvoir (1948, 81) defines oppression precisely as the situation wherein one cannot respond to an appeal, or when one makes such an appeal it falls uselessly back on itself. In other words, there is no encounter and hence no freedom. Such a situation is never "natural"; "man is never oppressed by things; in any case, unless he is a naïve child who hits stones or a mad prince who orders the sea to be thrashed, he does not rebel against things, but only against other men" (81). It is not just interdependence that makes conditions political but also our embodied exposure to and encounter with each other that constitutes "the risk implied by every step" (82). Explaining further, she writes:

> It is this interdependence which explains why oppression is possible and why it is hateful. As we have seen, my freedom, in order to fulfill itself, requires that it emerge into an open future: it is other men who open the future to me, it is they who, setting up the world of tomorrow, define my future; but if, instead of allowing me to participate in this constructive moment, they oblige me to consume my transcendence in vain, if they keep me below the level which they have conquered and on the basis of which new conquests will be achieved, then they are cutting me off from the future, they are changing me into a thing. (1948, 82)

Likewise only when all others are able to take up (or reject) our projects with us (and the projects are transformed via our interaction) are we fully free. As Beauvoir puts it, under conditions of oppression others may not be able to respond to my appeal nor take up my projects. Thus my freedom falls back on itself and is denied as well.

We can now see that Beauvoir's focus on what I call encounters captures a key dimension of politics that Arendt does not. Though like Arendt, Beauvoir holds individuals responsible for their actions in totalitarian and police states, she also directs our attention to the political sphere as specifically structured by embodiment, consciousness, inequality, and oppression. Hence the material situation of oppression as well as the myriad ways oppression plays out subjectively (e.g., in *The Second Sex* she explains that women must struggle for the desire to assume their freedom) offer a more robust sense of the requirements for and the constraints on freedom than does Arendt's account. The result of Eichmann's and Brasillach's actions was that Jews were denied the possibility of appearing on the earth, both in their "merely given" bodies and as "speaking and acting" beings able to exercise freedom. The "merely given" bodies of Jews were laden with political significance because of conditions of oppression and dehumanization. Another way of putting this is to say that the "mere bodily existence" of Jews, a category outside the realm of the political for Arendt, is for Beauvoir something we should be thinking about in the political register.

So while a failure to think or to embrace ambiguity within encounter can be classified as an ethical failure, Beauvoir forces us to think beyond the ethical to illuminate the political conditions in which unethical actions play out. It is worth noting that in *The Origins of Totalitarianism* Arendt (1966, 343) says those designated as "scum of the earth" were persons already cast out of political space and rendered stateless (and also without "human" rights as these were linked to citizenship). Beauvoir warns that even when and if people have rights as citizens, the ability to exercise these rights is situated by the meaning accorded to bodies, meanings that condition the thoughts and actions of both perpetrators and victims.

Thinking about Beauvoir's reading of the sub-man in the context of Eichmann's crimes and pairing this with her work on Brasillach's trial, we can see how avowing ambiguity within encounter meets our collective responsibility for working against oppression. Her focus helps us see that crimes like Eichmann's were made possible only by a prior and ongoing political interpretation of bodies, aided and abetted by writers like Brasillach. Beauvoir's appreciation of the political stakes for bodies in encounter informs her sense of solidarity with Brasillach's victims and her claim that "we" are trying to build a world where there is no room for people like Brasillach. As an observer of injustice, Beauvoir's "we" commits her to solidarity with its victims. This enactment of solidarity, from a position of privilege rather than necessity, is instructive for our own dark times as we face the political challenge of how to act and judge when we observe injustice from a safe distance. An example of this safe distance is the position of white allies in the struggle against state power to police and murder black Americans.[19]

Beauvoir's appeal to standing with individuals subject to derogatory meanings of embodiment offers us a way to carve a space for solidarity in a "we" not limited by identity. In the "Allies" section of this book, I develop her call to craft a political "we" out of the broken bodies of damaged selves formed in racist and colonial encounters. What we can say now is that Beauvoir's "we" contrasts with Arendt's more impersonal "we" of plurality. While the Arendtian "we" on behalf of worldly plurality should be interpreted as a commitment beyond a specifically Jewish solidarity, at the same time Arendt's focus on plurality remains an abstract formal condition for the possibility of politics rather than an embodied description of the pluralist human community actually engaged in political struggle.

Nevertheless there is much on which Arendt and Beauvoir agree. They both demonstrate a willingness to make judgments without recourse to overriding moral precepts, philosophical rules, and justifications within history or philosophy, thus affirming reflective judgment as central to political freedom.

In addition, they both seek to lay bare the stakes of the trials in their political contexts. Indeed both Arendt and Beauvoir were repulsed by the way the Israeli and the French courts manipulated the trials to teach lessons, garner authority for their fledgling national identities, and demonstrate that they could mete out justice. Analyzing the trials in their political contexts, seeing the crimes as failing to fit under existing moral or normative universalisms, and affirming the political act of judgment are lasting contributions of both Beauvoir's and Arendt's writings on these trials.

What this encounter also demonstrates, however, is that Beauvoir's theorization of ambiguity within encounters better captures the fragile, as well as daunting situation in which individuals act and in which collective freedom might be squandered or destroyed. Beauvoir's commitment to avowing ambiguity within encounter, particularly with a focus on the political meanings of embodiment, can guide our actions and how we judge them. Ambiguity is a phenomenological condition that we share as humans, in our self-expression through words and deeds and in our embodied encounters with others, who in turn interpret our actions and interactions. Like Arendt, Beauvoir holds individuals responsible for the effects of their actions on the world. Moving beyond Arendt, Beauvoir shows that engaging in collective action to alter conditions of oppression and inequality are political activities we must embrace as we negotiate all of our encounters, both large and small.

Adopting Beauvoir's and Arendt's practice of reflective judgment, I next bring Lars von Trier's film *Antichrist* into our conversation. Were we to judge this film by determinate rules of (feminist) ideology, it would merit no further mention beyond its especially derogatory portrayal of women as evil—indeed the heroine is positioned as the antichrist who must be burned at the stake. The experience of watching the film is described by one feminist critic (and this is a typical comment!) as "like having bad sex with someone you loathe—a hideous combination of sheer boredom and disgust."[20] Were we to accept her judgment, the film would be categorized as of interest to feminism only as an example (especially good? especially bad?) of pornography or horror, or pornographic horror. But if we are open to encounter, particularly encounters that test our reflective judgments and affirm our mutual freedom to judge, we might see that *Antichrist*'s target is not women but normative sexuality. I arrive at this conclusion by taking seriously Beauvoir's encounter with the Marquis de Sade, particularly Sade's traffic in bodies and body parts. When we are willing to engage in reflective judgment on aesthetic objects, even with those who appear to be misogynist enemies, we might see something new, something even *instructive* for feminist politics. Encouraging us to feel our way beyond patriarchy, von Trier's women characters tune our radar to notice and maybe even embrace "foreign existences" (Beauvoir's [(1952) 2012] term from "Must We Burn Sade?"), grotesque entities, and even acknowledge, à la Jane Bennett's (2010) *Vibrant Matter*, the agency of chestnuts, trees, and weird, wild, and deformed animals.

THE MARQUIS DE SADE'S BODIES IN LARS VON TRIER'S *ANTICHRIST*

We could say . . . that, for Sade, "the dick is the shortest path from one heart to another." —SIMONE DE BEAUVOIR, "Must We Burn Sade?"

Beauvoir's essay on the Marquis de Sade, "Must We Burn Sade?" published in *Les Temps Modernes* in 1952, inspires my framing of this chapter's encounter between Beauvoir and the film *Antichrist* by the controversial director Lars von Trier. In "Must We Burn Sade?" Beauvoir asks whether Sade's writing—in particular his defense of bodily cruelty and extreme sexual violence, reveals the secrets of patriarchy. She also ponders whether, for Sade, "the dick is the shortest path from one heart to another."[1] Yet she does not leave it there. She suggests that "the dick" is the means and method of connection and communication for Sade, but she also introduces the possibility that this might not be the whole story. Beauvoir ([1952] 2012, 61, 92) considers Sade's depiction of pain, abuse, collective debauchery, and cruelty to the body as a unique path toward discovering the "reality of foreign existences" and as a failed attempt at "genuine communication." Beauvoir's reading of Sade helps us to see that his writing points out the limits and constraints of bourgeois ideology and, with its emphasis on the body, fosters the desire to think and feel differently.

Condemned as pornography, as horror, or as justifying sexual violence and cruelty toward women, von Trier's *Antichrist*, more than any of his other films, is described as "Sadean" and is said to reveal his misogyny.[2] But inspired by Beauvoir's willingness to read Sade as grounding a different, embodied means of communication and connection, I suggest that although feminists may be rightly reluctant to embrace von Trier, we need not, and should not, burn him either. Instead we should be in conversation with him! What else is going on in *Antichrist*, aside from its seemingly obvious airing of the secrets of patriarchy? Von Trier's film helps us see questions of violence and politics when bodies encounter bodies differently from how we usually do. This is particularly the case when we put this film, in which bodies are so central, into conversation with Beauvoir's interpretation of Sade's bodies, which are themselves transformed in their encounter with Beauvoir's penetrating attention.

Judith Butler (2003, 187) sees Beauvoir's essay on Sade as an effort to comprehend the "full range of human possibility." In her view Beauvoir is saying that "to understand the ethical significance of Sade, one must suspend judgment about him and adopt the critical sympathy of the biographer" (187). I interpret Beauvoir's essay differently. I believe Beauvoir circumvents ethical and moral registers of interpretation not by showing that the Other is to be fully understood (or that we must "know" Sade to see the full range of the human). Instead she invites us to a more political register, one that involves both "the reality of foreign existences" and genuine communication regardless of full knowledge.

What if we consider *Antichrist* from a similarly capacious feminist perspective? In *Antichrist* the features that attract Beauvoir to Sade are in full view. The "realities of foreign existences" are wildly and vividly present, and they may even be seen to be a condition of genuine communication; indeed to not acknowledge the "foreign" results in a complete failure of communication, and certainly a failure of freedom. Most important in the film, foreign existences move within, throughout, and beyond the human: they include women who are grotesque within the patriarchal frame, a vibrant and pulsing nature in which animals and plants morph with the human and attempt to communicate, and human bodies in the grips of excessive emotion and pain. I argue that the film tries to communicate a politics via Sadean, corporeal images of the aberrant, the grotesque, and the excessive. Von Trier's attempt at communication fails for those who read the film as misogynist, but if we follow Beauvoir's reading of Sade's "failed attempt at genuine communication" we may find something quite promising within the failure.

Drawing on *The Second Sex* in addition to Beauvoir's reading of Sade, I stage an encounter between von Trier and Beauvoir that invites us to examine how we feel (or fail to feel) under patriarchy as well as how we might feel our way beyond it.[3] I suggest *Antichrist* treats prevailing conventions and ideologies, including and especially patriarchy, as dead ends. In a fascination with the feminine, von Trier seizes on foreign existences such as the aberrant, the grotesque, and the excessive as his film urges us to feel our way toward something else.

THE ABERRANT: FAILED FEMININITY

James Joyce once remarked, I am the foolish author of a wise book. Perhaps von Trier is the misogynist author of a feminist film. —LINDSAY ZOLADZ, on *Melancholia*

In the hyperstylized series of black-and-white slow-motion images that open *Antichrist* and are marked as the prologue, explicit sexual images between HE (played by Willem Dafoe) and SHE (played by Charlotte Gainsbourg) are set against images of innocence and bourgeois normalcy, even beauty: a child's puzzle, a balloon carrying a teddy bear, clothes tumbling in the washing machine.[4] These parents have neglected their responsibilities: the baby monitor is off, the window is unlatched and blows open, SHE even plants her derriere on the child's puzzle while having sex. Left to his own devices, the cherubic child ably climbs out of his crib, past small iron icons of grief, pain, and despair (affects that also organize the chapters of the film), opens the child safety gate, witnesses his parents having sex, pushes a chair to the window, deliberately climbs up, pushes the little statues of grief, pain, and despair off the table, and toddles out onto the snowy ledge. The next event is predictable, horrific, or maybe even funny, depending on your perspective, but beautifully filmed and accompanied by a Handel aria.[5] Holding his teddy bear, the boy plunges to his death just as his mother climaxes and the clothes in the washer cease their tumbling.

The rest of the film (this was just the prologue!) might be read as exploring how SHE deals with her grief. In fact the whole film could be interpreted through this lens: Is her grief excessive? Is it mourning or melancholia? Is it some deformed sort of grieving assisted by witchcraft and the weird and wild agency of plants and animals? Is her commune with nature inspired by divine or supernatural revenge? Did she kill her child, intentionally or unintentionally, in a way that was prepared for by her dissertation topic on witchcraft and gynocide? Read as exclusively concerned with the aftermath of the child's death, however, the film is confined to a realism that affirms a return to or reconciliation with the norm. This is not my approach.[6]

What we can say for certain is that SHE is not the ideal mother. And within von Trier's film repertoire, SHE has plenty of company. Most recently von Trier's volume 2 of his 2013 film *Nymphomaniac* uses the same music from the prologue in *Antichrist*, Handel's aria ("Let me weep over my cruel fate and that I long for freedom!"), to transport viewers back to this original trauma. Provoking anxiety in viewers who are forced to remember the tragic events of *Antichrist*, our hearts beat faster as we watch another toddler venture out of his crib and onto a perilous ledge. His mother, Joe, is the nymphomaniac of the title (also played by Gainsbourg) who leaves her little son alone for hours night after night to visit a sadist sex club where she is whipped into sexual ecstasy by a man called K (Jamie Bell). An even more compromised mother than SHE, Joe leaves her husband and child—on Christmas Eve, no less—when given an ultimatum by her husband. Joe seems relieved, and later sexually ecstatic, to spend the sacred holiday getting whipped by K, who ceremoniously gives her the whip as a Christmas gift. It is marked with her new name, Fido.

Von Trier has several aberrant wives and mothers in his film repertoire, but unlike Selma (Björk) from *Dancer in the Dark*, for instance, or Bess (Emily Watson) from *Breaking the Waves*, SHE and the aberrant women from von Trier's "Depression" trilogy (*Antichrist*, 2009; *Melancholia*, 2011; and *Nymphomaniac*, 2013) do not become symbols of abnegation, sacrifice, or ultimate victimhood.[7] As Magdalena Zolkos (2011, 186) points out, von Trier moves beyond the trope of "sacralised femininities" in *Antichrist* to depict this heroine, SHE, as "free from the forms of self-victimizing and self-destructive love." Free of self-victimizing love, can women in patriarchy love at all?

Female characters whose love does not take the expected (demanded) form of self-abnegation and self-sacrifice, particularly when they are mothers, are generally depicted in film as freaks of nature.[8] In the *Film Quarterly* discussion of *Antichrist* between Rob White and Nina Power (2009), Power assumes that the son's death is the mother's fault. She cites specific images as evidence: "the helium balloon tantalizing Nic [the toddler] to reach for it, the baby monitor on silent, the reversed shoes, the windows opening twice to let in the acorns and let out her son." Power asks, "Is there anything more frightening than the idea that mothers may wish to commit infanticide?" Referencing von Trier's "fascination with female violence," Power argues that the film is a "fascinated yet horrified disquisition on the ambiguity of witchcraft." SHE is wracked by grief over the death of her son, but it is unclear whether SHE has deliberately or unconsciously contributed to his death or how that might have happened. As is true of von Trier's *Medea* (1988), the viewer of *Antichrist* is never certain about what motivates the action, and the meaning of tragic events shifts as our perspective shifts from one character to another.[9] SHE might be an irresponsible, possibly even evil or monstrous mother who intentionally cripples or even kills her own child(ren); SHE might be suffering from severe trauma; or like Medea, as well as Justine from *Melancholia*, SHE may be exacting or embracing a cosmic vengeance that will put the world right.[10] We are never quite sure.

Viewers are certain, though, that SHE's identity as a mother is unstable—if we limit the mother role to care, sacrifice, and maternal instinct. Von Trier's images indicate that SHE herself wonders what it means to be a mother, and this makes his viewers also question this role. SHE's self-perceived deviation from the socially mandated mother role and the guilt and grief that result from this (failing to be the mother who rejects her sexual desire, failing to obsess over her child's safety, failing all the requirements of standard bourgeois parenthood) manifest in her body's reactions. Von Trier uses images of distinct body parts and the body in pain to convey how these states of desperation *feel*. These images in *Antichrist* demonstrate SHE's intense feeling of grief and anxiety and provoke affective responses in the viewer. In this case von Trier's images force us to feel this mother's intense grief by capturing the spectator's sight, skin, and gut. Whatever the cause—loss of her son, guilt concerning her role in this loss, socially induced guilt and anxiety about not being the "right" kind of mother, or some combination—the psychic and physical grief is physically felt and seen in images of the body.

Gender roles seem to be reversed as the couple walk behind their son's small coffin: SHE looks masculine and stoic and HE is feminine and crying (figure 3.1).[11] But just after this SHE faints; SHE wails that it hurts, and that she wants to die too.

Following a conversation with her husband in which she accuses him of being "distant," "very, very distant," "indifferent as to whether [his] child is dead or alive," and accusing him of calling her thesis on misogyny "glib" and then making it seem to her that it was "glib, or even worse, a kind of lie," SHE wakes up with an anxiety attack.

First we see an image of a burned-out forest that we will later recognize as part of Eden. Immediately following this we see close-up grainy photos of her eye, her ear, her throat, her beating heart, her twitching fingers, her veins, and the back of her head (figures 3.2 and 3.3).

SHE wakes up, breathing hard, and HE tries to calm her by calling up another image: "Imagine you are blowing on your thistle blooms," HE says,

FIGURE 3.1. Walking behind their dead son's coffin in *Antichrist.*

and we see her, with her son in the background, doing so. SHE says, "This is physical! It's dangerous!" With her we feel what HE names as her symptoms: dizzy spells, dry mouth, distorted hearing, trembling, fast pulse, nausea.

Von Trier employs specific and searing images in his "Depression" trilogy, linking the corporeal experience of his heroines to their nonconformity to bourgeois femininity. In *Melancholia*, Justine (Kirsten Dunst) can barely suffer through what her family keeps telling her should be the happiest day of her life, her wedding day. In the slow-motion shots that are the film's prologue, we see a close-up of her face: her smile begins to form as dead birds rain down behind her (figure 3.4).

Another image from the prologue shows Justine in her wedding gown; this time she is walking through a forest, slowed by vines freakishly grabbing her ankles, the bottom of her dress pulled back by clinging vines as she struggles to move forward (figure 3.5).

In the first part of the film, at her wedding party, Justine's bodily comportment screams resistance: she oscillates between utter exhaustion and frenzied activity. Trying to act properly, the best she can muster at the party is to drink too much, disappear for long stretches, and act out or misbehave when she is (though she rarely is) present and accounted for.

Joe in *Nymphomaniac*, whom we will meet again in chapter 6, also struggles with patriarchy's demands. One of the most powerful and memorable images is of Joe frantically slapping her "cunt," desperate because she is not able to achieve orgasm. Note that Joe loses all sexual feeling when having sex not with numerous strangers but with her husband. Domesticity and love

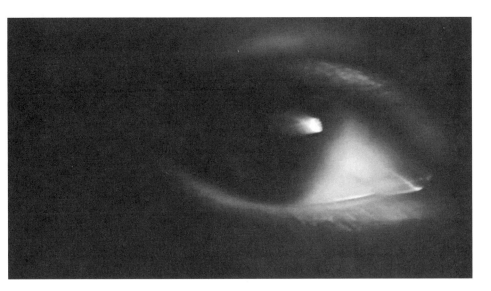

FIGURE 3.2. SHE's eye in *Antichrist.*

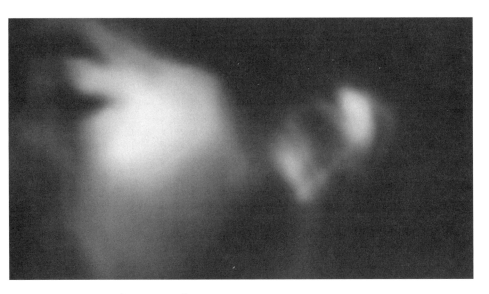

FIGURE 3.3. SHE's ear in *Antichrist.*

FIGURE 3.4. Justine with dead birds in *Melancholia*.

FIGURE 3.5. Justine and the clinging vines in *Melancholia*.

are the enemies of sensation; as soon as Joe falls in love, she loses her ability to have an orgasm. This is hardly peculiar to Joe; in *The Second Sex* Beauvoir cites too many instances to mention. Von Trier plays with this classic feminist trope to present Justine as an aberrant bride, Joe as an aberrant wife, and SHE as an aberrant mother. The roles—wife, mother, bride—are patriarchy's, but these women's habitations of them and their ways of being inhabited by them point elsewhere. Their bodily suffering and pathological symptoms (depression, melancholia, nymphomania, anxiety, fear) are linked to an inability or unwillingness to conform to society's bourgeois and patriarchal expectations.

Reading these images alongside the countless experiences of women documented by Beauvoir in *The Second Sex*, we may see that Beauvoir and von Trier are making a similar wager: readers and viewers can see and feel "private" or "personal" feelings as constructed by political and social contexts. Beauvoir directly connects women's affective ailments and psychic symptoms with patriarchal expectations around femininity. She brings attention to the figure of the melancholic woman by diagnosing the condition as a response to a particular situation. Take the following passage, for instance, which evokes the image of von Trier's vines pulling on Justine:

> The chains of marriage are heavy. . . . A wife has to find a way of coming to grips with a situation she cannot escape. Some, as we have seen, are puffed up with importance and become tyrannical matrons and shrews. Others take refuge in the role of the victim, they make themselves their husbands' and children's pathetic slaves and find a masochistic joy in it. Others perpetuate the narcissistic behavior we have described in relation to the young girl: they also suffer from not realizing themselves in any undertaking, and being able to do nothing, they are nothing; undefined, they feel undetermined and consider themselves misunderstood; they worship melancholy; they take refuge in dreams, playacting, illnesses, fads, scenes; they create problems around them or close themselves up in an imaginary world. ([1949] 2011, 515)

In another passage Beauvoir explicitly names lack of freedom ("empty freedom") as the instigator of the melancholy women often experience. Here freedom is the lost object women cannot identify. Beauvoir also diagnoses "worry" as a lack of freedom. "Worrying" because she is prevented from "doing" anything, she experiences "long, despondent ruminations" as the "specter of her own powerlessness" ([1949] 2011, 645–46). Beauvoir argues that, though at first the wife "lulls herself with illusions," eventually her "true feelings emerge" (519). Her feelings are a direct result of the loss of freedom:

"The home no longer protects her from her empty freedom; she finds herself alone, abandoned, a subject, and she finds nothing to do with herself. Affections and habits can still be of great help, but not salvation. All sincere women writers have noted this melancholy that inhabits the heart of 'thirty-year-old women'; this is a characteristic common to the heroines of Katherine Mansfield, Dorothy Parker, and Virginia Woolf" (519).

Beauvoir insistently associates affective behaviors and bodily experiences with societal expectations and values. She says, for example, that the young girl assumed to be "ashamed" of urinating in a squatting position and the male whose penis expresses his "pride" should make us examine our assumptions concerning "how the subject's aspirations can be embodied in an object" ([1949] 2011, 55). Affects appear on particular bodies, and individual people experience emotions and pathologies generated by social norms, but it is the failure of emotions to be located *solely* in a particular body or object that allows them to reproduce and generate the effects they do. In another example linking bodily affects with society's expectations, Beauvoir describes the "pathological melancholy" that some women feel after having an abortion as a feeling of guilt induced by the atmosphere of affects circulating in and through bodies that condemn the woman who makes this difficult choice (531).

While Beauvoir accumulates a multitude of women's experiences to force us to see the "truth" of women's lives beyond the myth of "Woman," von Trier goes even further in seeking to completely shatter expectations of what is normal. He unapologetically focuses his camera on women's intense experiences of joy, pain, grief, anger, cruelty, melancholy, violence, desperation, pleasure, humor, and ecstasy. If he is seen as a misogynist, that is because his refusal to look away from or remediate such feelings, his commitment to record and explore them, is mistaken for patriarchal pleasure rather than a critique of patriarchy's effects. But that risk, that we take pleasure in the cruelty we document, is endemic to such explorations. One piece of evidence in favor of reading von Trier as not only noticing and documenting but critiquing is the proximity he solicits between audiences and his women characters and the distance he generates from his men characters, in this case HE. Von Trier wants us to feel the women's suffering.

Images of SHE and her body parts encourage us to feel her bodily sensations, while images of HE maintain and increase the spectator's distance. Additionally, dialogue spoken by HE prompts either disgust or outright laughter. HE is clueless, misguided at best, or a rational methodical torturer at worst. Immediately following the close-up images of SHE's eye, throat, ear, fingers,

FIGURE 3.6. SHE at the toilet in *Antichrist*.

veins, and the back of her head, SHE initiates sex with HE. HE rebuffs her: "Never screw your therapist! Do the breathing." His next brilliant idea is to make a list of the things she fears. He seems to have forgotten, or never knew, that one key thing feared by mothers—the death of a child—has already occurred. SHE insists that she doesn't have a list: "Can't I just be afraid without a definite object?" Nina Power reads our distance from HE as von Trier's way to undermine "modern rationality" and "the flat use of technology." Rob White adds, "What a misfortune it would be to arrive in his consulting room!" As the film suggests, we have *all* arrived in his consulting room. In a subsequent series of images, we see SHE shaking, drinking, and writhing on the floor of the bathroom. Finally and desperately, she beats her head on the toilet seat (figure 3.6).

Power concludes, "The toilet she both bashes her head against and throws her pills down has the seat up, as if, for all his liberal caring humanism, he knows in the end it's a man's world." But it may not be for long. SHE warns her husband, "You're so damn arrogant! But this may not last—ever thought of that?"[12]

THE GROTESQUE: NATURE'S FEMININE

The woman who maintained her independence through all her servitudes will ardently love her own freedom in Nature. —SIMONE DE BEAUVOIR, *The Second Sex*

Highlighting the instability of marriage at this point of the film also highlights the instability of patriarchy as well as the instability of the categories and taxonomies in which it traffics and by which it is sustained. SHE as failed mother can be seen as a grotesque form of the feminine. Discussing the history of the grotesque in visual culture, Frances Connelly (2003, 2) argues that the "aberrant grotesque" exists as "the misshapen, ugly, exaggerated, or even formless": "This type runs the gamut from the deliberate exaggerations of caricature, to the unintended aberrations, accidents, and failures of the everyday world represented in realist imagery, to the dissolution of bodies, forms, and categories."[13] Rather than simply recirculating grotesque images to shore up "normal" categories or reinforce the importance of the human-culture over the animal-nature hierarchy, *Antichrist* plays with several cultural tropes, institutions, and ideas (the Church, Satan, evil, witches, femininity, masculinity, nature) to create rapturous foils, a grotesque practice that dislodges our sense of knowing, being, and feeling.

Thinking of *Antichrist* via the grotesque again brings Beauvoir and von Trier together. Beauvoir ([1949] 2011, 166) notes that male-created myths associate women not with nature generally but more specifically with "maternal darkness, a cave, an abyss, a hell." Thus she alerts us to *Antichrist*'s images of the female grotesque: these images refuse the conflation of female sexual organs with the cave, abyss, and complete darkness. For von Trier female sexuality and immanence do not threaten the abyss; they instead direct us toward what Beauvoir calls the existence of "foreign realities." At the very least his images show our world as much stranger than previously realized, and this portrayal of the natural world's generative creativity and inexhaustible novelty has several notable effects. It challenges an anthropocentric bias, showing nature as animated, vibrant, verdant, changing, pulsing, and breathing. The images defy our expectations and make us question our knowledge by showing nature as distorted, communicative, merging death and life, and always encroaching on "culture." Most important, *Antichrist* depicts women in special communication with the natural world. Indeed several of von Trier's films depict women conversing and merging with immanent features of the natural world not formerly seen or noticed and rarely recorded this way in film.

FIGURE 3.7. SHE turning green in *Antichrist*.

FIGURE 3.8. Justine and the lily pads in *Melancholia*.

FIGURE 3.9. SHE masturbating in nature in *Antichrist*.

FIGURE 3.10. Justine bathing in the light of the aberrant planet in *Melancholia*.

FIGURE 3.11. Young Joe lying in a field in *Nymphomaniac.*

FIGURE 3.12. Young Joe lifted to the heavens by her orgasm in *Nymphomaniac.*

When SHE and HE go to Eden, traveling there by train, *Antichrist* gets significantly weirder and wilder. On the train HE begins a series of cognitive-behavioral therapy exercises designed to help her face her fears. HE wants her to touch and feel the woods as her source of fear, to somehow overcome fear via proximity. In the first exercise HE initiates on the train, they begin work "on her expectations" by having her imagine her approach to Eden. SHE speaks as the viewer encounters several images. Crossing the bridge (where everything looks dead; it's shot in black and white, and there is no greenery),

SHE says, "It's evening. No birds can be heard. Darkness comes early down here. . . . I walk into it. . . . [There is the] old fox hole, among the trees. . . . [It should be] easy passing, and yet, it's like walking through mud. . . . The trunk is thick. The tree rots so slowly. It has some strange kind of personality. I've always felt that." As SHE approaches Eden in her imagination, HE directs her to lie down on the tall grass, to "melt into the green," to "just turn green." Color suddenly emerges: we see her full body in the grass, facing the sky, eyes closed, and then SHE disappears, slowly absorbed into the grass (figure 3.7).

This image of a woman supine against a natural backdrop is one von Trier also employs in *Melancholia* and *Nymphomaniac*. Indeed the main poster image for *Melancholia* is of Justine in her wedding dress, evoking Ophelia drowning: lying on her back in the water, holding a bouquet of flowers, veil flowing behind her head, against a natural green background (grass, lily pads, moss; figure 3.8).[14]

Nature is linked to female sexuality and its immanent, possibly evil features in several images of this type. In *Antichrist*, after begging HE to hit her during sex, when HE does not comply SHE masturbates outdoors lying in a field (figure 3.9). Strange noises accompany her self-arousal, and later, when HE joins her, hitting her over and over, SHE speaks in Latin and we glimpse distorted surreal bodies and hands surrounding her head. In *Melancholia* we see Justine bathing in the light of the aberrant planet Melancholia, her face portraying enchantment, pleasure, maybe even sexual feeling or contentment (figure 3.10). And in *Nymphomaniac*, Joe tells Seligman (played by Stellan Skarsgård) about a spontaneous orgasm when she was younger and lying in a field (figure 3.11). We see the orgasm literally lift her above the ground toward the heavens (figure 3.12).

These images encourage viewers to join the unleashed power of female pleasure with nature, the cosmos, immanence.[15] These may or may not have to do with evil but, importantly, they have nothing to do with nothingness or the abyss. Lack of feeling is not generally the female complaint for von Trier's heroines, although he also notices "ugly feelings" (Ngai 2005) such as anxiety, boredom, and anger that invade when patriarchy shuts down the possibility for women's sexual freedom. For von Trier's women characters, just as for Beauvoir's women, the point is that feeling is not derived from patriarchy's usual delivery systems. Note how Beauvoir ([1949] 2011, 657) describes free women's commune with nature: "Slave to her husband, children, and home, she finds it intoxicating to be alone, sovereign on the hillside; she is no longer spouse, mother, housewife, but a human being; she contemplates the passive world: and she recalls that she is a whole consciousness, an irreducible free-

FIGURE 3.13. Deer with dead fetus in *Antichrist*.

FIGURE 3.14. Fox with its innards exposed in *Antichrist*.

dom. In front of the mystery of water and the mountain summit's thrust, male supremacy is abolished; walking through the heather, dipping her hand in the river, she lives not for others but for herself."

"Sovereign on the hillside"! What better captures von Trier's images? Von Trier knows what Beauvoir is talking about: living for themselves, absorbing nature's power, gives women new feelings of freedom and maybe supports new forms of agency or even a grotesque form of sovereignty. In *Antichrist* SHE seems to absorb and redirect the power of nature even though nature initially frightened her. (When pressed, SHE told HE that the woods was a place she feared, but viewers do not know why.) The film might be described as increasingly grotesque as it pits the impotent rational aggression of HE against the increasing desire for revenge and retribution on the part of SHE in collaboration with nature and its powers, once HE and SHE settle in at Eden. Von Trier's grotesque images, almost always feminized, permeate the consciousness and imagination of the viewer and challenge our sense of certainty in perception. The images are surreal and impossible: they breach the boundaries between human and nonhuman, death and life, nature and civilization, reality and fantasy, divine and secular. Trees blend with human bodies and communicate with SHE; HE spots a fox losing its innards and a deer staring out at us with a dead fetus hanging from its body (figures 3.13 and 3.14); the same raven reappears again and again in spite of what should have been more than enough violence to cause its death; an eagle eats its own offspring that have fallen or been pushed out of the nest.

Von Trier makes it clear that nature does not underwrite the maternal bond: in nature the young die too, sometimes at the hand of their mother. He insists that the maternal is not natural, but his images also prompt viewers to reconsider the lines between what is real and what is fantastical, and to question the limits, methods, and possibilities of communication—between humans, between humans and animals, even between humans and acorns or humans and trees, given that SHE can "feel the tree's strange personality." We also further question what we can know and control, as events and grotesque images challenge our ability to process them. And sometimes the images are simply funny.

When HE asks SHE to touch, feel, and blend with nature as part of the therapeutic process, HE gets more than HE bargained for. The nature HE is thinking of can be known, controlled, enjoyed in bits, safely kept at bay. In this HE is just like Claire's husband (played by Kiefer Sutherland), John, in *Melancholia*, with his telescope and his confident citations of scientists and their predictions. John will be proven wrong, and so will HE. In the mind of

FIGURE 3.15. HE's hand covered with lichen in *Antichrist*.

HE there is a clear demarcation between the cabin and the woods, but as the film progresses, this line is breached not only for her but for him too, in spite of his best rational efforts. When SHE tells him she understands a new reality, that she knows "everything that used to be beautiful was perhaps hideous" and that she can now hear "the cry of all the things that are about to die," HE responds, "It would all be very touching if it were a children's book, but acorns don't cry, you know that as well as I do. Thoughts distort reality, not the other way around."

But HE's thoughts do not protect him from reality. The (in)famous talking fox delivers the message "Chaos reigns" to HE, not to SHE. Nature encroaches on the cabin from the moment of their arrival at Eden, looking progressively more deformed and frightening to HE. Indeed male hysteria sets in![16] HE is visibly disconcerted by the sound of acorns hitting the ceiling. It is SHE who must assure her husband, "It's just the stupid acorns." In the next shot we see his hand out the window covered with lichen (figure 3.15).

HE is horror-struck as he pulls his hand in and picks off the lichen, drawing blood. HE slams the window shut, but this does not keep the danger at bay. Immediately after this HE forces SHE to set her feet down on the grass (and here the viewer sees the grass pulsing, vibrating, and deeply weird) to conquer her fears. At the same time we see birds falling from the trees and a baby bird covered with ants, left to a raven for its feast. Death and danger are everywhere. SHE concludes, "Nature is Satan's Church." But the next morning SHE proclaims her good health: "I'm cured! You're so clever! I'm fine!" Just after her announcement of good health, HE sees something shaking in the distance and, walking forward, parts the grass to reveal the bleeding, talking fox.

The pronouncement "Chaos reigns," uttered by the self-eating and talking fox, takes on meaning as the narrative progressively links nature, immanence, the cosmos, and all that we cannot know or control with the feminine, particularly in the mind of SHE but also in the increasing worries of HE, and this in spite of the fact that worrying is what *women* do, as Beauvoir observes. When SHE proclaims that she is cured, viewers may well wonder where the film is headed. It is an ironic, even humorous moment, and we note the sarcasm in her voice when she chirps, "You're so clever!" Doubting her restoration to full health, HE continues the exercises, this time playing the role of nature (SHE calls him MR. NATURE). The therapy session culminates in the discovery that what SHE learned from her thesis on gynocide and witch burnings is that "female nature" is the "nature of all the sisters"; "women do not control their own bodies; nature does." HE is horrified by this conclusion: "The literature you discovered in your books was about evil conducted against women, but you read it as the proof of evil *of* women. You were supposed to be critical, that was your thesis, but instead you embrace it! Do you know what you're saying?"

THE EXCESSIVE: CRUSHING THE DICK

It's tiring to kill a man! —Charlotte Rampling's character Sarah Norton in FRANÇOIS OZON, *Swimming Pool*

The naïve liberal humanism of HE, summed up by his patronizing condemnation of the evils committed against women, will not go unpunished. Viewing this interaction between SHE and HE, we are struck by how abstractions such as bourgeois morality, humanism, and faith in progressive politics exact their own forms of violence, often most forcefully on female bodies. Beauvoir and von Trier share a similar sensibility in rejecting such abstractions in ethics and politics. In her essay on Sade we learn that Beauvoir is most attracted to Sade's total rejection of bourgeois conventions, the empty and meaningless clichés and comforts this ideology promises, and the violent forms it takes. She suggests Sade "chose the imaginary," rejecting the "blandness and ennui of virtue," exiting "this world, both boring and threatening, which offered him nothing of value; he would go seek his truth elsewhere" ([1952] 2012, 49–51).

In *Antichrist* the images of violence to genitals, of the abuse of HE and the self-abuse of SHE, and of SHE burning at the stake, all have been remarked upon as the most misogynist of the film, paralleling those analyses of Sade that reduce his literature to pornography, misogyny, or misanthropy. Much of the action of the last parts of the film involve SHE trying to kill HE, or at least make him suffer horribly, by using the tools of patriarchal masculinity—saws, hammers, giant metal objects—to sever his body parts, and then her own. In some of the more horrifying (or maybe funny) parts, SHE crushes HE's penis and buries him alive. Maybe, contra Audre Lorde, the master's tools can be used to dismantle the master's house, after all? Although SHE does not succeed in killing HE (as Ozon's script declares, "it's tiring to kill a man"), and although SHE is crucified at the end, we might see the film as pointing beyond patriarchy and beyond a reading of the ending as a scene of female "punishment."[17]

Most critics disagree and see *Antichrist* as affirming the ultimate tyranny of reasonable men over evil and crazy women. One critic describes the film as confronting "the director's intertwined fears of primal nature and female sexuality"; another, more vehemently, says the film is "like having bad sex with someone you loathe—a hideous combination of sheer boredom and disgust"; another says, "It's pretty damning about the whole of human nature, and, of course, the woman gets it in the end; of all the to-dos you could have, there's a demonized mother, [and] a witch who seems to prioritize her own sexual fulfillment over the safety of her child."[18] At the end of the film, after their battle with a drill, saw, scissors, shovel, grindstone, wrenches, and large pieces of metal used as weapons to mutilate both bodies, HE burns SHE at the stake as though she were a witch. These powerful, unrealistic, grotesque images of extreme and excessive acts of violence on the body have led many to conclude that when HE suffocates and strangles SHE and then burns her to death, the tyranny of men over women and nature is rightfully reestablished or reclaimed. However, I think these grotesque images of nature, the body, and women exceed such reclamation. They do not simply return us to misogyny and business as usual. They are not so easily recovered. They stay with us and press us to reconsider not only our values but also our usual forms and means of political association.

Readers of *The Second Sex* might expect Beauvoir to categorize Sade as the kind of male writer who replicates myths of women as solely immanent and trapped in their body, while casting men as capable of transcendence and sovereignty. Beauvoir considers this reading, but she does not develop it.[19] Nor does she allow the body to become a merely incidental occasion of or metaphor for a more abstract politics, as do those who treat Sade as ironizing the social contract with his consent-based practices of cruelty. Beauvoir is attracted to Sade's writings precisely because of the fact that his politics begin and end with the body. She sees the body's centrality in Sade, and in particular the body's centrality to his politics, and she works to keep it the focus of attention in her reading. In his insistent focus on the body, in particular on the body in excess and pain, Beauvoir's Sade critiques bourgeois normalcy and moves us to feel something different or to experience feeling differently. Sade's writing thus exceeds the categories of horror or pornography. While it may provide pleasure for the voyeur, it also provokes us to feel in a context where feeling is subjected to the deadening force of the conventional. Beauvoir ([1952] 2012, 54) writes, "One must truly misunderstand Sade to be surprised that instead of requesting a post as a commissary of the people in the provinces, which would have enabled him to torture and kill, he was discredited by his humanity. Do we imagine that Sade 'loved blood' as one loves the mountains or the sea? 'To make blood flow' was an act whose significance for him could be exalting in certain circumstances; but what he essentially required of cruelty was that both singular individuals and his own existence be revealed to him at once as consciousness and freedom and as flesh."

What especially captivates Beauvoir in Sade's images of violence, sexuality, corporeality, and bodies in pain is what also captivates us in von Trier's images in *Antichrist*: it is the way certain images and depictions of sexuality and corporeality deploy and then shatter our expectations of horror and suffering to capture another possible dimension of human connection exceeding ideology.[20] It is this method of mingling, the particular practice of interaction through bodies, and Sade's elevation of what is traditionally considered vile, filthy, or disgusting, breaking all taboos, that captures Beauvoir's ([1952] 2012, 63) attention: "Beauty is too simple; we grasp it with an intellectual judgment that does not tear consciousness from its solitude or the body from its indifference. Instead of being degraded by vileness, the man who has commerce with filth, like the one who wounds or is wounded, realizes himself as flesh; and in his wretchedness and his humiliation he becomes an abyss where the spirit is engulfed and where separate individuals are joined." In Beauvoir's reading, sexuality and violence—or the commingling of bodies via their permeability in corporeality—is for Sade the only true way to community, and hence the only way to politics. This is in part a critique of other promised but false ways to community. Sade's heroes and heroines do not attempt to get lost in immanence just for a moment of sexual ecstasy. Rather they see these moments as the only true moments of existence.

We see, then, that in Beauvoir's ([1952] 2012, 73) hands Sade's writing becomes proto-existential: "He opened for us, with surprising depth, insights into the relationship between sexuality and existence." But even so Beauvoir ultimately says that Sade's writing replicates troubling versions of sovereignty, tyranny, and aristocratic individuality: "He considered the outcome he chose for himself to be valid for all, and at the exclusion of any other outcome" (73). She concludes that Sade's work gets trapped in the logic of sovereignty that risks inauthenticity, disavows ambiguity, and affirms tyranny and abuse.

Beauvoir ([1952] 2012, 73) is also critical of some technical aspects of Sade's literature, such as his setting the scenes outside of time and place: "Not only do the orgies to which he invites us take place nowhere, in no time, but what is even more serious, no persons are brought into play. The victims are frozen in their tearful abjection, the torturers in their frenzy. Sade complacently dreams himself in them rather than lending them his living depth." She adds, "The debauches that Sade presents in minute detail systematically exhaust the anatomical possibilities of the human body rather than uncovering its singular affective complexes" (73). *Antichrist* may be said to suffer from the same flaws, but there they are potentially generative and creative rather than restrictive. Here von Trier may have something to teach Beauvoir. Like Sade's novels, von Trier's films most often negate place, time, and identity. HE and SHE are types rather than individuals; Eden is the post-Genesis woods where HE and SHE discover that evil resides not outside us but within us and is resurrected in the female form. This could be any moment, any wooded venue, any male and female interacting in mythical time and space. More recently *Nymphomaniac* too has been criticized for not situating characters in time and place. One critic says, for example, "Disconcertingly, *Nymphomaniac* lacks any sense of period or place. At times, we seem to be in early 70s Britain. However, the alleyway in which Joe is beaten up is obviously a studio set. So is Seligman's barely furnished apartment. The accents of the main characters do nothing to clarify matters. As Jerome, Joe's first lover, Shia LaBoeuf speaks with a Dick van Dyke–like English accent while Skarsgård still has a middle-European ring to his voice."[21] Disconcerting, yes. But is that a bad thing? One critic says that in *Antichrist* time is canceled and "we are in absolute or immediate time," which is "typical of the devil. . . . [The] birth-giving deer, the self-destructive fox, as well as the eternally returning raven all belong to the Dionysiac-cyclical understanding of time, which threatens chronological-linear time" (Thomsen 2009, 5). But rather than simply replace linear with cyclical time, von Trier may be doing something else. It could be that the abstraction from context brings the realities of foreign existences more clearly into view. What possibilities are opened by the vertiginous sense of placelessness and timelessness? Maybe the lack of firm place helps keep the focus on the body as the only emplacement we can identify. It may in fact be part of what makes the body so central.

FEELING OUR WAY BEYOND PATRIARCHY

There is a whole region of human experience that the male deliberately chooses to ignore because he fails to think it: this experience, the woman lives it. —SIMONE DE BEAUVOIR, *The Second Sex*

The final scene in *Antichrist* is of HE limping out of the woods, passing by the dead tree, collecting berries, and then noticing the deer, the fox, and the raven materialize out of the woods, completely innocent and normal-looking now, as a flock of faceless women in black and white images gather around him. The Handel aria that accompanied the prologue also marks the end. HE is the last man standing after a battle to the death, but is he triumphant? As I suggested earlier, the images von Trier generates in this film are not so easily reclaimed. We might notice that he has failed to leave this feral fecund hellscape behind to reclaim masculine order; instead HE brings some sisters along with him who have terrified and unsettled masculine boundaries.[22] When critics interpret the end of the film as affirming HE's triumph or as SHE getting her comeuppance, we have to wonder what motivates this moral of the story when all along the film draws our sympathy and perspective to her. How do we end up in HE's shoes?

In a statement called "Director's Confessions," von Trier says the following about the making of *Antichrist*:

> The work on the script did not follow my usual modus operandi. Scenes were added for no reason. Images were composed free of logic or dramatic thinking. They often came from dreams I was having at the time, or dreams I'd had earlier in my life.
>
> Once again, the subject was "Nature," but in a different and more direct way than before. In a more personal way.
>
> The film does not contain any specific moral code and only has what some might call "the bare necessities" in the way of a plot.[23]

We might conclude that if there is no moral code, there is no moral. With Beauvoir we are invited to see that von Trier is not asking us to condone violence but is instead exposing the regularity and invisibility of everyday systemized violence by forcing us to witness its excessive forms. It appears from the film that the only way to make a connection with another human being under patriarchy is by entering into extreme situations or by inflicting the most horrific forms of violence on the body. It is as if this is the only thing that will make us feel again or anew. But this is less a comment on us than on the ideological apparatus in question, which is unfeeling and deadens feeling.

What we know from the film is that our current existence is bankrupt. All that we regularly assume to be possible, real, and worth preserving is challenged or discredited. While Beauvoir says that we must keep working toward freedom in spite of (almost certain) failure, von Trier makes us confront the deadening effects and affects of this world without promising another. But as I have shown, the spectator is drawn to SHE's perspective throughout the film; HE is discredited, mocked, and shown to be insensitive, patronizing, and controlling. From SHE's point of view, we see the world differently than ever before. Our "normal" sensibility is shattered and opened up for possible renewal. With SHE we feel the tree's strange personality, we sense the intentions of acorns, and we feel a conflicted desire for both revenge against and communion with the husband who crushes her creativity and threatens to leave her completely alone and bereft.

The precipitating event for the film's action, the responsibility for and meaning of the death of the child, remains a mystery. We see that mothers are not always self-sacrificing and they sometimes enjoy sex. But notice that SHE is at exactly the age when Beauvoir says women stop enjoying sex with their husband and start to wonder what the hell is going on in their marriage. Maybe the death of the child is a metaphor for the death of feeling wrought by bourgeois marriage. Or maybe SHE is saved from the death of feeling by the death of her child, which introduces a swerve into her patriarchal life trajectory. Or maybe she willed her child to die. Willing does not mean wanting, however: in patriarchal culture, mothering and authoring, mothering and sex, are incompatible. But the film suggests they are not incompatible as such.

Whatever the meaning of the child's death, our couple finds it impossible to grieve together. They turn on each other, but not in the usual ways. Just before her vicious demise, strangulation at the hands of her husband, SHE drills holes into HE's leg to attach a grindstone and sexually mutilates him, crushing his penis. Later SHE masturbates with HE's limp hand. Weeping, SHE remembers sex with her husband as her boy fell to his death, and then she begs him to hold her as she cuts off her clitoris.

Why crush the dick and cut off the clitoris? The questions cannot be answered in only one way. But Beauvoir and von Trier suggest that we must get past the usual, prescribed pleasures of bourgeois family and heteronormative sex. These body parts, that is to say, stand for the cruel promises that bind us to regimes of unfeeling and the death of real sensation. Ironically these are the body parts most invested with the idea of sensation. But remembering what we have learned from Beauvoir, we may see how *Antichrist* moves us to want to feel our way, in solidarity with SHE and von Trier's other suffering and vengeful heroines, beyond patriarchy.

PART II. ALLIES
ANTINOMIES OF ACTION IN CONDITIONS OF VIOLENCE

The two chapters on enemies, read in the context of Beauvoir's textual encounters with enemies in "Right-Wing Thought Today" and *The Second Sex*, alert us to the material bases and affective motivations of ideology and the way ideologies themselves motivate affects and change material conditions; they also warn us of the very real and too proximate possibility that violence can erupt at any time, is unpredictable, and cannot be controlled. Beauvoir and Arendt are resolute in stressing that in spite of the fact that Brasillach's and Eichmann's actions played out at some distance from the actual killing machines of the Holocaust, they need to be held responsible and face execution for what they did and didn't do: for their role in the death of millions of human beings. Sade and von Trier do not allow us to turn away from what the destruction of bodies looks and feels like. There is pleasure in violence, a deeply erotic lure of its power and danger that cannot be ignored if we are to think honestly about political affective histories of violence and their effect on bodies, nations, and psyches.

Chapter 4 takes up the task of distinguishing among physical, structural, linguistic, and intimate forms of political violence, but by putting Beauvoir in conversation with Frantz Fanon, I am most interested in exploring how the violence(s) of language, geography, and mandated activity (labor, housework) shape bodies, physically and psychically. Products of colonial, patriarchal, and intimate histories of violence, different political subjects even have diverse experiences of time, space, and their relationship to history.

Because Beauvoir prioritizes encounter as the site and space of freedom, and because encounters always involve risk, she does not think violence can be completely eliminated from our lives, although she insists that we should organize politically in ways that will likely minimize it. She stops short of saying that we can disentangle violence from politics; for her even intimate relations are indelibly marked by violence, and she cannot point to a relationship that escapes the dynamic of power, where violence is always lurking. While careful to mark their differences, Beauvoir sees all forms of violence as political; it is the regrettable but inevitable result of struggles over interpreting a contingent and shifting reality and attempts to control our place in it. Here she would disagree with Arendt, who claims that violence marks the end of politics, as well as with scholars who argue that violence *could* be eliminated from politics were we to see its ontology as itself contingent and historical (see, e.g., Oksala 2012). Contrarily Beauvoir goes so far as to say that the oppressed, and those on the side of the oppressed, are justified in the instrumental use of violence when it opens up the future, even though it can never be contained or controlled and might involve doing violence to others (see "Antinomies of Action" in Beauvoir 1948).

Chapter 4 begins by recounting the situation in which the conversation between Fanon and Beauvoir began, in the midst of urgent questions and mounting tensions over France's colonial war in Algeria. In addition to the proxy wars precipitated by the power struggle between the United States and the Soviet Union, it was the French wars in Morocco, Tunisia, and Algeria that moved Beauvoir ([1963] 1992, 330) and the *Les Temps Modernes* group to try to articulate "distinctions between our real allies and our adversaries in this new 'Left.'"[1] This new Left, as she calls it, "was proposing to remodel capitalism and colonialism in order to bring them into line with a new technocracy: really no more than a right wing policy with a face lift" (330). Algeria, a heavily settled colony, was far more difficult than either Morocco or Tunisia for the French to relinquish, even for Camus, who was unable to support Algerian national sovereignty.[2] The situation, particularly the cruelty, injustice, and bloody consequences of French policy, specifically the use of torture and terrorism, caused Beauvoir enormous grief. She says, "It was not of my own free will, nor with any lightness of heart, that I allowed the war in Algeria to invade my thoughts, my sleep, my every mood" (377). When she was asked by Djamila Boupacha's lawyer in 1961 to intervene on Boupacha's behalf, Beauvoir was eager to seize an opportunity to speak out on the case of a female Algerian militant raped by French soldiers.

Emboldened by the scene of SHE crushing HE's penis and cutting off her own clitoris, we can imagine the scene of Boupacha's rape: a bottle forced into her vagina by a French officer representing colonial and patriarchal power. In the *Le Monde* article that Beauvoir wrote to bring public attention to the case, she was forced to change the word *vagina* to *womb* so as not to scandalize readers, as if the revelation of the torture was not itself scandalous. She was also asked to excise the line "Djamila was a virgin," which she refused to do, knowing that this was a significant fact for a young Muslim woman.[3]

The day after the editorial was published (June 3, 1960), Beauvoir received a death threat. The next year brought violent demonstrations in France, assassination attempts against members of the French Left (French extremists planted a bomb above Sartre's apartment, at 42 rue Bonaparte, in early January 1962, causing a huge explosion), and increasing violence in Algeria. Sarah Bakewell (2016) reports that it was a miracle no one was hurt in the explosion in Sartre's apartment building, and although Camus was worried about his mother in Algeria, it was Sartre who now had to worry about his mother, as she lived with him and hence was suddenly in danger too. Nevertheless, "Sartre did not let the attack stop his campaigning: he and Beauvoir continued to speak at demonstrations, write articles, and give evidence in support of those accused of terrorist activity" (277). Beauvoir writes in *Force of Circumstance* that in the chaos and worry of all this violence they learned that Fanon was dead. Claude Lanzmann received a cable from Josie Fanon, who wrote from Washington, DC, where Fanon was being treated for his leukemia. Beauvoir ([1963] 1992, 621) gravely recounts, "Fanon had lived every moment of his death and savagely refused to accept it; his aggressive sensitivity had cast off all restraint in his deathbed fantasies; he loathed the Americans, all racists in his eyes, and distrusted the entire hospital staff."

Tragically Fanon died surrounded by those he considered his enemies. With Fanon in chapter 4, Beauvoir asks whether, how, and under what conditions suffering and wounded bodies might join together to challenge enemies rather than turning on each other or inadvertently acting out perverse protests in the form of bodily symptoms. I return to the question of how to redirect what Beauvoir calls "perverse forms of protest" in chapter 6, but first I ask, through Beauvoir's encounter with Richard Wright, how we might, as Beauvoir puts it, make "distinctions between our real allies and our adversaries" and whether allies have to look like ourselves.

Chapter 5 recalls Beauvoir's four-month visit to the United States in 1947, marvelously documented in her (philosophical and chatty, always insightful) travel diary, *America Day by Day* ([1948] 2000). She had met Wright in Paris and was "delighted" to see him again. Wright hosted her in New York City, taking her to the Savoy in Harlem, where she saw his "friendship, his presence at my side, [a]s a kind of absolution" after her solitary walk through Harlem, where she felt the color of her eyes signified "injustice, arrogance, and hatred" (36–37). She was worried that her body and even the color of her eyes, a feature usually unnoticed (and mostly not politicized), might draw suspicion in Harlem and make her into an enemy. In an uncharacteristic move, Beauvoir refuses the encounter. She says, "I'm white, whatever I say and do, this curse weighs on me. . . . I dare not smile at the children in the squares; I don't feel I have the right to stroll in the streets" (36).

But Wright became her ally, and he accompanied her all over the city—to the Abyssinian Baptist Church, where the sermon was led by Adam Clayton Powell, to the Bowery, to flophouses, and through Greenwich Village, where Wright lived with his wife and daughter. Discouraged by the entrenchment of racism in the United States, Wright and his family moved to France later in 1947, where he and Beauvoir deepened their friendship and continued their conversations about writing, race, violence, gender, colonization, and family, until Wright's death at the age of fifty-two in 1960. There is no question that Beauvoir considered Fanon and Wright to be "real allies," and they probably felt the same, even though Beauvoir was far more eager to transform or alter her thinking (as well as cite their influence on her) than they were. Informed by Beauvoir's thinking with Fanon on pathological behaviors, ugly feelings, and the way identities emerge as much from wounds and deep scars as from autonomy or agency, her conversation with Wright on the history of racial violence in America, the decolonization struggle in Ghana, and the adoption of *négritude* as a potentially liberating political strategy is motivated by one of the questions that haunts *The Second Sex*: Why do women not say *we*? What Beauvoir hopes for is not only that women will learn to say *we* (I return to this central problematic in Beauvoir's thought in part III, "Friends") but also that women will seek encounters with potential allies, both like and unlike ourselves. Beauvoir and Wright's conversation takes us some distance along that road.

VIOLENCE, PATHOLOGIES, AND
RESISTANCE IN FRANTZ FANON

In June 1960 Beauvoir published a short editorial in *Le Monde* titled "In De-fense of Djamila Boupacha." Boupacha, a female Algerian militant accused of planting a bomb, was tortured and raped by French officials in an effort to extract a confession. Although there was extensive evidence in France of the use of torture as a systematic practice, as well as the increasing militancy and resistance of the Algerian population, the French chose to ignore their complicity in the organized violence of colonization. Beauvoir, who at this time was quite well known and well regarded in French intellectual circles, put these issues center stage in her public intervention into Boupacha's case.

Frantz Fanon, originally from Martinique, had been documenting the specific harms and violence of colonization since 1952, when he published *White Skin, Black Masks* in France. Continuing this work via an appoint-ment as a psychoanalyst at the Blida Clinic in Algiers, Fanon joined the Al-gerian resistance and published his observations and analysis of the war in *A Dying Colonialism* (1959) and *The Wretched of the Earth* (1963). Fanon worked closely with Sartre (who wrote the preface to *Wretched of the Earth*) and met Beauvoir and Sartre in Italy in 1961. Beauvoir ([1963] 1992, 318–19) remarks in her autobiography *Force of Circumstance* that she was particularly struck by Fanon's observation that "all political leaders should be psychiatrists," and her impression that although he was ill with leukemia, he was so passionately alive.

In *What Fanon Said*, Lewis R. Gordon (2015, 32) laments Fanon's "failure to articulate his indebtedness to Beauvoir." I bring Beauvoir and Fanon into the same space in this chapter as a way to extend the conversations they were already having and to acknowledge the interconnections in fighting oppression within colonial, patriarchal, raced, and classed networks of power. Noting that Beauvoir and Fanon were already in conversation, even if not explicitly, about the many and related aspects of the structural violence of colonialism, in this chapter I read their work together regarding female agency and the highly publicized case of Boupacha. I then return to certain key sections of *The Second Sex* to read these insights in conjunction with *The Wretched of the Earth*. I am interested in illuminating passages in Fanon that concern ordinary and widespread practices of embodied violence and thinking of these with Beauvoir's focus on pathological and symptomatic behaviors of women under patriarchy.

In *The Wretched of the Earth*, published two years after his premature death, Fanon ([1963] 2004) argues that violence directed against the colonizers is a redemptive reversal of the symptomatic practices of violence that the colonized typically direct toward each other. Repetitive and ecstatic ritualistic practices, and even the symptoms of melancholy, are redirected to a higher purpose in the anticolonial struggle, wherein the colonized turn the violence away from themselves and toward their oppressors. *The Wretched of the Earth* documents the violence that colonization exacts on the colonized (and even the colonizers in making them unreflective and brutal masters) while also instancing multiple examples of successful resistance. Reading *The Wretched of the Earth*, one undoubtedly feels that the time and prerogative of the colonizers is over, history is changing, and freedom will be seized.

Beauvoir also is attentive to embodied pathologies that women experience under patriarchy, but unlike Fanon she mostly does not identify these practices as potential sites of liberation. According to Beauvoir, many women try but fail to find their freedom through these bad-faith practices, such as the repetitive rituals of housework or women's impoverished relationship to time, that encourage them to more fully embrace alienated forms of femininity. Unlike Fanon, Beauvoir does not see a way to link these behaviors to collective forms of resistance other than to encourage encounters, through her writings, among potential female readers of her text. This is a literary-political technique I introduced in chapter 1 and to which I return in more detail in chapter 7, on feminist friendship.

With Fanon and Beauvoir I ask whether and how what they both identify as alienated embodied practices might become sites of critical, although limited and contradictory, agency. In my analysis of von Trier's *Antichrist* we saw how images of body parts—violated sexual body parts, and grotesque figures that signal the presence of what Beauvoir calls "foreign existences"—are utilized to move film spectators toward critical affective encounters. In this chapter, I ask what Fanon's and Beauvoir's attention to oppression's marks on the body might portend for thinking about resistance and freedom. Read with Fanon's insights on redirecting pathological violence, Beauvoir's extensive writing on women's situation in regard to repetition and the particularly oppressive effects of time on women's bodies under patriarchy takes on new and different meanings. Thinking of the simultaneity of repressive and generative power, we might uncover the experiences of those who are relatively powerless as still expressing forms of dissent that could potentially be mobilized for fuller political agency. I hope to open up new ways to read the symptoms caused by what, in 1955, Aimé Césaire called "colonial trauma," and what I would expand to call patriarchal and colonial trauma, as varieties of dissent.

One goal of this chapter is to notice how Fanon and Beauvoir see oppression as expressed somatically in repetition, melancholy, and a relationship to time as immanent, contingent, and unable to be fully known and controlled. Though they each cautiously explore psychoanalytic explanations for pathological embodied symptoms, Fanon and Beauvoir share a criticism of forms of metaphysics and metatheories that impose a predetermined meaning on obscure events experienced immanently. Rather than adopt psychoanalysis wholesale as a narrative explaining the hidden meanings of action and the unfolding of one's life, their existentialist lens orients them, each differently, to be attuned to theorizing experience as it is lived: as disjointed, irrational, and nonlinear. Additionally they orient us to a collective rather than simply an individual unconscious and describe it as unfolding within and shaped by material and social circumstances. Finally, each brings our attention to the fact that collective psychic wounds appearing on individual bodies (many a result of these metatheoretical narratives) are revealed and repeated in behavior and affects.

While sharing these insights in common, however, the two thinkers differ on several counts. Reading Fanon with the help of Beauvoir encourages us to imagine the anticolonial subjectivity and revolutionary activity of women and locate the individual woman against the masses. Beauvoir also helps us see why embracing freedom in encounter by acknowledging ambiguity helps us to temper hubristic quests for transcendence and sovereignty. Reading

Beauvoir with the help of Fanon we look again to see if what appears to be pathological symptoms or alienated femininity (what Beauvoir calls bad faith or womanly nihilism) might express a microversion of agency, dissent, or potential resistance that could be mobilized to collective action, a possibility I develop further in chapter 5, on Beauvoir's encounter with Richard Wright.

Most important, I emphasize that in spite of the tendency toward repetition of pathological behaviors, Beauvoir and Fanon retain a focus on the possibility and indeed the potential of seizing freedom within collectivity. Both depict individuals as responsive (in Beauvoir's case, being responsive within the encounter is the only way to grasp freedom) and able to choose and enact change. This shared philosophical orientation sharpens their focus on embodiment, situation, and becoming, while keeping the need for transformation and the attainment of freedom with others in view. Reaching back to them, I offer a reading that reframes their joint contribution as one that helps us see pathologies not as individual ailments but as social symptoms that offer a poignant critique of political conditions. Fanon and Beauvoir also share a unique intellectual perspective that is existentialist in being focused on individual and collective freedom, while also attentive to but poised to convert key insights of the psychoanalytic tradition in their attention to reading symptoms on the body as conveying information that is available for interpretation.[1]

My return to these two thinkers complements, but also challenges, new work being done in political theory that is likewise attentive to embodiment, but in different ways. Integrating perspectives from diverse fields of scholarship, including chaos theory, neurobiology, and affect theory, contributions such as Bill Connolly's *Neuropolitics* (2002) and *A World of Becoming* (2011) and Davide Panagia's *The Political Life of Sensation* (2009) share some ground in common with Fanon and Beauvoir in their commitment to theorize experience as it is lived: as contingent, as immanent, as resistant to any larger or linear narrative, and as disjointed and without clear meaning. Yet there are important ways that Beauvoir's and Fanon's perspectives differ from new work in political theory focused on bodily affects and immanent aspects of experience. Beauvoir and Fanon each rework insights from psychoanalytic frameworks that explore a collective political unconscious, and they retain a vision of individual agents as responsible political actors in the midst of disjointed experiences.

There are differences and debates between affect theorists, and to engage them in detail would take me too far afield. The argument I develop here is that Beauvoir's reading of feelings and emotion challenges any claim that we might see affects primarily as biological or separate them from political, social, and linguistic interpretations.[2] The view of affects as discrete, for example, and as limited to nine biological categories in the work of the American psychologist Silvan Tomkins is not in keeping with the way Fanon or Beauvoir theorize the relationship between bodies, emotions, and political formations. Tomkins's work is taken up productively and in a more expansive way by Eve Kosofsky Sedgwick and Adam Frank in "Shame in the Cybernetic Fold: Reading Silvan Tomkins" (2003). They provocatively admit that they "can't convince [them]selves that, for instance, the formidably rich phenomenology of emotions in Tomkins is in any accidental or separable relation to his highly suspect scientism" (94). I am open to Tomkins's work as Sedgwick and Frank parse it, and yet their charge that theory distances itself from biology in direct relationship to claims to creativity, performance, and change does not apply as a critique of the work of either Beauvoir or Fanon. Both of them interpret bodily affects to try to decipher the complex links among biology, structure, language, consciousness, and intention and to try to motivate new directions and new forms of affect that might help us, in the political struggle to create what gets materialized as ontology, see and feel "reality" differently.

When we return to Beauvoir and Fanon we see that oppression itself is lived immanently and chaotically, is imprinted on bodies in comportment and repetitive habits, and yet can nevertheless be consciously (and narratively) rethought and redirected, even rejected by individuals and collectives to create something different and better. Most important, Beauvoir and Fanon never lose sight of agency as constituted in and through political life. While it is important to recognize, as Connolly (2011, 25) explains, that "limits to human agency flow from the proto-agency of other systems and the strains and limits built into the jerry-built character of human agency itself," Fanon and Beauvoir theorize how, when, and why human agency is both made possible and constrained by political life, including structures, language, economies, and the accumulation of a collective unconscious about the meaning of certain forms of embodiment.

Fanon and Beauvoir together help us think about how political actors, as individuals motivated toward collective action, can move from submission and the behaviors and affects that follow from submission, to resistance and a transformation of the political and social situation that makes new forms of collective life possible.[3] I read these thinkers together as they illuminate ways to understand repetitive behaviors and our relationship to time, and how the body's symptoms as they manifest in these registers might signal potential dissent. This reading shows that the body is the central focus of analysis for both thinkers, but it is not the body read only via science (although Beauvoir does include a fascinating discussion on the contingency of sex and the ontology of violence in her chapter "Biological Data" in *The Second Sex*, which I also discuss) or only via the appearance of affects. They read the body as both somatic and situation, as afflicted by affective political symptoms, to offer us new ways to mobilize resistance in seemingly hopeless situations. Most important, Fanon and Beauvoir always have an eye on the need and potential to *transform* situations, to imagine and create new political configurations and alliances that make collective freedom a meaningful and viable possibility.

COLONIAL AND PATRIARCHAL VIOLENCE

Before turning in detail to my reading of *The Wretched of the Earth* with *The Second Sex*, I reconstruct and situate the conversation in which Fanon and Beauvoir were engaged about state violence in a colonial and patriarchal context. To this end I focus first on "Algeria Unveiled," the first chapter in Fanon's 1959 text, *A Dying Colonialism*, alongside Beauvoir's introduction to the 1962 text, written with Gisèle Halimi (Boupacha's lawyer), of *Djamila Boupacha: The Story of the Torture of a Young Algerian Girl Which Shocked Liberal French Opinion*. Beauvoir's introduction is an extended version of her 1960 *Le Monde* editorial publicizing Boupacha's torture and rape by French officials. From my reading of these two pieces I extract the conversation concerning French violence in Algeria and point to how Beauvoir and Fanon theorized women's anticolonial subjectivity differently.

In "Algeria Unveiled," written at the beginning of the Algerian Revolution, Fanon ([1959] 1965) discusses French and Algerian attitudes toward the practice of female veiling. This is a remarkable text to read in the early twenty-first century, remembering that U.S. justification for war and occupation in both Iraq and Afghanistan was partly focused on the education and "freeing" of women, with the wearing of the veil becoming a primary fetish for Western analysts (see Abu-Lughod 2002; Marso 2007). Reading Fanon now reveals that very little has changed in the familiar pattern of Western eyes exoticizing and instrumentalizing women in foreign cultures (see Narayan 1997). As Joan Scott (2007) explains, controversial issues around veiling, often referred to in contemporary discourse as "headscarf controversies," are still entrenched at the center of debates about French identity and the presumed "resistance" of Islam to modernity. French officials claiming to "emancipate" girls with the 2004 ban on wearing the headscarf in school talked about the girls as "victims of their families or dupes of radical political Islamists" (148).

Fanon ([1959] 1965, 37) takes us back to the early 1930s, when officials of the French administration in Algeria concentrated their "efforts on the wearing of the veil, which was looked upon at this juncture as a symbol of the status of Algerian women." According to Fanon, this was a variant of the "well-known formula, 'Let's win over the women and the rest will follow'" (37). He argues that this policy was the brainchild of sociologists, ethnologists, and other pseudo-scientists leading to the situation wherein

> the dominant administration solemnly undertook to defend this woman, pictured as humiliated, sequestered, cloistered. . . . It described the immense possibilities of woman, unfortunately transformed by the Algerian man into an inert, demonized, indeed dehumanized object. The behavior of the Algerian was very firmly denounced and described as medieval and barbaric. With infinite science, a blanket indictment against the "sadistic and vampirish" Algerian attitude toward women was prepared and drawn up. Around the family life of the Algerian, the occupier piled up a whole mass of judgments, appraisals, reasons, accumulated anecdotes and edifying examples, thus attempting to confine the Algerian within a circle of guilt. (38)

Fanon ([1959] 1965, 41) argues that the French mistake this marker of distinct identity as "religious, magical, fanatical behavior." He returns to the revolutionary potential of the religious, the magical, and the fanatical in *The Wretched of the Earth*. We see here that for Fanon and Algerian nationalism, veiling carries the weight of tradition and dignity while the colonizer sees it as exotic, mysterious, and alluring. As Fanon puts it, "The rape of the Algerian woman in the dream of a European is always preceded by a rending of the veil. We here witness a double deflowering. Likewise, the woman's conduct is never one of consent or acceptance, but of abject humility" (45).

Fanon ([1959] 1965) offers a sophisticated reading of the way the French impose a distinct form of cultural violence in their static interpretation of Algerian women as simply and always oppressed by the veil. But he is less aware of the way he too does violence to the subjectivity of Algerian women by depicting them as an undifferentiated mass whose choice in dress reflects the pride of the nation, or in other instances, reducing women's dress and behavior to a reflection on male subjectivity. Fanon cites the situation wherein the Algerian man living in France is asked by his boss to bring his "little family" for a social occasion. "If he comes with his wife, it means admitting defeat, it means 'prostituting his wife,' exhibiting her, abandoning a mode of resistance; on the other hand, going alone means refusing to give satisfaction to the boss; it means running the risk of being out of a job" (40).

He goes on to tell the history of the meaning of veiling under coloniza-tion and decolonization as subject to many transformations and mutations. Outside the gaze of the French, however, veiling seems to exist for Fanon only as an innocent mark of tradition or culture rather than being enmeshed in a complex nexus of gendered national politics. His insight into how the French disrupt the patriarchal power of Algerian men recognizes but at the same time disavows that a gendered politics existed prior to colonization; the meaning of the veil shifts again outside the colony when Algerians live in the mother country, as Fanon clearly understands. Focusing his critical lens only on the French and as an inducement to Algerian male pride or shame dissuades Fanon from thoroughly exploring the gendered politics of Algerian men and women and why the veil, in particular, bears the burden of national identity.

From the perspectives Fanon investigates—those of French authorities, the Algerian nation, and the individual Algerian man—individual Algerian women's complex or contradictory reasons for veiling, or for rejecting the veil, are obscured. Yet although Fanon occludes women's subjectivity by ren-dering it secondary to the nation and male subjectivity (French or Algerian), he also very consciously highlights the importance, both strategically and morally, of Algerian women's revolutionary contribution. In Fanon's analysis the veil becomes a device that can be reoriented toward advancing revolt and revolution. As such, while the French perception of the veil remained mostly static, attitudes of colonized Algerians toward this item of clothing were transformed repeatedly. Early on in the revolution, for example, French assumptions about the veil and its meaning (as oppressing women, as ex-pressing religious beliefs and modesty) were used against the French in clever tactical ways by Algerian militants. For the Algerians veiling became a sign of resistance, and both veiling and not veiling were used as a mask for revo-lutionary activity.

In his film *The Battle of Algiers* (1966), Gillo Pontecorvo brilliantly visu-alizes the phenomena that Fanon outlines in his chapter. Veiled women pass easily through French barriers to the Kasbah ("Don't touch their women," the French police say to each other); veiled women pass guns to militants who turn them against French and colonial authorities; and unveiled women in European garb hide bombs in their purses to detonate in the European quar-ters. And yet, Anne McClintock (1999) points out that, for Fanon, women's agency begins only at men's invitation. Fanon fails to offer any reason women would join the revolutionary war or become militants of their own accord. Rather men bring them in when the time is right. Fanon presents women's revolutionary activity either as a product of a mechanized unfolding of the uprising or as pursuant to male revolutionary strategy. McClintock parses the text of "Algeria Unveiled" thus: "Female militancy, in short, is simply a passive offspring of male agency and the structural necessity of war. . . . The problem of women's agency, so brilliantly raised as a question, is abruptly foreclosed" (291).

I reopen the question of women's agency for Fanon by bringing Beauvoir into the conversation. As Beauvoir ([1963] 1992) recounts in *Force of Circumstance*, the war in Algeria grew in importance in her consciousness and her politics from 1957 onward. *Les Tempes Modernes* published exposés by French soldiers as early as 1957 and continued publishing several articles and editorials denouncing torture conducted by the French in Algeria and denouncing colonialism tout court (89). In *Force of Circumstance*, which Beauvoir was writing in 1960 and published in 1963, she recalls 1957 as the time she realized the *pied noirs* "lynched anyone they could get their hands on," that the "press had become a lie factory," and that the "vast majority of the French people" "failed to realize the depth of their racist attitude" (87–88). She writes, "In 1957, the broken bones, the burns on the faces, on the genitals, the torn out nails, the impalements, the cries of pain, the convulsions, they reached me, all right" (89). As Beauvoir describes it, France's role in Algeria was structurally and institutionally deeply corrupt, for which opinion she was labeled "anti-French" (90).

In 1960, when Halimi contacted Beauvoir about the case of Djamila Boupacha, Beauvoir seized the opportunity to make her own intervention. Deepening and extending Fanon's insights, she takes the agency and revolutionary activity of an individual female militant seriously in their own right. Beauvoir makes it obvious that the French exercised a specifically gendered form of torture—forcing a bottle into Boupacha's vagina—and that Boupacha's rape and torture was not a lone case. Beauvoir does not explain why or how Boupacha became a member of the resistance, but she does repeatedly highlight Boupacha's agency in her self-assertion of her right to personhood and dignity. Most important, Beauvoir demonstrates how Boupacha moves beyond shame to agency. As Beauvoir puts it, in spite of being left in a state of "abject traumatic shock after the savage treatment she had received," Boupacha possessed the courage it took to make a clear demand: "I have been tortured. I insist on a medical examination" (Beauvoir and Halimi 1962, 12).

Boupacha's resolve initiated a series of events. Her actions (or what we might see as her willingness to speak back after a rape that was intended to turn her into a thing and fix her in the place of the Other) began a struggle with the French authorities that would eventually lead not quite to justice or freedom, but it least would get her closer. Boupacha persevered with her case in spite of intense harassment and the duplicity of medical examiners and psychiatrists who sought to discredit the evidence of rape and torture and worked with police authorities offering to drop charges against her in exchange for the withdrawal of her accusations. Despite these obstacles and with the help of her French attorney, Halimi, as well as Beauvoir and a special committee organized on her behalf, Boupacha's case was brought to the attention of the French public. On the strength of Boupacha's determination and resolve, the case wove its way through a state bureaucracy determined to cover up evidence, lie about every level of involvement, and protect all representatives and agents of the colonial apparatus. In 1962, upon Algeria's independence and under the conditions of the Évian agreement, all charges against militants were dropped and the Boupacha case ended without her torturers ever facing justice.

What is remarkable about Beauvoir's analysis, in addition to emphasizing Boupacha's tenacity and agency, is her insistence that moral indignation about the vast bureaucracy that condones and hides torture is not an adequate or even appropriate response. As Beauvoir puts it, "In a war of this sort morality as such has no place" (Beauvoir and Halimi 1962, 19). Revulsion against this form of suffering does nothing; it lacks "concrete reality unless it takes the form of political action" (20). In her final paragraphs of her introduction she condemns the "willing and facile grief" of the French over "past horrors" such as "the death of Anne Frank" (20). Instead she calls on the French to not "content [them]selves with a mere token of horrified sympathy" and align themselves with "our contemporary butchers rather than their victims" (21, 20). Echoing Césaire's ([1955] 2000) argument in *Discourse on Colonialism*, Beauvoir sees contemporary colonial violence as much the same in both practice and motivation as that practiced by the Nazis. Likewise she concludes that just as sorrow and moral indignation failed to defeat fascism, collective political action is necessary to counter colonial crimes.

BEAUVOIR'S THEORY OF VIOLENCE

Beauvoir targets the complacent French as her audience in the Boupacha essay, seeking to rally public opinion to political action to force the French out of Algeria. In "Algeria Unveiled" Fanon has different aims. His work in *A Dying Colonialism* documents violence as well as resistance in the early years of the revolutionary struggle to show the multiple ways Algerians used

French discourse concerning the veil, and even modern devices such as the radio, against them.

Earlier I noted that while Fanon is astute in reading the mutations of the meaning of the veil for both the French and the Algerians, at the same time he denies Algerian women outright agency even though their behavior, comportment, and consciousness were changing as revolutionary circumstances changed. Beauvoir, on the other hand, documents Boupacha's assertion of her agency following her torture but does not talk at all about what brought her to the point of resistance and direct involvement in the Algerian struggle. To be sure this is partly because Beauvoir's essay is directed to the French. Yet there are similar absences in *The Second Sex*. While Beauvoir documents the denial of freedom without specifying how one might get to the point of resistance, Fanon is always searching for resistance in behaviors that might initially look like compliance and moving us to see how changing bodily and habitual behaviors can change consciousness too.

A feature of women's revolutionary activity that goes unremarked by both Beauvoir and Fanon is their willingness to engage in violence. Neither thinker finds it surprising or alarming that women join revolutionary activity and engage in violent resistance. Beauvoir and Fanon agree that violence *can* be justified, although neither advocate it (as has sometimes mistakenly been assumed—by Arendt, for example, in reading Sartre's preface to *The Wretched of the Earth* as ventriloquizing Fanon). While Fanon's position on violence has been extensively debated and discussed, Beauvoir's position is less studied. She addresses several explicit instances of the political use of violence, such as the violence of occupation (*The Blood of Others*, *The Mandarins*, "An Eye for an Eye," *Force of Circumstance*), the violence of colonization ("In Defense of Djamila Boupacha" and *Force of Circumstance*), and the ethical responsibility of individuals considering the political use of violence to counter occupation and systemic oppression (*The Blood of Others* and *The Ethics of Ambiguity*). In each case she argues that the instrumental use of violence—by states, groups, and individual actors, legitimately or not, to achieve political goals—is an affront to the human condition of ambiguity. Yet while she claims that the use of violence denies ambiguity by freezing both violator (tyrant or subject) and violated (thing or object) into ossified positions, she still does not take a wholly pacifist stand. She says in *The Ethics of Ambiguity*, for example, that violence can still sometimes be ethically defended in movements for liberation (1948, 97), and in "An Eye for An Eye" ([1949] 2004), as we saw in chapter 2, she justifies the execution of a Nazi criminal by the French state.

Beauvoir says less about the international organization of power through violence, such as how states organize to deploy violence by building arsenals of weapons, by investing in technology to initiate and perpetuate the destruction of communities and individuals, and by training armies in the use of such weapons and methods of mass destruction. When she does speak of the concentration of weapons and armies by states attempting to assure domination or effect a certain outcome, she emphasizes the paradoxes haunting any struggle for sovereignty and the inability to predict or control actions set in motion: "The more widespread their mastery of the world, the more they find themselves crushed by uncontrollable forces; though they are masters of the atomic bomb, yet it is created only to destroy them" (1948, 9). In all of her writings she argues that whenever violence is deployed, the outcomes are always unpredictable, other than to know that every action contains an "element of failure": "No action can be generated for man without it immediately being generated against men" (99).

Often theories of violence, such as in the Hegelian, Kantian, and utilitarian traditions, discuss the uses and abuses of violence primarily as an instrument and attempt to theorize ways to counter or control its unethical use and deleterious effects. To Beauvoir's mind, however, not only must we acknowledge the unpredictability and uncontrollability of violent actions and counter actions, but we must also recognize that violence is a complex, fluid, and affective force. Beauvoir insists that violence is present not only on the national and international scene but also as part of everyday life in the very way language and all relations of interpersonal subjectivity operate. So rather than simply deploring or condemning violence, we have to understand that violence delineates and manifests in all our relationships and representations. In this sense violence cannot be eliminated from existence, although we must distinguish between its several forms and minimize its impacts.

Violence is embedded in our body and muscles, in language, speech, and writing, in intimate and distant relationships, and in processes and forces in nature. We are always exposed to each other, connected as much by potential cruelty as by generosity or kindness, and violence is always possible. While Beauvoir's theory of violence avows ontological conditions—such as nature's irrational cruelty, our servitude to reproduction of the species, the fact of finitude and mortality, the precariousness and fragility of life, and the vicissitudes of chance—she finds no innate justification for structural and political conditions of oppression emanating from these facts of nature. Human relationships of oppression situate us as systematically and unequally exposed to violent injury and premature death and as unequally able to nourish a creative and flourishing life, and these are never justified by ontology.

For example, Beauvoir condemns ideologies claiming that nature justifies relationships of oppression such as in Nazism, colonial claims to superiority, or capitalist boasts of "the survival of the fittest." She describes the gendered use of violence manifest in the everyday harms and more extreme instances of violence against women and other groups of politically vulnerable subjects. Noticing and theorizing these intersections—among instrumental, ontological, structural, and affective workings of violence—are the key contributions of Beauvoir's political theory of violence.

We can see these features in the chapter "Biological Data" in *The Second Sex*. When, for example, Beauvoir turns to biological data to ponder the origin of sexual difference, she demonstrates that linguistic violence is always present in the political interpretation of biological "facts"—in the marking and categorizing of two sexes and their capabilities and potential. The deadly violence that ensues within, upon, and through reproductive practices does not necessarily give rise to judgments concerning the perpetual existence (or not) of violence, does not reveal the secrets that could "explain" sexual difference, and does not and should not direct or dictate social organization or political meaning. Beauvoir's analysis finds physical violence to be a fluid and affective force in nature that also operates in and through language and representation, again as a fluid and affective force, to identify and fix how we "see" nature. Violence is thus *both* nature and construct: violence in natural processes, violence as the brutal forces of time and space, and violence as it manifests in the continual sacrifice of individuals to species perpetuation all are facts of existence. Most damaging are the political meanings, and here Beauvoir is most attentive to gendered meanings that circulate and are said to be justified by nature.

In the traditional view of social contract theory, as one key example where meaning is derived from nature, theorists return to the idea of nature, or to a construct of the state of nature, in order to legitimate their specific version of the social contract and discern the origins of current political and social practices. Whether and where these thinkers identify the existence and manifestation of violence in the state of nature legitimates a state that will control people's violent proclivities (Hobbes, Locke) or bring out their better nature (Rousseau). Violence is theorized as prepolitical in the social contract tradition, in that we seek to escape conditions of "natural" violence by engaging instead in politics. Beauvoir challenges this return to nature to legitimate social organization, particularly as a way to authorize the categorization of women as other. Moreover she alerts us to the intersection of violence and politics by insisting that "all authority is violence" and "no one governs innocently"

(1948, 108). She also urges us to think more skeptically as well as more creatively about what nature does and does not authorize.

Asserting that "humanity is always in the making," Beauvoir ([1949] 2011, 44, 45) posits that we are a "becoming," that "*possibilities* have to be defined" rather than being reduced to the past or the present. She invests in the future anterior, a future that has yet to take place, to argue that the world *could* look otherwise. What our capacities *might* be will "manifest themselves clearly only when they have been realized. . . . When one considers a being who is transcendence and surpassing, it is never possible to close the books" (46).

Thus we are cautioned to foreswear making judgments that look to nature or ontology to confirm a "*natural* hierarchy of values" or that engage in "psychophysiological parallelism" ([1949] 2011, 45). Studies that "confuse a vague naturalism with an even vaguer ethic or aesthetic are pure verbiage" (45). So when we see violence in nature, we must tread carefully in reaching conclusions concerning what such violence means for human relationships and our relationship to the facticity and materiality of the world.

According to Beauvoir, we can nevertheless see the force of violence in nature, even at the very bottom of the species ladder. At lower levels of development living organisms are mostly slaves to the maintenance of the species, dying immediately after coitus or after fertilization. Death comes rapidly after the "next generation's future has been assured" ([1949] 2011, 32) and it happens mechanically. Violence is ever present, but never employed by conscious agents. As we move up the species ladder, more ugly events appear with increasing resistance by individuals against the species, but no conscious agent or actor, other than the force of species preservation, can be held responsible. We can see in Beauvoir's language that even she is lured by the temptation to assign volition. She says, for example, that after the queen termite lays her last eggs and becomes sterile, she is "pitilessly massacred." In bee and ant matriarchies "males are intruders that are massacred each season." Male ants are "killed" or they "starve to death" after being refused entry to female encampments. The fertilized female ant has no better fate having to "dig herself into the earth alone" and "die from exhaustion"; if she manages to make a new colony, she is "imprisoned for twelve years laying eggs ceaselessly" (all quotes on 32). The female spider "devours" the male after coupling. The praying mantis "assassinates" her spouse. The male "attacks, palpates, seizes her and imposes coitus on her." Sometimes "he has to fight off other males" (all quotes on 33). The drone bee "that catches the queen in her wedding flight crashes to the ground eviscerated" (33). When in heat, fish and cetaceans "isolate themselves and become aggressive toward other males" (37).

Even though Beauvoir ([1949] 2011, 38) herself employs language that makes it seem as if agents are consciously enacting violence, she explicitly cautions against interpreting too quickly or broadly from these observations other than to realize that "in nature nothing is ever completely clear." To see "in these facts the harbinger of the 'battle of the sexes' that sets individuals as such against each other is just rambling" (33). She insists that assigning human meaning to the facts of nature reveals the most egregious anthropomorphizing. Although she says it seems true that the male of several species "imposes himself on [the female]" and that "it is he who *takes* her" and "she is *taken*," "the male does not *do* violence to the species, because the species can only perpetuate itself by renewal; it would perish if ova and sperm did not meet" (35). The *processes themselves* are affective and active, propelling and impacting other processes and energy flows.

To Beauvoir's mind, to read *human* desire and consciousness into processes of complex and multidirectional biological relationships illuminates not the "battle of the sexes" but rather the opposite: the political and social violence that occurs when nature is said to legitimate constructed familial and social arrangements. For example, because the male is seen to be more violent and aggressive in nature, human boys are schooled in the lessons of violence and girls are not. But there is plenty of counterevidence that challenges the certainty of male violence. Feminine and masculine activities in nature do not simply or cleanly map onto the opposition of "passivity and activity" ([1949] 2011, 38). Nevertheless social situations often assume these oppositions: "Much of masculine behavior arises in a setting of potential violence: on every street corner skirmishes are waiting to happen; in most cases they are aborted; but it is enough for the man to feel in his fists his will for self-affirmation for him to feel confirmed in his sovereignty" (343). In contrast "these conquering actions are not permitted to the girl, and violence in particular is not permitted to her"; girls "are banned from exploring, daring, pushing back the limits of the possible" (343). Beauvoir declares that to argue that nature justifies sexual hierarchy is total nonsense: males and females are not even "always sharply distinguished," and the division into sexes is often "absolutely contingent" (38). "Biological data take on [only] those values the existent confers on them" (47).

So what can we conclude about the presence of violence in nature? Beauvoir ([1949] 2011, 46) states, "In truth these facts cannot be denied: but they do not carry their meaning in themselves." For different types in nature, the "active operations" (not passive female and active male, but two active operations) of "maintenance and creation" realize the "synthesis of becoming" differently (38). How we respond to and act within the constraints of biology—in this case the violence that portends from our being enslaved to reproduction in different ways for the male and the female—becomes a political struggle. We can confirm or deny ambiguity and potential freedom, but we cannot eliminate the fact that violence exists in nature and perpetuates itself in the reproduction of all species. The meaning that biological data is given, the very partition of beings into two distinct types—male and female, in hierarchical arrangement—is itself an act of linguistic violence which is made material and physical in structures and bodies.

Beauvoir's acknowledgment of conditions of violence in the reproduction of the species signals her unwillingness to simply reject or condemn violence outright. Instead she points out that violence is a force that is harnessed when we identify or even challenge its existence, such as when authors turn to biological data to justify the "battle of the sexes," the confinement of women to the home, women's maternal instincts, the rapacious and aggressive "nature" of men, or the superiority of one race or civilization over another. Beauvoir's theorization of violence as a politicized ontology, as well as her focus on violence being intrinsic to partitioning in language and representation, makes her even more attentive to the many manifestations and kinds of violence we see in more extreme, more physical, and more obviously political circumstances, such as the Boupacha case and her support for the anticolonial struggle in Algeria.

REPETITION AND RELATIONSHIP TO TIME

Beauvoir and Fanon both are attentive to how colonial and patriarchal violence is registered on bodies to change behaviors and sense of self and possibility. An orientation to the world that Beauvoir's women and Fanon's colonized share is the sensation of being outside of linear time. In contrast, men in Beauvoir's text and the colonist in Fanon's are characterized as seeking to master time, to make history, to always move forward. As Fanon ([1963] 2004, 14) simply puts it, "[The colonist's] life is an epic, an odyssey"; Beauvoir ([1949] 2011, 73) adds, "To appropriate the world's treasures, he annexes the world itself. . . . He spills over the present and opens up the future." Women and the colonized experience time differently: as repetition, as destiny, as nonlinear, obscure, and cyclical. Their relationship to time condemns them to immanence, orienting them toward the past and present rather than transcendence and the future. Fanon and Beauvoir share a two-pronged, sometimes internally contradictory approach to articulating the implications of this dynamic. On the one hand they imply that because the oppressed are stuck in repetition, their relationship to time is impoverished. On the other hand they depict the oppressed as seeming to understand something the conquerors don't: that time ultimately cannot be mastered, that nature has a power that cannot be controlled, and that we must be responsive to and act within the immutable and immanent aspects of time.

Beauvoir articulates this last point more clearly than does Fanon, in her explanation of why we must embrace ambiguity in order to enhance the conditions of freedom for everyone. Because the act of accepting ambiguity—through consciousness of ourselves as both subject and object, simultaneously transcendence and immanence—is centrally prized in her politics as the first step toward freedom, Beauvoir insists that when men foolishly seek to control and master time, they violate life's human parameters and debase the conditions of true freedom. One way men violate ambiguity is in trying to always be transcendent, consequently pinning immanence solely on women's bodies and not their own. Man's existential crisis, his fear of living in a limited and confined body, his fears of aging and death, his revolt against his "carnal condition" feed his desire to make slaves of women:

> He considers himself a fallen god: his curse is to have fallen from a luminous and orderly heaven into the chaotic obscurity of the mother's womb. He desires to see himself in this fire, this active and pure breath, and it is woman who imprisons him in the mud of the earth. He would like himself to be as necessary as pure Idea, as One, All, absolute Spirit; and he finds himself enclosed in a limited body, in a time and place he did not choose, to which he was not called, useless, awkward, absurd. His very being is carnal contingence to which he is subjected in his isolation, in his unjustifiable gratuitousness. It also dooms him to death. ([1949] 2011, 164–65)

Men seek freedom from their bodies by assigning the body in all its obscurity and mystery to the idea of Woman in her role as wife: "The wife perpetrates the immutable species; she ensures the even rhythm of the days and the permanence of the home she guards with locked doors; she is given no direct grasp on the future, nor on the universe; she goes beyond herself toward the group only through her husband as mouthpiece" ([1949] 2011, 443). This, however, is a bad-faith form of freedom. As Beauvoir insists, freedom does not equal transcendence; freedom happens only in encounter. To achieve freedom we must acknowledge and live ambiguity by resisting the temptation, even when you possess the power or agency, to turn people into things through a violation of their potential for transcendence: "In truth, all human existence is transcendence and immanence at the same time; to go beyond itself, it must maintain itself; to thrust itself toward the future, it must integrate the past into itself; and while relating to others, it must confirm itself in itself" (443).

Just as they violate ambiguity by creating myths that fix women as being in communion with nature, linked to the species, and a naturally submissive consciousness ([1949] 2011, 161), men violate ambiguity again when they assign certain tasks and duties of immanence to women as their "natural" role. Passages in *The Second Sex* where Beauvoir describes the rituals of housework, its endless repetition and drudgery, are some of the most depressing in the book, although we will see in chapter 6 that she also says there can be a certain form of pleasure in these tasks. But there is always repetition. The dishes are washed only to get dirty again; the child is fed but is hungry in two hours; the mud is cleaned from the floor just before someone brings more mud into the house. Not only are these tasks repetitive in themselves; they also repeat through history and across cultures, seeming to deny creativity and block the emergence of anything new. But sometimes novelty emerges from repetition.

Interpreting these passages, Penelope Deutscher (2008, 95–96) says that Beauvoir also condemns the repetitive life of the worker, expanding this Marxist-inspired analysis in her portrayal of the life of the housewife. Insofar as Beauvoir explicitly and straightforwardly condemns repetition, Deutscher finds her argument less interesting than when Beauvoir seems to indicate the possibility that there may be something beyond simple repetition of the same or that reproducing a norm may not always simply reproduce a norm. As she discovers elsewhere in the text, Deutscher says that Beauvoir's examples sometimes speak counter to or in ways more diverse than the conclusions she draws (110). Since Beauvoir includes so many kinds of activities under the rubric of repetition—housework, reproduction, imitating norms of femininity—the term itself becomes destabilized. I look to some of these examples below, then move to a comparison with the way Fanon describes repetition to ask whether and how we might locate dissent or critique within repetition (a theme I return to in chapter 6), how changing the context helps us to see something potentially new emerging from the background of repeated pathologies, and whether the relationship the oppressed have to time is one that teaches us how we might better find freedom within the more immanent aspects of existence, such as the effect that time has on our bodies.

Beauvoir recognizes that having an impoverished relationship to time that is imposed, such as the way men impose housework and maternity on women as their destiny, is different, more oppressive, than the acknowledgment that time itself is immanent and imposes its somewhat obscure rules and conditions on us against our will. This latter aspect, a recognition of ambiguity, is something that the oppressed experience in having a different relationship to time; strangely they are both *less* and *more* able to fool themselves about the possibility of conquering time or of having sovereignty over nature. Less able to fool themselves because they feel equally powerless against all things: "volcanoes, policemen, employers, or men" ([1949] 2011, 642). "The world seems governed by an obscure destiny against which it is presumptuous to react" (643). But sometimes it seems they are more able to fool themselves: in response to perceived chaos and an imposed destiny, housewives create a strict routine. Routine and repetition create order in a self-imposed mechanized existence that housewives slavishly obey. This precipitates a meticulous adherence to the schedule and rhythm of daily life. While this can be comforting and offers its own sensual and bodily delights, it is also delusional to attempt to exercise sovereignty over a world of things. As Beauvoir well realizes, objects often resist our sovereignty over them.

Not because of any natural proclivity but rather due to their structural position, women are thus closer to immanence.[4] Indeed the women described in *The Second Sex* might be said to be in tune with what Deleuze and Guattari (1987) call "radical immanence": they experience objects as potentially having control over them, they do not experience transcendence or reasons for existence, and everything (but their routine) seems outside of their control. As Beauvoir ([1949] 2011, 472) puts it, housework "makes the woman grapple with matter, and she finds an intimacy in objects that is the revelation of being that consequently enriches her." Oppressed and bored women "console [themselves] with creamy sauces, heady wines, velvets, the caresses of water, sun, a woman friend, or a young lover" (643). When woman battles in her world, attempts to exert sovereignty or take control, it is to no larger end: "Mainly because she has never experienced the powers of liberty . . . she does not believe in liberation" (643). "The house, the bedroom, the dirty laundry, the wooden floors, are fixed things: she can do no more than rout out indefinitely the foul causes that creep in; she attacks the dust, stains, mud, and filth; she fights sin, she fights with Satan" ([1949] 2011, 476). Women learn that with some kinds of tasks, waiting is better: "Respectful of duration that no haste can conquer, they do not measure their time" (642). "As the woman does not take part in history, she does not understand its necessities; she mistrusts the future and wants to stop time" (641).

Read in conversation with Fanon's description of repetition in the lives of the colonized, the following long quote from *The Second Sex* is revealing:

> She introduces primitive superstitions into religion—candles, ex-votos, and such—she embodies ancient spirits of nature in the saints—this one protects travelers, that one women who have just given birth, another one finds lost objects—and of course no marvel surprises her. Her attitude will be that of conjuration and prayer; to obtain a certain result, she will follow certain time-tested rites. It is easy to understand why she is ruled by routine; time has no dimension of novelty for her, it is not a creative spring; because she is doomed to repetition, she does not see in the future anything but a duplication of the past; if one knows the word and the recipe, duration is allied with the powers of fecundity; but this too obeys the rhythm of months and seasons; the cycle of each pregnancy, of each flowering, reproduces the preceding one identically; in this circular movement, time's sole becoming is slow degradation: it eats at furniture and clothes just as it disfigures the face; fertile powers are destroyed little by little by the flight of years. So the woman does not trust this force driven to destroy. ([1949] 2011, 640)

As Beauvoir describes it, women's relationship to time, and the embodiment of that oppression in habits and rituals, precipitates and perpetuates a process of self-destruction for women (sometimes erupting in meaningless and futile violence, as we will see in chapter 6) but maintenance of the status quo for men. Focused inwardly on what she *thinks* she can control (the dust, the mud, the appropriate temperature and time for boiling the potatoes, the way she does her hair, her weight and beauty rituals) and asking for help from saints for what she knows she cannot control (illness, the likelihood of more pregnancies, the well-being of her children, destructive weather), the woman is always poised toward narcissism. She focuses on herself and her immediate enclosed world, making it far less likely that she might turn her gaze back onto her oppressors, onto those who have enshrined her in myths and *created* her self-destructive behaviors and habits. As I argue in part III, barring some contingent shift in historical conditions (a possibility introduced by Fanon and discussed in chapter 5 in conversation with Wright), it seems like the only thing that can save isolated women from their fate is collective political action (freedom in encounter).

Likewise the colonized turn their aggression toward themselves and each other rather than against their collective enemies. As Fanon ([1963] 2004, 15–16) describes him, the colonized man is a man penned in, forced to contain an aggression that is "sedimented in his muscles" and has no outlet: "This is the period when black turns on black, and police officers and magistrates don't know which way to turn when faced with the surprising surge of North African criminality." Just as women under patriarchy direct gossip and ill will toward each other (see Beauvoir [1967] 1969), the colonized too mistake who their enemies really are. As Fanon ([1963] 2004, 17) eloquently puts it, "Whereas the colonist or police officer can beat the colonized subject day in and day out, insult him and shove him to his knees, it is not uncommon to see the colonized subject draw his knife at the slightest hostile or aggressive look from another colonized subject."

This violence toward each other is sometimes siphoned off by religion, magic, and rituals of dance and possession. "Malevolent spirits" exist to hold the colonized in check: "leopard men, snake men, six-legged dogs, zombies, a whole never-ending gamut of animalcules or giants that encircle the colonized with a realm of taboos, barriers, and inhibitions far more terrifying than the colonialist world" (Fanon [1963] 2004, 18). Rituals and repetition of certain dances and rites also serve to "protect and empower" (20). "Organized séances of possession and dispossession" such as "vampirism, possession by djinns, by zombies, and by Legba, the illustrious god of voodoo" (20) are rituals repeated again and again, serving to keep the colonized focused on themselves, their internal and enclosed world. The comparison to Beauvoir's description of women's rituals under patriarchy is striking: the constant repetition of the tasks of housework, the focus on rituals of beauty and cleanliness for the house and oneself, and the belief in spirits and destiny all drain female energy away from a critique of patriarchy.

Fanon ([1963] 2004, 21), however, is not hopeless: "The challenge now is to seize this violence as it realigns itself. Whereas it once reveled in myths and contrived ways to commit collective suicide, a fresh set of circumstances will now enable it to change directions." What are these circumstances? It is partly the increased violence of the colonizers: "With his back to the wall, the knife at his throat, or to be more exact the electrode on his genitals, the colonized subject is bound to stop telling stories" (20). The discourse of the nationalist political parties, in spite of their desire to avoid violence, also contributes to putting the revolution in motion. Naming of the colonized "We blacks, We Arabs" stirs up "subversive feelings" and "raise[s] the people's hopes," and "the imagination is allowed to roam outside the colonial order" (29). Stories about "role models" killing police officers, committing suicide rather than "giving up" their comrades, also stir the violence "rippling under the skin" (30–31). The penetration of the modern world convinces the masses that "they have been robbed" (34). According to Fanon, in no way are the colonized afraid of violence. Surrounded by and directly subjected to the violence of the modern world, "for once they are in tune with their time" (40).

"For once they are in tune with their time." Fanon is certainly right that objective historical circumstances changed. The Algerians were part of a larger historical process in winning self-determination; they were one of many formerly colonized nations seizing their freedom, with a variety of methods, in the mid-twentieth century. But possibly because he died before *The Wretched of the Earth* was published, Fanon does not recognize the depth of the wounds of colonialism; nor does he theorize that these wounds will repeat, reopen, scar over, only to be exposed again and again. The behaviors and symptoms of oppression, of lack of autonomy, of submission and dehumanization are not easily healed, certainly never erased. As Pontecorvo puts in the mouth of one of his revolutionary fighters in *Battle of Algiers*, the hardest part is not winning the revolution, but comes after the victory.

Fanon's optimism is mostly absent from *The Second Sex*. As I discussed in chapter 1, the hope that Beauvoir has for the future comes from her affective appeal to us as readers to think differently about new possibilities, a hope that is pitched as a bid for feminist friendship in chapter 7 of this book and in chapter 5 is developed as the search for political allies across identity boundaries. A pessimistic reading of *The Second Sex*, however, might conclude that women seem to be forever out of tune with their time and that there is no reason to hope for the transformed circumstances or the new alliances that make change possible. When Beauvoir makes any predictions at all about the future, something she is philosophically reticent to do, she only makes a half-hearted nod to early Soviet politics that valued women's public work and female suffrage. In part we might attribute her position that women seem always to be out of tune with their time to her sophisticated analysis of the history, intimacy, depth, and breadth of gender oppression. At the same time, though, racism and colonialism too are intimate, indeed sexual, as well as deep and broad. One difference between the two situations is that women's resistance tends toward individual rather than collective action, although Beauvoir repeatedly warns that any real change must be conducted on the level of the collective. While collective violence against men sometimes happens, absent the possibility for freedom in the encounter it is far more likely that violence will erupt in individual cases, as we will see in chapter 6.

Possibly even more unfortunate, patriarchy permeates the consciousness of revolutionary militants as pervasively as it does colonial occupiers. As one sobering example, we can think again about Djamila Boupacha. Having asserted her agency as a militant attempting to bring the French who tortured her to justice, Boupacha continued to assert her agency in her wish to not return to Algeria following her release from a French prison in 1962. Eerily prescient about the direction the newly independent state might take in regard to women, Boupacha wished to stay in France rather than return to her now independent country. Her worries were justified: in spite of the 1962 Algerian Constitution's guarantee of the vote to all over the age of nineteen, the country's shift to an Islamic identity with a focus on religion, marriage, and family imposed strict social guidelines on women's dress and comportment, gave rights to husbands, and denied women political input.

In sum, although Fanon tells us we can shift our relationship to time by directing violence against the oppressors, he worries that the violence might turn back onto itself in yet another repetition. As history reveals, initial hope turns into despair as women are victimized in revolutionary Algeria and the nation-state form reveals its own violent proclivities and habits. Is this the defeat of resistance, or just an indication that pathologies lodged materially, fixed through habits on bodies, remain as all too easily reopened wounds?

Fanon suggests that were we to regard freedom as the lost and unarticulated object of a melancholic collective, we might see melancholy itself as expressing a deep and abiding dissatisfaction, even dissent, toward the status quo. Rather than help individual subjects achieve alignment with an oppressive body politic, could we harness symptoms to move in another direction? This is what Beauvoir says must be done in order to achieve freedom and Fanon hopes to accomplish as a psychoanalyst.

NEW FORMS OF REFUSAL?

While Beauvoir indicates that sometimes women's pathologies can be read as unconscious forms of protest, Fanon ([1963] 2004, 220) says explicitly that "the colonized's indolence is a *conscious* way of sabotaging the colonial machine" (emphasis added). To barely work or to put forth minimal effort is for the colonized subject "who has not yet arrived at a political consciousness or a decision to reject the oppressor" a way of resisting as "non-cooperation" or "at least minimal cooperation" (220). This move can be read as a form of refusal, maybe akin to Bartleby's "I would prefer not to": a version of dysfunctionality, inoperativity, or what, with Beauvoir, I call "perverse protests."

When we turn to Fanon to explore these questions as compared with Beauvoir, we see in his work a more explicit embrace of psychoanalysis as technique and interpretive tool, but it is an embrace that is tempered by what we might call a conversion or reconfiguration. His observations and conclusions are a result of his clinical work in the Blida Clinic in Algiers, where he worked as a psychiatrist with both North African and European patients. At the end of *The Wretched of the Earth*, Fanon ([1963] 2004, 181) acknowledges that his "notes on psychiatry" may seem "out of place or untimely" in "a book like this." His simple retort: "There is absolutely nothing we can do about that" (181). The colonists brought the methods and tools of psychiatry to the colonized hoping to "cure" the "colonized subject correctly, in other words making him thoroughly fit into a social environment of the colonial type" (181–82). Fanon says that the hospitals were filled with patients during colonial rule and that the "all-out national war of liberation" also has become a "breeding ground for mental disorders" (182–83). He adds in a note that "France's human legacy in Algeria" is "an entire generation of Algerians steeped in collective, gratuitous homicide with all the psychosomatic consequences this entails" (183n22).

After discussing several case studies of individuals, both Algerian and French, Fanon ([1963] 2004, 215–16) claims that the "pathology of the entire atmosphere in Algeria" induces pathologies with psychic origins wherein the disorder is both "symptom and cure." This manifestation of the disorder is the only way the body can cope, but we also might see it as the body's refusal. The only real cure, given that these illnesses stem from the "daily humiliations inflicted on man by colonial oppression" (219), is the war of national liberation. These imprecise symptoms—stomach ulcers, hypersomnia, tachycardia, premature hair whitening, and muscular stiffness—are another way of refusing the colonial order, just as what Beauvoir sees as women's ailments (anxiety, depression, melancholy, narcissism, general bitchiness) are also a form of refusal. Symptoms are the body's way of responding to cultural confusion, humiliation, and even loss of the potential for freedom or loss of a future, but they also are a way of refusing. As a cure, Fanon says, the militant is charged with hunting down not only "enemy forces" but also "the core of despair crystallized in the body of the colonized" (219).

Theorizing these affects and symptoms imprinted on the body as emerging from a social and political as well as emotional and psychological situation, the encounter between Fanon and Beauvoir directs our attention to the potential resistance, or at least forms of dissent, that might be registered in these affects; it also prompts us to ask how we might address them collectively and politically. With this reading we have new insight into Beauvoir's keen interest in the Boupacha case, why she so consistently highlights Boupacha's own agency, as well as why and how she seeks to understand individual women's attempts to find freedom in alienated forms of femininity, even in situations where, because of structural oppression, agency seems impossible.[5] Fanon's work, in contrast, helps us to see collective and revolutionary dissent, but at the same time it tends to obscure individuals, erasing the subjectivity of individual Algerian women and even the individual's pathologies in always seeing them as being the result of collective ailments or collective needs. Additionally Fanon (mistakenly, to my mind) values transcendence and sovereignty over immanence and ambiguity in spite of his worries about the potential repetition of violence in acts of sovereign power following decolonization.

In light of these differences in emphases and insights, putting Beauvoir and Fanon together in this conversational encounter enhances their individual contributions. One truth they share is their observation that individual affects and behaviors are often the manifestation of collective existence ruled by oppression, and yet individuals still have the potential for agency. Highlighting the political in the work of these two thinkers helps us to notice forms of agency, however compromised or confused, and redirect it toward collective action. Heeding Beauvoir's insights concerning the dangers of disavowing ambiguity, linked with Fanon's nagging worry about the future forms of violence potentially repeated in the nation-state, we can conclude that collective agency should be directed not toward transcendence and sovereignty but rather toward imagining and creating a different form of politics. Beauvoir's encounter with Richard Wright helps us think about the forms this politics might take.

IN SOLIDARITY WITH
RICHARD WRIGHT

Richard Wright's speech to the Paris Congress of 1956 ignited a firestorm of debate within black political and intellectual circles.[1] Claiming freedom as the ability to break away from identities formed by culture, religion, and tradition and create possibilities for new forms of collective action, Wright challenged the idea of reclaiming "blackness" as a politically liberating identity. His speech raises urgent questions about identity, freedom, and action, both for his time and ours. This chapter offers a concrete example of how theorizing freedom, collective action, and solidarity does not occur in isolation but emerges from conversations between people committed to challenging various forms of oppression. Wright enhanced the scope as well as the meaning of his work on racism in conversation with Beauvoir, whose challenge to patriarchy was likewise deeply enriched by their intellectual friendship.

Assembled as blacks, the participants at the Paris Congress, hosted by the journal *Présence Africaine,* included American, African, European, and Caribbean black intellectuals and artists.[2] Wright, arguably the most well known black intellectual in the world at this juncture, was expected to speak in the voice he had made famous in *Black Boy* (1945) and *Native Son* (1940). These two books, by this time translated into several languages and very popular in France, fixed Wright for many of his contemporaries as an authentic black son, born and raised in Mississippi, and thus able to represent the "true" African American experience.[3]

But Wright was no longer focused on Bigger Thomas's individual, misogynist, and ultimately futile resistance to white supremacy.[4] He had moved on from the perspective of the oppressed psyche of the American black male to consider the possibility of broader, worldly, collective political action.[5] In fact he was determined to connect the African American experience to that of oppressed peoples in Africa and beyond. Disheartened by racism in the United States, Wright had voluntarily exiled himself and his family to Paris in 1947. At the time of the Paris Congress he had recently returned from sojourns in Argentina, Haiti, and Spain, as well as Nkrumah's revolutionary Ghana (called the Gold Coast during colonization), where he collected material for his book *Black Power*, and Indonesia, where he reported on the 1955 Bandung Conference of Third World Nations.[6]

Wright said to those assembled in Paris that Third World peoples, joined in solidarity, needed to seize freedom by rejecting their "traditional" cultural and religious identities. This message shocked the participants. Although Wright was respected by his contemporaries as the author of *Native Son*, when he stepped up to the podium to deliver his speech, the audience wasn't quite sure what to expect. Though a committed leftist and anti-imperialist, Wright could not be counted on to toe any party or ideological line. His politics was very much his own, and he could be unpredictable. Differing from most of his peers at the Congress, he did not present himself as an ideological radical seeking to overthrow modernity.[7] He also refused to take on the role of "authentic" black man and chose instead to identify as one contesting racism, colonialism, and, as we will see in his encounter with Beauvoir, even patriarchal oppression. He lamented the absence of women and female voices at the Paris Congress and commented extensively on the role of women in revolutionary Ghana.[8]

Moving beyond the national frame, Wright wanted to connect the experiences of black Americans to the experiences of other oppressed people. By the time of the Paris Congress he was articulating three main ideas in this effort: that there is nothing essential to black identity; that blacks can and should cross the color line and join in solidarity with other oppressed groups; and that blacks must embrace modern ways of being in the world, and thus embrace their own emerging collective political subjectivity, in order to be free. Beauvoir's work traces a surprisingly similar path. By theorizing her own experiences as a woman understood in comparison to as well as inextricably linked to the lives of other women, she interrogates the category of "women" itself. Rejecting forms of desire that are bound up with "femininity" because they are born from wounds and mired in pathologies, Beauvoir imagines alternative ways of being a woman in the world as she simultaneously envisions new forms of solidarity.

Wright's early emphasis on the primacy of freedom had situated him in a universe of existentialist thought long before he began to rub shoulders with intellectuals in Paris. Wright and Beauvoir's mutual friends and philosophical and political interests brought them together even earlier. Beauvoir had met Wright when he traveled to France in 1946, so when Beauvoir went to the United States in 1947 he and his wife Ellen Poplar hosted her. While many have discussed the friendship between Beauvoir and Wright, I demonstrate their intellectual synergy by putting Beauvoir's ([1949] 2011) *The Second Sex* into conversation with Wright's ([1941] 2008) essay and photodocumentary, *12 Million Black Voices*. In these two works especially, but supported by their larger oeuvres, we can interpret their mutual rejection of tradition, religion, and oppressive identities as a move toward a more expansive and creative form of political solidarity that emphasizes collective action. They each acknowledge the sediment of a collective cultural otherness defined by political meanings attached to race, gender, and historically rooted habits of behavior and thinking (thus acknowledging the power of situation in constructing and constraining freedom), and they prize agency for the individual. Yet my reading of *The Second Sex* with *12 Million Black Voices* demonstrates that collective political action is the key to grasping freedom. Reading their work in concert we see that nurturing a political subjectivity via freedom in encounter gives us the opportunity to reject normative identity categories and stimulate the imagination of alternative futures.

When we bring Wright into conversation with Beauvoir, we see that both theorize freedom as constrained by the particulars of contingent, historical, embodied experiences rather than as unhinged, disembodied, and universal or as ontologically untouched by situation. And yet they both reject the notion that solidarity is born from or forged by habits, experience, and ways of knowing attached to alienation and pathology as a result of oppression. Like Fanon, who looked to the decolonization struggle for options and answers, Wright agrees that we must reject identities born out of oppressive discourses and contexts and make something new. Together Beauvoir and Wright assert that a new political world cannot be won by inscribing new meaning onto identities, practices, and habits that held the oppressed hostage in the past and that were endowed with negative meaning by the old order. Rather we express freedom by seeing and describing the world differently, forging political bonds across identity categories, and acting in concert with other oppressed peoples to claim a new future.

THE "ROT" OF TRADITION AND CULTURE

In Wright's (2008, 718) speech to the Paris Congress titled "Tradition and Industrialization," he cites the "smashing" of the "irrational ties of religion and custom and tradition in Asia and Africa" as "the central historic fact" resulting from colonial ventures. Surprisingly he says this should be celebrated. It was an "unconscious and unintentional" result of Western exploitation, to be sure, but one we can work with and build on (718). As Wright describes it, the onset of colonization can be understood as "irrationalism [meeting] irrationalism" (717). Europe called its adventure "the spread of civilization, missions of glory, of service, of destiny even," urged on by an imperial desire rationalized as the "consecrated duty of converting or enslaving all infidels" (717, 712). As a result, "today, a *knowing* black, brown, or yellow man can say: 'Thank you, Mr. White Man, for freeing me from the rot of my irrational traditions and customs, though you are still the victim of your own irrational customs and traditions!'" (719).

It was bold, to say the least, for Wright to call the traditions and customs of Asia and Africa "rot." The Paris Congress was organized partly to consider the dignity of these same traditions and cultures, to celebrate the contributions of African civilization, and to reclaim and rebuild blackness as a distinct way of being in the world to challenge the emptiness, alienation, and bankruptcy of Western thought. Wright's speech struck participants as discordant with the more romantic versions of *négritude* such as the one affirmed by the Senegalese poet Léopold Sédar Senghor, who advanced "black values" as the embrace of precolonial, communal Africa.[9] Although Wright recognized, *insisted* even, that being black was a central category of modern politics and social history, he consistently rejected anything he regarded as approaching a "racialist" perspective and preached a qualified affirmation of modernity. Ironically he invokes his own experience as helping him move beyond any fixed identity. Identifying himself as a Western man of color, Wright (2008, 704–5) establishes the "generality" and "reasonableness" of his argument as rooted in the fact that he is both black and a "man of the West." Situated in both arenas, and noting his hybrid identity as a modern man, Wright claims a "double-vision" that renders him "chronically skeptical," "restless," "eager, urgent," and "irredeemably critical" (704–5).

Pointedly Wright (2008, 706) admits to his colleagues that he is "offended" by the "teeming religions gripping the minds and the consciousness of Asians and Africans," although he adds that his sympathies are "unavoidably with, and unashamedly for, them." He has no kinder words for the religion, customs, and traditions of white people living in industrialized nations. He portrays white history and its consequences as a "ghastly racial tragedy" (721). In the fallout resulting from enslavement and colonial adventures, whites have grasped onto their own version of "rot" by taking refuge in a new religion of racism. The "Western environment is soaked in and stained with the most blatant racism the world knows," a racism that has become "another kind of religion" (706–7). This is the religion of the "materially disposed and the culturally disinherited," but "what a shabby, vile, and cheap home the white heart finds when it seeks shelter in racism" (706–7). Thus we have, in Wright's analysis, the irrationalism of the masses of the Third World facing the intense and sustaining irrationalism of the masses of the West on the historical stage.

But Wright sees the future unfolding in Third World terms. At the same time that he explicitly condemns colonial and imperialist ventures around the world, he also maintains that these ventures created possibilities for Third World peoples to seize freedom. He urges his comrades to consider their common plight *and* to reject blackness as a way to ground politics. Manthia Diawara (1998, 64) argues that Wright's dramatic opening phrase to his speech, "The hour is late and I am pressed for time," is framed to refer not only to the late hour and the exhaustion of the participants but also to make the participants aware of their place in time and in history and the importance of seizing the moment.[10] In telling the "men of Europe" to "give that elite [leaders such as Nkrumah] the tools and let it finish the job," Wright anticipates Fanon's ([1963] 2004, 59) argument in *The Wretched of the Earth* that aid to Africa is not charity but "reparation," the "final stage of a dual consciousness—the consciousness of the colonized that *it is their due* and the consciousness of the capitalist powers that effectively *they must pay up*."[11]

Wright died in 1960, spared from witnessing how hard the future would be for Africa. As early as 1964 "the bloom had come off the rose of Ghana's celebratory moment" as Nkrumah and the Conventional People's Party, arguably in response to Western hostility, had become increasingly authoritarian, bureaucratic, and divorced from the Ghanaian people who had supported his rise to power.[12] More broadly, other new nations on the African continent were also struggling with internal problems and civil unrest while trying to negotiate their relationship to the West and to the Soviets. In 1960, the year of Wright's death, seventeen African nations declared their independence from Britain, France, and Belgium, but by 1968 there had been sixty-four coups or coup attempts in these new nations.[13] Each nationalist leader was at risk and under pressure; the Congo leader Patrice Lumumba's murder in 1961 by Katangese secessionists allied with Belgians only increased deep concern about Africa's future and enhanced African suspicion and distrust of Westerners. Obviously the future Wright hoped for and worked to achieve, in which both collective and individual freedom for Africans was key, became the path not taken. But can this occluded future offer a critical purchase on forms of political subjectivity that we should advance today? To consider this question it is necessary to detour first through Wright's trip to Nkrumah's revolutionary Ghana, a trip on which he deepened his philosophical commitment to existential freedom as well as his political commitment to carving a place for blacks in and through modern forms of political collective action.

RACE MATTERS, BUT HOW? WRIGHT'S TRIP TO GHANA

Like many African Americans who traveled to the African continent in the mid-twentieth century, Wright wanted not only to see Africa but also to take stock of his own identity as an African American. After his boat docks in Ghana, he is guided through the crowds by a personal friend of Nkrumah, and the first thing he notices is that "black life was everywhere" (2008, 52). Fascinated by the bare feet, the richly colored cloth, and the fact that the "whole of life that met the eyes was black," Wright is startled when he sees a European family "threading its way through the black crowd" (53). His host comments, "It's good *not* to be a minority for once, eh?" (53), and Wright admits the truth in this. But the next minute he is confronted by an African salesman in a shop who immediately recognizes Wright as an American and asks which part of Africa he came from. Startled and upset by this question, one he will confront again, Wright says, "Well, you know, you fellows who sold us and the white men who bought us didn't keep any records" (54).

From the outset Wright admits his perspective is that of a *Western* man of color, and this outlook is reinforced at every turn. The distance he feels from his African heritage, his disassociation with this identity, is confirmed by his reaction to seeing Africans wearing few clothes, dancing, singing, and drumming, and taking part in traditional ceremonies. He seems critical of life lived too publicly: women with babies strapped to their back, nursing them as they are walking, people urinating and bathing in the open, the constant beat of drums in drum circles, deformed beggars making heart-rending appeals, and all this under the constant sun, the oppressive and cloying heat. He writes,

"The intimacy of the African communal life can be witnessed in all of its innocence as it clusters about an outdoor hydrant" (2008, 71).

Throughout his travels Wright (2008, 59) remains hyperaware, with a desire but without the ability to understand what he is seeing: "Faced with the absolute otherness and inaccessibility of this new world, I was prey to a vague sense of mild panic, an oppressive burden of alertness which I could not shake off." This "panic" and "alertness" clearly stem from his trying to figure out his heritage, his ties to a continent that confuses him yet stakes a claim on his identity. Wright admits he was left cold when his black friends would boast, "We have a *special* gift for music, dancing, rhythm and movement. . . . We have a genius of our own. We were civilized in Africa when white men were still living in caves in Europe." He explains, "Talk of that sort had always seemed beside the point; I had always taken for granted the humanity of Africans as well as that of other people" (20). Maybe because Wright does not feel any natural tie to the continent, he also does not see any essential or special genius, ethics, or talent in black blood. For him race portends nothing about belonging to humanity; neither does it point toward privileged knowledge of how to change humanity for the better.

Thus although Wright argues that racism plays a primary role as one of the most important, if not the most important historical forces in the oppression of people worldwide, he also contends that race itself tells us nothing about identity, solidarity, or even the roots of oppression. For example, he does not point to social or political beliefs about racial inferiority to explain the original reasons for slavery. Studying what he calls the "many-centuries-war waged by the peninsula of Europe, with the sanction of Catholicism, against the continent of Africa," he argues that "slavery was not put into practice because of racial theories; racial theories sprang up in the wake of slavery, to justify it" (2008, 23–24). What interests him is the *effect* of slavery on blacks, both Africans and those in the diaspora. He does not accept that the resiliency of tribal behaviors, primitive or pagan customs, and religious (even Christian) fervor in both Africa and the United States indicate an essential quality to being black or a racial link between African Americans and Africans on the continent; therefore he is shocked to see some surface similarities between the behavior of Africans and some African Americans he knew in the South. Wright is especially unsettled when watching the dancing in Ghana for he remembers he had seen the "same snakelike, veering dances before. . . . Where? Oh, God yes; in America, in storefront churches, in Holy Roller Tabernacles, in God's Temples, in unpainted wooden prayer-meeting houses on the plantations of the Deep South. . . . And here I was seeing it all again against a background of a surging nationalist political movement! How could that be?" (78). Later in the narrative Wright contends that the resiliency and resemblance of these traditions on both continents points not to an essential quality to blackness but rather to the way oppression manifests on the bodies and behaviors of all kinds of people.[14] Here Wright moves toward articulating that modernity works to create the very concept and practices of what we call tradition, that these behaviors and customs are part of the displaced core of modernity itself.

Thus what some read as marks of positive racial qualities and deeper connection, Wright sees as varieties of pathology that coexist with other pathologies, all stemming from oppressive social and political conditions. Consistent with his other work, Wright identifies systematic oppression with a distinctly negative influence on the psyches of its victims. In Ghana, for example, he sees this impact in several of his interactions with people; he finds them suspicious, distrustful, and on guard and concludes, "A sodden distrust was lodged deep in the African heart" (2008, 128).

This intellectual and emotional distance from Africans gives Wright a sympathetic, albeit critical perspective on Nkrumah's efforts to create a modern political movement out of a tribal culture and competing traditional religions. Wright is impressed by Nkrumah. Directly defying the suggestion that Africans cannot rule themselves or must "learn" Western behaviors of citizenship, Nkrumah and the Convention People's Party demonstrate that self-rule can happen now. Most striking to Wright (2008, 76) is that the people of Ghana understand the meaning of freedom more deeply and urgently than Westerners:

> It meant the right to public assembly, the right to physical movement, the right to make known [their] views, the right to elect men of [their] choice to public office, and the right to recall them if they failed in their promises. At a time when the Western world grew embarrassed at the sound of the word "freedom," these people knew that it meant the right to shape their own destiny as they wished. Of that they had no doubt, and no threats could intimidate them about it; they might be cowed by guns and planes, but they'd not change their minds about the concrete nature of the freedom that they wanted and were willing to die for.

Though mainly tribal, from diverse tribes, and illiterate, four million people had organized themselves into a *we* demanding freedom from an alien flag and sovereignty over their own land. Here the peasants, in spite of their lack of formal education, were already acting as free citizens: "They had melted their tribal differences into an instrument to form a bridge between tribalism and twentieth-century forms of political mass organization; the women who danced and shouted were washerwomen, cooks, housewives, etc." (2008, 76). The Convention People's Party channeled citizens' "wild and liquid emotion" away from religion and into a new outlet: "Mass nationalist movements were, indeed, a new kind of religion. They were politics *plus*!" (77–78). Wright congratulates Nkrumah, exclaiming, "You've done what the Western world has said is impossible" (85).

Not surprisingly Wright (2008, 417) urges Nkrumah to reject both the West and the communists and follow a distinctly African path: to forge a secular religion and build a social structure that would offer "emotional sustenance" and allow escape from "the domination of foreigners." As Diawara (1998, 68) puts it, Wright understood that "for Nkrumah to realize his dream of independence, these West Africans would also have to be freed from themselves, from tribal religions which formed a psychological barrier between them and the modern world, and from the chiefs who had usurped a godlike position." Although we know now what Wright didn't know but suspected—that this would not be a path taken by new African nations—his reflections on Ghana may help us think about solidarity and collective political subjectivity today.

To explore this line of thinking further, I return to Wright's theorization of how to forge a collectivity beyond identity among blacks in the United States. Wright was already in conversation with French existentialists, particularly Beauvoir, before he left his home, and this encounter can help us think productively about these questions.

FREEDOM AND SOLIDARITY BEYOND IDENTITY
AND ACROSS BORDERS: SAYING "WE" WITH BEAUVOIR

Fifteen years prior to traveling to Ghana and addressing the Paris Congress, Wright was thinking about these same questions in the United States. His work resonated so deeply with Beauvoir that when she went to the United States in 1947 to travel for four months, she and Wright became close friends. Wright had already met Beauvoir and Sartre in 1946, on a visit to France by invitation of the French government initiated by Gertrude Stein and supported by Sartre and Marc Chagall; a year later Wright took Beauvoir to Harlem, showed her his favorite places in New York City, and helped her to think about women's situation as not so unique when studied in relationship to racial oppression. Most important, the work of Beauvoir and Wright offers an especially attractive variant of existentialism since they both theorize freedom as experienced collectively, in encounter, and their work is deeply informed by the diverse voices of the excluded and oppressed as expressed by the desire to embrace freedom.

Though Beauvoir's many references to Wright's work and friendship have been recorded, their intellectual relationship has not been explored in any real depth. When the friendship is studied, Wright's influence on Beauvoir is usually considered positive, as opening her eyes to racism, although Beauvoir had already read extensively about the Jim Crow South in preparation for her travels. In contrast Wright's interest in existentialism is most often read as negative such that it clouded, complicated, or even destroyed his authentic black voice (Gilroy 1993, 186). Lamenting the fact that Wright is remembered and venerated for his exploration of the "authentic" black American experience, while his later (and related) work from France is dismissed as having nothing to say to those studying race and black identity, Paul Gilroy urges study of the intellectual ties between Wright and Beauvoir that transgress the boundaries of nationality and ethnicity.[15] Extending the conversation between Wright and Beauvoir additionally helps us recognize that Western feminist and Third World antiracist liberation projects need not be seen as distinct, and certainly not as opposed, endeavors.

A few scholars have taken up Gilroy's call. Arguing against the position that Beauvoir references racial suffering in order to enhance her argument about the significance of gender, thus erasing the position of the black woman, Vikki Bell (2000) reads Beauvoir's engagement with Wright's work as helping her to demonstrate that women's suffering is *not* unique, that alterity is a *shared*, indeed a social experience. Likewise Margaret Simons (2001) credits Wright's influence on Beauvoir as moving her toward theorizing freedom as always situated, as well as toward thinking about sex, gender, and race through the lens of social caste rather than biology. Inspired by this work, I will show that Beauvoir and Wright portrayed subjectivity and identity as constructed yet not fixed, and they theorized and explicitly linked the experiences of oppressed groups across nations and oceans as well as across identity boundaries.

Reading their work together I notice the intellectual synergy between Wright and Beauvoir, so important for theorizing the affinities and interrelationships between sexed and raced identity and the situated agency of every subject. Both authors portray subjectivity as inherently porous, constrained as well as enabled by a web of relationships and connections (in other words, as constituted by situation). While the oppressed are subject to structural constraints that are internalized psychologically, both Beauvoir and Wright argue that the oppressed collectivity, as well as each individual subject, is nevertheless able to exercise agency and act in ways that exceed the assigned character-istics of collective identity. While remaining acutely attentive to relationships of power and oppression in (de)forming the psyches of subjects, Beauvoir and Wright also argue that oppressed peoples are able to forge bonds of solidarity, initiate change, and express their immanent freedom through these actions.

A final important feature common to Beauvoir's and Wright's work is their detailed attention to the varieties of experience *within* communities of blacks and *within* communities of women. Each stresses that differences between groups (men and women, black and white) are viewed as more pronounced when we fail to take account of the diversity of experiences inside these cate-gories. Wright and Beauvoir foreswear identity to pluralize perspectives, while still constructing a political *we* that defines a concrete alternative to the false universalism of the American national story and the patriarchal norm.

In 1941 Wright was invited to compose a text to accompany Farm Security Administration photos of rural and urban poverty. The result of this effort, *12 Million Black Voices*, can be productively paired with Beauvoir's *The Second Sex*. Each author sharply criticizes the construction of a false universal while also calling an alternative into being. How does Wright produce a *we* out of 12 million individual black voices, particularly since he is so attentive to noticing how oppression and violence affect blacks *perversely* as well as *differently* de-pending upon the situation—most notably location, generation, religion, and sex? How does Beauvoir do the same for women while also noting women's di-vision by class, age, religion, and nation? To show precisely how will illustrate Beauvoir's and Wright's productive articulation of the relationships between oppressed identities and the potential to initiate transformative freedom in encounter. Studying *12 Million Black Voices* as situated in a transatlantic con-versation with *The Second Sex* also illuminates the lasting contribution of Wright's speech to the Paris Congress as well as his work from Ghana.

Wright announces in the preface to *12 Million Black Voices* that he wishes to seize upon what is "qualitative and abiding in Negro experience." His soli-darity is "with the countless black millions who made up the bulk of the slave population during the seventeenth, eighteenth, and nineteenth centuries; those teeming black millions who endured the physical and spiritual ravages of serfdom; those legions of nameless blacks who felt the shock and hope of sudden emancipation; those terrified black folk who withstood the brutal wrath of the Ku Klux Klan, and who fled the cotton and tobacco plantations to seek refuge in northern and southern cities coincident with the decline of cotton culture of the Old South" ([1941] 2008, xx–xxi). His poignant narrative, moving through slavery, Jim Crow, and the great migration to urban poverty and discrimination in the North, is accompanied by photos taken by Dorothea Lange, Walker Evans, Edwin Rosskam, Russell Lee, and Wright himself. The photos were commissioned as a New Deal project to document suffering and its alleviation by New Deal agencies.[16] After working with photographers to capture over 1,500 images of Chicago's South Side alone, Wright selected 86 images for the book. Wright was a skilled photographer at this point, and he continued his interest in photography throughout his life. In the 1950s, when he traveled to Spain and to Ghana and took extensive photographs of these trips, he was fully aware of the danger of exoticizing his subjects and acutely attentive to his subject position as a Western man of color.[17] But even as early as *12 Million Black Voices*, Wright thought a great deal about the subjectivity of the photographer (himself and others), about how the image should be framed, and what his words should express and even where they should be placed on the page. His attention to rhetorical strategies and multiple readers' interpretations is revealed in his anticipation of what the viewer and reader might see in the image and how the reader and viewer might interpret the photos as reflected through their "naturalized" identity as white or black.

For example, Wright takes great care in framing what he wants to emerge as the meaning of the photos via his accompanying text, which addresses white and black readers at different moments. The opening paragraph of the first chapter, titled "Our Strange Birth," is placed directly below a photo of an older black man looking straight into the camera, his face marked by deep lines (figure 5.1). Wright's ([1941] 2008, 10) words evoke deep divisions in the national *we* as he addresses whites: "Each day when you see us black folk upon the dusty land of the farms or upon the hard pavement of the city streets, you usually take us for granted and think you know us, but our history is far stranger than you suspect, and we are not what we seem."

In this powerful opening passage, Wright addresses white readers as pupils, arguing that what "you" assume about black people is wrong. He demands that whites acknowledge blacks as a collectivity whose existence challenges any claim to a universal white nationality and avow that blacks are individuals whose diverse experiences defy caricatures of the presumed Negro character.[18] Doing so Wright deconstructs any claim to national unity (or common interest) by addressing readers as black or white. He chastises whites and simultaneously draws attention to the population of all too visible, and yet hidden, black Americans, a *we* of "millions of black folk who live in this land" ([1941] 2008, 12). Black Americans are part of "Western civilization" but subject to an especially "weird and paradoxical birth" (12), forced to this nation on slave ships.

FIGURE 5.1. Sharecropper, Georgia. Photo by Jack Delano, Farm Security Administration.

This *we* of black Americans, however, is also fractured and in no way naturally unified. Products of multiple forms of oppression, violence, and provincialism, American blacks are themselves internally divided. Dividing his audience into black and white readers, and then fracturing this *we* even further, Wright indicates that we can never assume a national unity, that what was said to be true of blacks is in fact an invention by whites, and that blacks themselves are divided and fractured and have to work to create any unity that could oppose and change this situation. The *we* that Wright hopes to create is not readily or easily available and has nothing inherently in common. It is the structural history of slavery and current experiences of oppression that bring American blacks together, but only potentially. Blacks may potentially constitute a *we* of 12 million black voices, but it has to be *produced* rather than assumed: "Our outward guise still carries the old familiar aspect which three hundred years of oppression in America have given us, but beneath the garb of the black laborer, the black cook, and the black elevator operator lies an uneasily tied knot of pain and hope whose snarled strands converge *from many points of time and space*" ([1941] 2008, 11, emphasis added).

Using a similar strategy Beauvoir destroys the illusion of the universal *we*, showing it to be a male invention from a male perspective, while at the same time producing a new and revolutionary *we* by positing a collective of women that previously did not exist. Just as Wright rejects the expectation that he will identify with all Africans or black Americans simply because he is black, Beauvoir experiences a disjuncture and a distance from the idea of Woman as written in science, literature, and psychoanalysis and creates, rather than naturally discovers, political bonds to women in the world. The introductory chapter to *The Second Sex* frames her theoretical goals: to show how women have been defined as "Other" to the universal and to "describe the world from the woman's point of view such as it is offered to her" ([1949] 2011, 17). As we saw in chapter 1, volume 1 of *The Second Sex* recounts how in science, psychoanalysis, literature, history, and myth, women are invented as fixed, natural, essential, unchanging, and codified under the idea of Woman. This wrongly assigns a stable meaning to sexual difference, which is always inherently *unstable*, and in doing so aids and abets women's second-class status. Volume 2 recounts experiences and creates multiple conversations across women's lives via the compilation of thousands of individual stories, extracted and borrowed from the lives of Beauvoir's acquaintances, from her own life, from autobiographies and biographies of famous women, and from literature.

In everyday life too Beauvoir notices the disjuncture between what is expected of her as Woman and the diversity of human life and the meanings assigned to it. She writes, "If I want to define myself, I first have to say, 'I am a woman'"; all other assertions will arise from this basic truth. There is "an absolute human type that is masculine," but a woman's "ovaries and uterus" are the "particular conditions that lock her in her subjectivity" ([1949] 2011, 5). Beauvoir's women, then, also have a "weird and paradoxical" relationship to the universal. Women's road to freedom is blocked by their material conditions, their own psychologically produced visions of what they can accomplish, and their previous inability throughout history to adequately say *we* primarily due to the concrete material differences in their lives. Women are a *we* that must be produced rather than discovered:

> Women—except in certain abstract gatherings such as Congresses—do not use "we"; men say "women," and women adopt this word to refer to themselves; but they do not posit themselves authentically as Subjects. . . . They have no past, no history, no religion of their own. . . . They live dispersed among men, tied by homes, work, economic interests, and social conditions to certain men—fathers or husbands—

more closely than to other women. As bourgeois women, they are in solidarity with bourgeois men and not with women proletarians; as white women, they are in solidarity with white men and not with black women. ([1949] 2011, 8)

Wright and Beauvoir share a commitment to existentialist freedom witnessed in the claim that modernity, though it has created oppressed subjects, has failed to embrace them or enable their political subjectivity. The two also share the insight that enormous energy goes into the creation of the subordinated status of the other to shore up a whitened and masculinized self to whom history, transcendence, and sovereignty rightly belong. As we saw so clearly in Fanon, the whitened masculinized self assigns immanence, ambiguity, mortality, and embodiment to the created other and insists that repetitive, alienated, flexible, and low-paid labor is naturally appropriate and ideally suited for the temperaments and talents of women and colonized, enslaved, and nonwhite peoples.

Producing a counter to this false subject, a collective *we* produced from the lived experience of individual women, constrained and enabled by their particular situations, is the challenge Beauvoir takes up in *The Second Sex*. Like Wright, she unveils the particularity of the male self as well as the ideal of Woman. She demonstrates that men make assumptions about women via belief in and perpetuation of the myths proclaimed about women, while knowing little of women's lives. And like Wright, Beauvoir counters these myths by creating an alternative collective. This alternative, though, does not fall into the trap of assuming any identity prior to experience and it does not run roughshod over the individual voices making up the potential collectivity. Wright's and Beauvoir's call for an as yet unimagined political collectivity produces political solidarity out of the diverse lived experiences of oppression, across borders and across ethnic, racial, and gender boundaries.

Offering numerous and specific details of individual lived experience, Beauvoir and Wright illuminate the daily materiality of oppression, as does Fanon in his work with colonized Algerians. For example, Beauvoir argues that motherhood as currently mandated to be women's destiny and the ultimate fulfillment of feminine desire is inherently oppressive. But she also argues that the oppressive norms of motherhood vary by culture, by ethnicity, by class, and throughout history and that women experience this demand within these locations very differently. She contends that "pregnancy and motherhood are experienced in very different ways depending on whether they take place in revolt, resignation, satisfaction, or enthusiasm" ([1949] 2011,

533). A woman who had desperately wanted a child might be surprised to find that she experiences motherhood as a burden, and another woman might find in her child "the satisfaction of secretly harbored dreams" (533). Beauvoir's main contention concerning motherhood is that it should truly be a choice rather than an obligation or a natural "destiny": "To have a child is to take on a commitment; if the mother shrinks from it, she commits an offense against human existence, against a freedom; but no one can impose it on her" (566). Although Beauvoir never discusses the experiences of slave women in *The Second Sex*, her sensitivity to women's differing experiences of motherhood, and her consistent critique of the bourgeois white ideal of the mother, shows Beauvoir's writing as a precursor to the work of Hortense Spillers, for example, who shows that conventional gender categories were unavailable to black women under slavery and their work of mothering fell outside the very category of motherhood (Spillers 1987). Filled with thousands of anecdotes about girlhood, sexual initiation, menstruation, marriage, motherhood, prostitution, lesbian relationships, aging, and more, Beauvoir's almost eight hundred pages link these diverse experiences within and as constituted by "demands of femininity" (Marso 2006).

While Beauvoir ([1949] 2011, 567) recounts stories from individual lives to document the falseness of the idea of Woman, illuminated in one instance by the claims of mothers that "maternal love has nothing natural about it," in *12 Million Black Voices* Wright lays bare the invention of the Negro by collecting the photos of individual blacks. For example, here is Wright ([1941] 2008, 18) denouncing the "American attitude" toward blacks: "Compounded of a love of gold and God, was the beginning of America's paternalistic code toward her black maid, her black industrial worker, her black stevedore, her black dancer, her black waiter, her black sharecropper; it was a code of casual cruelty, of brutal kindness, of genial despotism, a code which has survived, grown, spread, and congealed into a national tradition that dominates in small or large measure, all black and white relations throughout the nation until this day." Juxtaposed to the categories of "*the* black maid," "*the* black industrial worker," "*the* black stevedore," and so on are photos featuring *individual* blacks performing these tasks. These individual faces expose the lie of the kindness, geniality, and benevolence of white supremacy as well as the lie of inherent servitude, the cheerful nature of the black domestic worker, the natural inferiority of blacks. As Wright tells and shows the story of both individual and collective black experience in America, he exposes the lies whites tell about black people, documents the several and different ways racism is

FIGURE 5.2. Interior of kitchenette, Chicago. Photo by Russell Lee, Farm Security Administration.

made material, and calls on blacks to build a solidarity not from identity but from collective action.

A good example showing how racism manifests differently for different blacks emerges from Wright's narrative and photos recording black lives lived in kitchenettes in northern urban areas. As Wright ([1941] 2008, 104) recounts, "Bosses of the Buildings" of northern cities rent out kitchenettes to blacks for vastly higher profits than they would make from white tenants. These crowded, filthy, one-room apartments, "havens from the plantations in the South," are also "our prison, our death sentence without a trial, the new

FIGURE 5.3. Interior, Washington, DC. Photo by Arthur Rothstein, Farm Security Administration.

form of mob violence that assaults not only the lone individual, but all of us, in its ceaseless attacks" (105, 106). But while life in the kitchenette affects all badly, it also affects them differently: "The kitchenette jams our farm girls, while still in their teens, into rooms with men who are restless and stimulated by the noise and lights of the city; and more of our girls have bastard babies than the girls in any other sections of the city" (110). This text is accompanied by a photo of a young mother holding a baby, with two young girls by her side (figure 5.2). On the opposite page is a photo of a young black male staring into the camera: "The kitchenette fills our black boys with longing and restlessness, urging them to run off from home, to join together with other restless black boys in gangs, that brutal form of city courage" (111; figure 5.3).

In *12 Million Black Voices* and *The Second Sex*, Wright and Beauvoir never assume commonality; instead they attempt to forge solidarity by imagining the collectivity built differently. By recounting individual and collective lived experience they reveal the deceit of a presumed universality and yield an alternative base for formulating a common life. Rather than call on the experience of oppressed subjects to show an ever widening and more inclusive universalism (to include blacks in the American story, or women in philosophy and history, for example), Wright and Beauvoir criticize exclusion from the outside to produce a *we* that leads to somewhere else. The oppressed subjects cannot be folded back into the original and newly revealed false universal by an ever increasing circle of democratic inclusion; instead their experience demands a new way of producing the common and a new vision of progress. Having completely deconstructed any "natural" basis for "feminine" desire and "black" ways of being in the world, Beauvoir and Wright reject essentialism and commit to seizing a kind of freedom that is not rooted in identity or assumed from nature or tradition. How to respond to oppression experienced in and on the body and learn how to imagine and embrace freedom in encounter is the central political question for Beauvoir. In part III I will return to this question to explore the forms of violence in which some women engage as a "perverse protest" to oppression when they are isolated and alone. While allies can potentially change this response, as we learned from Beauvoir's encounters with Fanon, Boupacha, and Wright, I extend this conversation to ask what difference friends might make.

What version of freedom are Wright and Beauvoir advocating? Freedom entails siding with the oppressed and opening up the possibility of freedom for everyone. Also clear in the work of Wright and Beauvoir is their rejection of those values that can be understood as modernity's constitutive outside—feminine irrationality or passion, the "wisdom" or "ethics" of the black peasant, or the religion, traditions, customs, or folk intuition of the oppressed. While in *12 Million Black Voices* Wright ([1941] 2008, 75) does acknowledge the role of religion and of dancing, singing, and other ways of experiencing joy under oppression, he says they are "not enough to unify our fragile folk lives in this competitive world." For Wright, what potentially unifies blacks and moves them toward solidarity are the effects of some of the very intrusions from whites that had also brought oppression. Part of the story of modernity that Wright tells in *12 Million Black Voices* is of successive generations losing claim to the land that had oppressed them and learning about the possibility of seizing freedom by seeing their potential ties to others. Of the children of the sharecroppers, he writes, "Unlike us, they have been influenced by the movies, magazines, and glimpses of town life, and they lack the patience to wait for the consummation of God's promise as we do" (75). The impact of media as well as the impact of industrialization in the auto industry and steel factories move blacks away from their folk lives. Wright says "thundering tractors and cotton-picking machines" (79) are partly responsible for the great migration to the North, a migration that changed not only blacks' daily habits but their consciousness. New and contingent practices open up opportunities and change situations in unexpected ways. These insights indicate that it might be struggle and encounter with other people—enemies, allies, and friends—that can help us see our world differently, or it might be that an encounter with a changed situation, a contingent historical fact can shift our perspective as much as a shift in consciousness. We must be open to all these possibilities, and ready for them.

Just as Wright reinscribes modernity as holding greater promise for the oppressed than the old embrace of religion or tradition, Beauvoir's work follows this same trajectory as she explores the ways women's "feminine" desires link them to the past and to their oppression rather than opening up a future. Following upon the chapter titled "Biological Data" that demonstrates sexual difference as always unsettled and necessarily contingent, the five chapters on history in volume 1 of *The Second Sex* show that while normative categories of sexual difference signify relations of power and are constitutive in social relationships, various material changes—such as introducing or eliminating private property, female suffrage, access to abortion, even the rituals of courtly love—substantively change women's situation. While normative categories are an attempt to alleviate the psychic anxiety that sexual difference seems to always generate, for Beauvoir, as for Wright, the act of holding onto these same categories, even when coded positively, is the wrong way forward. For Wright and Beauvoir, leaving these categories open, unmoored, unsettled is one of the more promising interventions of modernity.

BLACK AND FEMALE VOICES CLAIMING FREEDOM

The final chapter of *12 Million Black Voices,* titled "Men in the Making," is introduced by a full-page photo of a black man dressed in the garb of an industrial worker, confidently returning the viewer's gaze (figure 5.4). Turning

FIGURE 5.4. Steel worker, Pennsylvania. Photo by
Arthur Rothstein, Farm Security Administration.

the page, we see a photo of four black women carrying signs in front of the
White House. They are delegates from Michigan, Massachusetts, Louisiana,
and Kentucky, protesting lynching (figure 5.5).

These two photos emphasize Wright's ([1941] 2008, 142–43) point that out
of oppression ("cultural devastation, slavery, physical suffering, unrequited
longing, abrupt emancipation, migration, disillusionment, bewilderment,
joblessness, and insecurity") "there are millions of us and we are moving in all
directions." These photos depict blacks seizing the strategies and instruments
of modern politics: the union, the picket line, the protest march. Later in the
chapter he cites the Great Depression as a time for blacks to see an "identity of
interests" with "many white workers" and understand the forces "that tended

FIGURE 5.5. Demonstration, Washington, DC. AP/Wide World Photos.

to reshape our folk consciousness." As Wright counsels, "we" blacks must accept the "death of our old folk lives," enabling us "to cross class and racial lines." Leaving our "folk lives" (by this Wright means premodern religion and culture, superstitions and intuitions) is the "death that made us free" (144).[19]

Nearing the end of *12 Million Black Voices* we detect a curious development that prefigures Wright's report from Ghana and his address to the Paris Congress. Having constituted a *we* from the fragmented lives of black Americans, Wright recommends leaving behind the culture and traditions that defined blacks as oppressed. So we might ask: Is there anything distinct about being black *other than* the history of oppression and the struggle against it? Although Wright depicts blacks with dignity, composure, and elegance, he has an ambivalent relationship to anything that might be described as black culture. Just as he is perplexed and baffled by ancestor worship and traditional explanations of life cycles and beliefs in Ghana, he is deeply critical of the evangelical and religious beliefs (as well as claims to being good dancers and singers) professed by African Americans. Not only does Wright think it a grave mistake to try to prove the humanity of blacks by celebrating early and extensive African culture; he also thinks it is a mistake to base solidarity and revolutionary potential on essential characteristics of a culture or a people.

Instead Wright moves in a different direction. At the very end of *12 Million Black Voices* he confirms his faith in political subjectivity and freedom as expressed in collective action. In spite of the resistance and violence of "Lords of the Land" and "Bosses of the Buildings" blacks are "winning our heritage," "crossing the line you dared us to cross, though we pay in the coin of death!" ([1941] 2008, 146–47). "The differences between black folk and white folk are not blood or color, and the ties that bind us are deeper than those that separate us. . . . Look at us and know us and you will know yourselves, for *we* are *you*, looking back at you from the dark mirror of our lives!" (146). Wright's final words: "Print compels us. Voices are speaking. Men are moving! And we shall be with them" (147). His message: though denied the freedom promised by modernity, blacks were born within modernity and will seize freedom, violently or otherwise, via modern forms of protest and politics. Blackness, though constitutive, is not definitive; human beings, blacks included, share much in common, most importantly the desire to be free.

Beauvoir ([1949] 2011, 750–51) closes *The Second Sex* in a similar manner:

> Once again, to explain [woman's] limits, we must refer to her situation and not to a mysterious essence. The future remains wide open. . . . The historical past cannot be considered as defining an eternal truth; it merely translates a situation that is showing itself to be historical precisely in that it is in the process of changing. . . . The free woman is just being born. . . . What is beyond doubt is that until now women's possibilities have been stifled and lost to humanity, and in her and everyone's interest it is high time she be left to take her own chances.

In the very final words of *The Second Sex*, echoing Wright's call to blacks and whites to move together, Beauvoir writes, "Within the given world, it is up to man to make the reign of freedom triumph; to carry off this supreme victory, men and women must, among other things and beyond their natural [biological] differentiations, unequivocally affirm their brotherhood" (766).[20]

Both Wright and Beauvoir conclude that the oppressed should leave identity, religion, culture, and tradition behind. For both of them, it is oppression—not race, gender, or any other form of identity—that links us in solidarity, across identities and across borders. Embracing modern forms of politics, as they see it, makes it possible for the oppressed to define their own future. Beauvoir and Wright value this embrace of freedom against remaining in traditional forms of community and repeating ways of life that confirm the status quo. For example, Wright sees Africans embracing national sovereignty in the same way Beauvoir sees women in the paid workforce: confronting the world in these ways is an important first step toward freedom, even though it is no guarantee of happiness and may not even alleviate oppression in the short term. These are not solutions; they are only steps. Embracing national sovereignty fails to recognize interconnected global conditions of inequality and domination, and to advocate women's entry into wage work fails to challenge the dominant legitimizing discourse of work (on the latter point see Weeks 2011, 13).

James Baldwin (1964) warns that the price of leaving religion and all other gimmicks, primarily racism, behind will undoubtedly be angst, loneliness, and rootlessness—all burdens accompanying the responsibilities and rewards of an existential freedom that refuses the comforts of falsehoods that help us get by in the world. Ultimately these gimmicks are too costly. White Americans are trapped in a history they don't understand and black Americans are trapped by anti-black racism. The loneliness we each endure in the wake of losing collective myths makes collective political action possible and necessary. The reward is the possibility of a new future, one brought about by new forms of solidarity that were previously unimagined or seemingly impossible.

Wright readily admits that his vision of moving beyond race, but also beyond religion, tradition, and the status quo, is not the path toward what we think of as happiness. Here again he shares the intellectual universe with Beauvoir, who consistently values freedom above religious or other mythic solace, too easy moral closure, and clear promises about the future. Beauvoir ([1949] 2011, 16) clarifies the point: "We cannot really know what the word 'happiness' means, and still what authentic values it covers; there is no way to measure the happiness of others, and it is always easy to call a situation that one would like to impose on others happy: in particular, we declare happy those condemned to stagnation, under the pretext that happiness is immobility." In *White Man Listen!* Wright (2008, 647) pointedly says, "Recently a young woman asked me: 'But would your ideas make people happy?' And, before I was aware of what I was saying, I heard myself answering with a degree of frankness that I rarely, in deference to politeness, permit myself in personal conversation: 'My dear, I do not deal in happiness; I deal in meaning.'"

HESITATIONS

In *On the Postcolony*, Achille Mbembe (2011, 6) argues that what is often missed in reflections on the African self is that "the African subject is like any other human being: he or she engages in *meaningful acts.*" Treating the other as any human subject longing for freedom, Beauvoir's and Wright's existential commitments allow them to see difference and plurality where others see identity and sameness, at the same time that they invoke a collective political subject united across many differences. We might see *12 Million Black Voices* and *The Second Sex* as calls to create community, to bring something new into existence where previously only a noxious community of sameness could be seen. In this way these texts are political actions that may result in the formation of politically liberating subjectivity.

Wright's and Beauvoir's articulations of modernity's promise to create new conditions of solidarity might be too sanguine. Wright invokes Third World, Asian-African solidarity in *The Color Curtain* in 1956, documenting his three-week visit to Indonesia for the Bandung Conference, though his report has been challenged as a far too rosy picture of what actually happened. One British journalist based in India, G. H. Jansen, offers a different perspective: "Two conferences were held at Bandung in April 1955. One was the real conference, about which not very much is known. . . . The other was a quite different conference, a crystallization of what people wanted to believe had happened which, as a myth, took on reality in . . . the Bandung Spirit" (quoted in Roberts and Foulcher 2016, 3). In their remarkable collection of historical documents written by Asian participants and commenters on the Bandung conference, newly translated from Indonesian and Dutch, the editors of *Indonesian Notebook: A Sourcebook on Richard Wright and the Bandung Conference* show what was ignored in invoking the romance of the "Bandung spirit." In a narrative of collectivity, too easy solidarity, and the move toward increasing freedom by joining with other oppressed peoples and nations, we erase the many competing state-building projects and logics and voices of dissent arguing that African American experiences are profoundly different from each other, to start with, and from those of citizens in decolonizing African nations, and that these, in turn, differ from the experiences of diverse Asian citizens with imperialism, colonialism, and efforts to decolonize and win freedom.

While these are profoundly important documents, and we must not forget diversity of experience and contingencies of identity, this is a quite familiar problem. Beauvoir too is criticized by feminist scholars who rightly claim that when solidarity and commonality of experience are too easily and quickly asserted, particular voices—usually nonwhite, marginalized voices—are silenced. Also, it is the assertion of identity as feminine difference (or cultural otherness) and black pride (in various offshoots of *négritude*) that have often been effective for mobilizing group action. Additionally Mbembe and others warn of the danger of reproducing the opposition (and thus the false choice) of an affirmation of identity via alignment with traditions or culture versus merging with and subsequent loss in modernity and its conditions of alienation.

But I think Wright and Beauvoir help us to move beyond this false choice. Though both thinkers urge the rejection of categories of identity that emerge from relations of inherent inequality, analyzing the weight of these identities in the current political moment remains at the heart of their vision of how to craft political alternatives. While some might argue that Wright and Beauvoir are too hopeful about bringing a group into existence where none had existed before, particularly since they do this through language and text, we might nevertheless admire their ability to be so astute in showing how identity categories shape history while insisting that we not get stuck in these limited dimensions of experience. Most inspirational is Wright's and Beauvoir's shared audacity to demand more freedom, more possibilities, and the shaping of as yet unimagined futures. In part III, I return to the ills of isolation and the false faith in individual agency and individual and group identity as a solution to conditions of unfreedom. And again I will argue that we can experience freedom only in encounter. Beauvoir urges us not only to struggle with enemies and allies but also to actively seek out friends. Her texts, and her commitment to encounter, are exemplary in this regard.

PART III. FRIENDS
CONVERSATIONS THAT CHANGE THE RULES

Chapters 2, 4, and 5 (on Arendt, Fanon, and Wright) moved among different levels of intimacy in encounter, demonstrating how structural, political, group, and historic encounters shape, make possible, or block intimate and bodily encounters and how encounters between bodies have the potential to put forces into motion on a larger historical or political scale. Beauvoir often moves among levels, extracting the political importance of intimate relationships within and with the power to change habits, manners, and modes of collectivity. Hers is a highly unusual method for a political thinker. While she sees differences and distinctions among modes of assemblage and contends that these differences certainly matter, she shifts back and forth and in between, such that we can see new connections and, most important, see *politics* where we used to see only love, sex, family, intimacy.

Chapter 3, on Sade and von Trier, destroys any assumptions we might have about love and intimacy as apolitical. HE and SHE are in love, and their relationship is intimate, but it is never shorn of power and agonism. Beauvoir's willingness to look relationships of love directly in the face to inquire into their political mechanisms challenges Arendt's characterization of love as apolitical. In *The Human Condition* Arendt (1958, 242) writes, "Love, by its very nature, is unworldly, and it is for this reason rather than its rarity that it is not only apolitical but antipolitical, perhaps the most powerful of all

FIGURE III.1. Alison Bechdel, "The Rule," *Dykes to Watch Out For*, 1985.

antipolitical human forces." As an alternative form of intimate relationship that might show plurality in microcosm, Arendt might turn to friendship.[1] Indeed in chapter 7 I explore Arendt's willingness to extend a form of feminist friendship to Rahel Varnhagen as she reaches across history to retell the story of her life.

While the first two sections of this book focus on enemies and allies, this one features the freedom-enhancing potential of feminist friendship. I highlight this intimate space to illuminate what is at stake for freedom in every encounter. To frame my discussion of several films in this last section and think about them in regard to feminist friendship, I turn to Alison Bechdel's "rule" for feminist film. The "Bechdel rule," referenced in 1985 in Bechdel's comic strip *Dykes to Watch Out For*, says a film is feminist only if it has at least two (named) female characters who talk to each other about something other than a man (figure III.1).

Bechdel is a 2014 recipient of the "Genius" MacArthur Foundation

Awards,[2] creator of the long-lived strip (1983–2008) *Dykes to Watch Out For* and the graphic memoirs *Fun Home: A Family Tragicomic* (2006), about the suicide of her closeted gay father, and, most recently, a Winnicottian-inspired exploration of her relationship with her mother, aptly titled *Are You My Mother? A Comic Drama* (2013). A memoirist who ties her story to that of her family members, friends, lovers, psychiatrists, and random life encounters that introduce swerves into her trajectory, Bechdel utilizes graphic memoir to present her autobiography in a sometimes melodramatic or excessive, non-narrative, and nonheroic way.[3] Her illustrations often do not match the narrative of the text, introducing spaces where the reader has to ponder meaning or even interject her own meaning. The way Bechdel renders bodies in motion, sometimes out of control and sometimes stubbornly stuck in place, continually challenges our desire to believe in sovereign action and control and coherent identity. Moreover Bechdel undermines the autobiographical form by refusing both the heroic storyline and the storyline portraying the stereotypical struggle to overcome obstacles. She consistently blurs boundaries, defies formal rules, and queers our expectations of family life and love. She also forgoes an end or closure to her story and often embraces failure as a route to new encounters and new ways of being. Most important, she depicts her life as bound up with the lives of others and their interventions in, as well as perceptions and descriptions of, her life. The way Bechdel tells her own story is closely linked with the stories of women's lives I now turn to.

I make the Bechdel rule my interpretive task, assessing various strategies by which we might meet, pass, negotiate, exceed, or break this rule. Doing so I raise questions about how narrative and aesthetic choices shape how we see the individual as well as the collective story, or competing stories, of women's lives in narratives and on screen. Guided by several of Beauvoir's short essays on literary style, I discuss how aesthetic features of texts and films, including narrative and form, play a key role in how we talk about freedom, sovereignty, and agency in women's lives and in feminist politics. Fostering encounters between women, those that begin new conversations, changes all the rules.

Adopting the Bechdel rule strictly has had mixed consequences. When extracted from its context in *Dykes to Watch Out For*, it has sometimes become a bar for liberal representation. The rule is taken out of the context of the queer comic strip to create a representational system that obscures the actual conversation between the two dykes. Doing so, it erases the two dykes from consciousness and proclaims a rule. Here is the rule—now we can forget the dykes! Thus shorn of its queer comic aesthetic, Bechdel's rule becomes a call to simply put more women on screen and get them to talk to each other.

While this might pass as a representation of women's lives, we have to ask if the conversations that are created only bend rather than break the rule of patriarchy.

I read the Bechdel rule both in and out of context. I remember its queer context but also take it out of context to enhance its queer potential by thinking about it with three very different films in chapter 6. All the films in chapter 6 fail when we apply a strict interpretation of the rule, but they succeed in what I take up as the Bechdel task. The female biopics and the biography I explore in chapter 7 all succeed the rule and the task, but each in a different way. Thus reading in and out of context, I bend the Bechdel rule to measure its measure in new ways: not to demand more women on screen or more progressive representation of women's lives (although that can be important too, as we will see) but to consider narrative and formal features of women's lives as having an impact on how we see and talk about the collective, competing stories of women's lives, the stories of feminism, and our ability to see anew how freedom is grasped or missed in encounters. Adopting the Bechdel rule as an *interpretive task* enhances its queer potential by surpassing the systematicity of rules to extend Bechdel's political claims about conversation into new spaces.

In chapter 6 I turn to Chantal Akerman's *Jeanne Dielman*, David Fincher's *Gone Girl*, and Lars von Trier's *Nymphomaniac*. Featuring isolated women, none of these films satisfies the rule in its strict reading. All three women are alone, dangerously alone, as it turns out, bereft of the company and counsel of other women. Violent consequences ensue. Reading with feminist film theorists and in conversation with key moments of *The Second Sex*, I show why Bechdel finds it so crucial for women to find friends: to speak together, to have conversations about something other than men, and for these conversations to be available (for viewing, reading, encountering) in public culture. Chapter 7 enacts Beauvoir's politics as encounter by showing what happens when Beauvoir reaches out to Violette Leduc, when Arendt reaches out to Rahel Varnhagen, and when Margarethe von Trotta reaches out to Arendt. These three encounters, read with each other, demonstrate how the rules of politics change when we do politics with Beauvoir and embrace freedom in the encounter.

PERVERSE PROTESTS
FROM CHANTAL AKERMAN
TO LARS VON TRIER

Capital has made and makes money out of our cooking, smiling, fucking. . . .
Our faces have become distorted from so much smiling, our feelings have got
lost from so much loving, our oversexualization has left us completely desex-
ualized. —SILVIA FEDERICI, *Revolution at Point Zero*

A woman combines *cooking* and the relentless rituals of housework with her
daily practice of prostituting herself in her own bedroom, one day murdering one of her clients with a pair of scissors. An especially beautiful woman
never stops *smiling*, even when she hits her face with a hammer to "fake" domestic abuse and implicate her husband. A self-proclaimed nymphomaniac,
addicted to *fucking*, loses all sexual feeling with her husband, deciding to
leave her toddler home alone while she frequents a sadomasochist sex club to
search for her lost libido.

These are brief plot summaries of Chantal Akerman's 1975 feminist classic
Jeanne Dielman, David Fincher's 2014 Hollywood blockbuster *Gone Girl*, and
Lars von Trier's 2013 two-volume European art-house film, *Nymphomaniac*.
The heroines in these films embody the characteristics of seemingly idealized
femininity—they are white, middle-class, heterosexual, and cosmopolitan—
and yet the eruption of female violence against a man, each time provoked

by a sexual act or a moment of pleasure, signals deep levels of dissatisfaction and anger. Like many of the women Beauvoir studies, who are marked by pathologies of femininity, the heroines in these films might easily be dismissed, even condemned by viewers as slutty, crazy, vengeful, and violent.

While the narratives have in common female violence against men, their intended audiences and artistic and aesthetic contexts are quite different. Directed by the female auteur Chantal Akerman, *Jeanne Dielman* is aesthetically avant-garde and appreciated by film scholars and feminist thinkers. *Gone Girl*, directed by David Fincher with a script by Gillian Flynn, is based on a book by Flynn that was on the *New York Times* best-seller list for eight weeks and sold over two million copies in the first year. The film was produced for profit and mass consumption and has been interpreted by several critics as misogynist in its depiction of female manipulation and power. *Nymphomaniac* is the most recent film from Lars von Trier. As I noted the chapter on *Antichrist*, while von Trier has directed several films with female experience at the center, he has nevertheless received an (at best) ambivalent response from feminist critics and academics.[1]

In my chapter on Beauvoir's encounter with Fanon, I concluded that she did not see much potential for collective resistance in pathological symptoms; in this chapter, following on Beauvoir's literary practice in volume 2 of *The Second Sex*, I stage an encounter of the three isolated women in these films to demonstrate that they are desperately in need of collectivity in order to experience freedom. To my mind, Jeanne's, Amy's, and Joe's actions signal a clear need for sororal bonds. When we see the heroines in conversation with each other and read the films in conversation with *The Second Sex*, we can discern how women's seemingly pathological feelings and acts of violence, produced in isolation and conditions of oppression, might productively be read as signs of resistance.

I extend and deepen Beauvoir's attention to women's feelings in each film's mise-en-scène by bringing Beauvoir's insights about women's experience to each film's materialized aesthetic. Doing so moves us away from an abstract existential condition to show the compromised conditions of freedom for women and what happens to freedom when women are isolated and their pathologies dictate their actions in encounter. Nevertheless women act. Even isolated women often exceed the limits of feminine identity and its mandated behaviors to resist oppression in perverted and yet discernible ways. Putting Beauvoir in conversation with Akerman I show that even activities that are oppressively associated with femininity, as well as the affects that are often a result of these activities, might produce pleasure and also cue us to notice surprising resources for resistance.

This chapter homes in on a particular conjunction of emotion: the relationship between pleasure and danger. I argue that each heroine is positioned to act at the apex of pleasure and danger in her relationship to the activities Federici names in this chapter's epigraph: cooking, smiling, and fucking. But while Federici suggests that women have lost the ability to feel, in the films I discuss, while oppressive mechanisms and institutions (marriage, motherhood, sex with husbands) do not deliver the promised feelings (satisfaction, fulfillment, happiness), women *do* feel things, just not *these* things or at least not at the right moments. These heroines feel pleasure when cooking, smiling, and fucking, but this pleasure positions them too close to danger. Like SHE in *Antichrist*, they suddenly feel too much, not in the "right" way, or at the wrong moment.

In conversation with each other and read through the lens of *The Second Sex*, the films urge us to think about a diverse range of women's feelings—anxiety, paranoia, revenge, wanton desire, and murderous intent—but especially zeros in on the surprising conjunction between feelings of pleasure and danger that seem to lead to violent acts and make these women look crazy and dangerous.[2] Motivated by new or increased intensities or sometimes the sudden absence of the emotions that sustain them (at the end of volume 1 of *Nymphomaniac* Joe laments, "I can't feel anything!"), the women act, or at least they act up. What they do might be seen as displaced, off-target, deviant, maybe even perverse or grotesque in its excess, and yet their actions move them from victimhood to something and somewhere else.[3] At a key moment in each film, driven by a range or intensity of feelings and linked to a sexual act,[4] the woman claims her (circumscribed) agency and commits an act of violence. Tellingly the way the heroines refuse the role of victim cannot be contained by the liberal feminist frame: these are not stories of the conventional feminist heroine who takes control, becomes empowered, or "leans in" to assert herself.[5] Agency in these films is significantly compromised or distorted, but nevertheless the possibility of agonistic actions appears in even the most narrow or negative spaces, though it would be better directed toward collective action.

COOKING

Cooking is more than penetrating and revealing the intimacy of substances. It reshapes and re-creates them. In working the dough, she experiences her power. . . . Done every day, this work becomes monotonous and mechanical; it is laden with waiting: waiting for the water to boil, for the roast to be cooked just right, for the laundry to dry; even if different tasks are well organized, there are long moments of passivity and emptiness; most of the time, they are accomplished in boredom. —SIMONE DE BEAUVOIR, *The Second Sex*

Akerman's, *Jeanne Dielman, 23, quai du Commerce 1080 Bruxelles*, premiered in 1975. Presented in what seems like real time, the film centers on a Belgian widow going about her day—peeling potatoes, washing dishes, making coffee, brushing her hair, taking a bath, cleaning the bathtub, straightening linens on the bed, shopping for a button, breading veal cutlets, making meatloaf, putting evening meals on the table for her teenage son, caring for a neighbor's child, eating lunch alone at the kitchen table, and servicing clients as a prostitute for a half hour each afternoon of the three days the film chronicles. The year of the film's release was, coincidentally, the same year Federici published her influential essay, "Wages against Housework," which I quote at the beginning of this chapter. Here Federici ([1975] 2012, 16) argues, "Not only is wages for housework a revolutionary perspective, but it is the only revolutionary perspective from a feminist viewpoint." Also that year Laura Mulvey (1989) published her influential, now-canonical and much criticized essay, "Visual Pleasure and Narrative Cinema," arguing that classic Hollywood film conventions are predicated on, as well as reproduce, the male gaze as subject and the female body as object.

Jeanne Dielman seemed perfectly poised to answer both Mulvey and Federici. The film challenges cinema's male gaze by breaking with Hollywood's conventions and instead utilizing long interior takes, very little dialogue, and a minimalist aesthetic that is narratively linear yet remarkably experimental.[6] Some argue that it also provides visual content to rally us to Federici's feminist revolution by revealing the daily grind of housework on screen. Attending to Mulvey's concern with formal aesthetic choices as well as Federici's focus on housework brings into view Beauvoir's theorization of women's structural position in the home as directly linked to somatic and emotional pleasures and dangers.

For example, as the three days in Jeanne's life unfold, viewers come to see her tasks and her relationship to them as mandated and determined by oppression (her structural position as woman in the home) but also as providing pleasure (they are ritualistic, aesthetic, bodily, and even sensual).[7] Although Jeanne displays almost no emotion throughout, speaking (when she does speak) in a deadpan voice and never changing her pleasant facial expression as she goes about her day's tasks, viewers do not get the feeling that she wholly resents maintaining her home or serving her son and servicing her clients. On the contrary she seems to take distinct pleasure in the accomplishment of these predictable rituals. But this is an odd kind of pleasure, if we can even call it that. Creating order in her day, and subsequently in her life, by tending to these jobs may keep more dangerous emotions and disorderly thoughts and feelings in check.

Beauvoir captures the ambiguous dimensions of how housework affirms and undermines women's sense of self in *The Second Sex*.[8] Likewise by portraying the details and work patterns of her day as affirming or at least maintaining Jeanne's identity, Akerman's formal choices and narrative frame refuse the simple reading of her heroine's life that would show housework only as drudgery and the female protagonist as victim. Beauvoir's text and Akerman's film demonstrate that although women are cast as other to male subjectivity, women's experiences do not situate them *only* as victims. Although Beauvoir has been misinterpreted as insisting that women must take up the male position, she instead affirms the embrace of ambiguity. Indeed, as I have already noted, Beauvoir reads the expression of ambiguity (here depicted as Jeanne's pleasure in her daily tasks that we might otherwise read as repetitive and oppressive) as a protest against structures and taxonomies that try to deny the fact that we are always self and other, immanence and transcendence, simultaneously. It is the trapping of the oppressed *solely* as immanent, as identified by the political meanings of their bodies, and as naturally suited to take up menial and repetitive tasks, that Beauvoir (and Fanon too, as we saw earlier) seeks to challenge.

In the epigraph that begins this section, Beauvoir says that housework is "monotonous" and "mechanical," that the housewife experiences long stretches of "passivity and emptiness," and that these tasks are accomplished in "boredom." She adds, however, that cooking "reshapes and re-creates substances." This recognition of creativity in housework is often overlooked by those who read Beauvoir as always condemning the work to which women are traditionally assigned (mothering, housework, repetitive jobs). Beauvoir writes, "Working the dough she experiences her power." Akerman's camera captures the pleasurable, sensual, aesthetic, and satisfying dimensions of "women's" work in the way she films Jeanne massaging the meatloaf, tidying the bed sheets, and perfectly setting the table. Echoing Beauvoir's ([1949] 2011, 472) language, Akerman's camera appeals to our senses—the touch and feel of "freshly ironed linens, of the whitening agents of soapy water, of white sheets, of shining copper."

Akerman's filming of Jeanne's work draws attention to its sensual dimensions, illuminating that some women get satisfaction, even pleasure from these tasks. Housework can even offer the illusion of sovereignty: "When she covers [jars of jam] with parchment paper and inscribes the date of her victory, it is triumph over time itself: she has captured the passage of time in the snare of sugar; she has put life in jars" (Beauvoir [1949] 2011, 480). But of course danger is present too, sitting alongside the pleasure. There is the danger of thinking that one actually *has* triumphed over time, a sovereigntist fantasy that, I should add, is a much greater danger for men because of their enhanced position of power. In the chapter "Myths" in volume 1 of *The Second Sex* Beauvoir describes how men indulge in dangerous and ultimately much more destructive fantasies by crowning themselves as transcendent beings who aspire to and should be granted control, even immortality. Seeking transcendence and hoping to escape finitude, myths created by men seek to pin immanence, as well as the body's messiness and the tasks and responsibilities associated with it, onto women. The housewife faces other perils. She worries that men or "things" will wrest away her small bit of power: "She is dependent on the soufflé, the roast, the butcher, the cook, the extra help; she is dependent on the husband, who frowns every time something goes wrong" (583). So the danger for women is ontological and existential, and it turns political when privileged women hire "help" to try to shield themselves from the reduced agency and demeaned tasks assigned to their sex.

Jeanne lives at the apex of such instances of pleasure and danger. In iconic images we see her peeling potatoes, hovering over pots on the stove, and bidding farewell to a john at the door (figures 6.1, 6.2, and 6.3).

After the second client (there are three) leaves the house, we notice a subtle but palpable shift in Jeanne's composure and routine. As she exits the bedroom, her bangs are just a bit out of place. This is the first time we see any small detail out of order in her appearance or routine, and the small disruption portends impending chaos. Jeanne fails to return the lid to the tureen in the middle of the dining room table, where she keeps cash earned from her sexual service. Minutes later she lets the potatoes boil too long. Carrying the pot around the apartment, searching for a place to dump the water, she looks like a madwoman, full of anxiety. As Ivone Margulies (2009) puts it, "We see Jeanne from the kitchen as she appears by its door, and this first shift in the camera's habitual position announces the character's unraveling. In one of the funniest choreographies ever of domestic terror, Jeanne carries the pot around the house, not knowing what to do with this evidence of mistiming." Asked directly about what precipitates the change in Jeanne's composure and strict comportment, Akerman replies that Jeanne has had her first orgasm with a john and that this displaced sexual feeling sets her on a course wherein everything veers out of control.[9] It is important that it is a new and unexpected sexual feeling, the orgasm, that sets Jeanne on the path to murder. It is as if she were so used to unfeeling, to the deadening and deadened effects of her small and straightened life, or to the small bit of control she had over her tasks, that this deadness and illusion of control kept danger away. As she explains one night to her son, she never thought to marry for love but only for a better situation. When her son asks her about sex, she cuts off the conversation, turns, and abruptly puts out the light; the message is: pleasure portends danger.

As viewers we feel the anticipation of bad things to come as Jeanne seems ever more unable to control her domestic sphere and keep dirt and grime, and its ally, chaos, at bay. Yet she perseveres and even finishes her chores ahead of time. As she sits in a chair with her feather duster, we see the anxiety building in her breathing and composed yet increasingly uncomfortable body. This is one of those "long moments of passivity and emptiness" that Beauvoir had warned of. Nearing the end of the film, and the late afternoon hours of the third day, Jeanne receives her third client in her bedroom. Again the encounter produces an orgasm, and this time the viewer is privy to it. Jeanne gets up from the bed, slowly and methodically dresses, takes a pair of scissors in her hand, walks over to the bed, and stabs her client (figure 6.4). The next image, and the last seven minutes of the film, are of Jeanne sitting at her dining-room table, her blouse splashed with blood, as the light from the window flashes across the screen, changing its contours as time passes (figure 6.5).

What are we to make of the distinctly disturbing feelings, the murderous intent, and the perverse version of agency as presented by Akerman? While the meaning of this film is deliberately ambiguous, *Jeanne Dielman*'s staging of the housewife-prostitute-murderess is a rich resource for thinking feminist politics. Although Beauvoir says that only collective action, not individual actions, can significantly alter the conditions of oppression in which we are situated, individual women living within the demands of femininity often rebel, exceeding imposed limits on their identity in varieties of creative and sometimes perverse or violent ways. See, for example, the way Beauvoir ([1949]

FIGURE 6.1. Jeanne peeling potatoes in *Jeanne Dielman*.

FIGURE 6.2. Jeanne in the kitchen in *Jeanne Dielman*.

I'll see you next week.

FIGURE 6.3. Jeanne at the door with a client in *Jeanne Dielman*.

2011, 515) describes perversions turning to violence in the following passage: "Shut up in provincial monotony with a boorish husband, with no chance to act or to love, she is devoured by the feeling of her life's emptiness and uselessness; she tries to find compensation in romantic musings, in the flowers she surrounds herself with, in her clothes, her person: her husband interferes even with these games. She ends up trying to kill him." "She" in the quote is the "smiling Mme Beudet" (515). Although Beauvoir does not reference the director Germaine Dulac in this passage, she may have been referring to the 1922 short silent film considered by many to be one of the first feminist films.[10] Beauvoir goes on to say, "The symbolic behavior into which the wife escapes can bring about perversions, and these obsessions can lead to crime" (515).

Beauvoir alerts us to the insight that even the tasks and situations that bind women to conditions of unfreedom provide surprising openings for pleasure and agency, even if in perverted form, to emerge. She insists that women's emotions are inextricably linked to patriarchal structures and ideologies, buttressing the obstruction of women's individual and collective political agency. Nevertheless women's experiences of the uglier range of these emotions— melancholy, narcissism, anxiety, shame, resentment, paranoia, and jealousy— also potentially signal dissent, or at the very least discomfort with the status quo. Rather than deny or demean negative emotions, their somatic expressions, and women's assigned structural location and tasks, Beauvoir studies

FIGURE 6.4. Jeanne stabbing the client in *Jeanne Dielman*.

FIGURE 6.5. Jeanne in her dining room after the murder in *Jeanne Dielman*.

them carefully to think about the ways they might be read as and harnessed for protest and disruption.

Abandoning both moralistic and redemptive framings, Jeanne is depicted as neither victim nor sovereign agent, and her strange behavior defies our ability to see her as a generic type. Instead we are offered a singular character defying categorization and a complex account of how the didactic poles (victim versus agent) operate. Reading the film with Beauvoir we can see that Jeanne is trapped somewhere in the murky in-between of thwarted agency and too obvious, easily condemned, and clichéd violence as she murders her john with scissors, the second most quintessential feminine weapon after knitting needles. Moreover her action is motivated by a feeling, sexual arousal, that was until then kept at bay by her pleasurable because deadening and yet increasingly dangerous routine. Returning to this classic film with insights gleaned from *The Second Sex* prepares us to better interpret two more recent films, each ambivalently situated in relationship to feminist politics.

SMILING

The social significance of the toilette allows woman to express her attitude to society by the way she dresses; subject to the established order, she confers on herself a discreet and tasteful personality; many nuances are possible: she will make herself fragile, childlike, mysterious, candid, austere, gay, poised, a little daring, self-effacing, as she chooses. Or, on the contrary, she will affirm her rejection of conventions by her originality. . . . She is like a painting, a statue, like an actor on stage, an analogon through which is suggested an absent subject who is her character but is not she. It is this confusion with an unreal object—necessary, perfect like a hero in a novel, like a portrait or bust—that flatters her; she strives to alienate herself in it and so to appear frozen, justified to herself. —SIMONE DE BEAUVOIR, *The Second Sex*

David Fincher's *Gone Girl*, a screen adaptation of the novel by the self-proclaimed feminist Gillian Flynn, is a whodunit that is structured narratively as a he-said, she-said mystery. Interpreted as misogynist (as well as lowbrow) by several critics, the novel that the film is based on was a best seller and favorite among female readers.[11] The mystery at its center is whether Amy's husband, Nick (played by Ben Affleck), is the culprit in her disappearance from their McMansion in the recession-suffering suburban Missouri hellscape. But as Beauvoir helps us to see, Amy (played by Rosamund Pike) is a "gone girl" long before she goes missing; while she is central to the film, she is an absent center, a sort of Beauvoirian "unreal object."

What we learn of Amy is revealed to be artifice layered upon artifice. When she was a child her handsome, bourgeois, East Coast, highly educated parents wrote an extremely successful book series featuring "Amazing Amy." Amazing Amy, the wildly popular and profitable fictional image, grows and changes with the real Amy from birth to marriage. Except, as Amy confides to Nick, first her boyfriend and then husband, Amy herself, although certainly amazing—she is beautiful, educated (a Harvard graduate), charming, and witty—is still never quite as amazing as the character in the books. Amy is, as in Beauvoir's description, "an absent subject who is her character but is not she."

Amy is an artifice crafted not only by her parents but also by Nick's imagination, by capitalist profit, by her own self-imposed expectations and perceived shortcomings. Throughout the film we see her embracing, albeit ambivalently, several of the distorted and pathological images with which she is forced to constantly negotiate. The film invites us to enter a space where reality will be judged against fantasy, and reality will always come up short. For Amy this shortcoming leads to her own bitterness and jealousy, and eventually paranoia and revenge, a host of difficult feelings that motivates some quite unattractive actions.

Accompanied by a voice-over from Amy's diary, early in the film we see Nick and Amy at a Manhattan party for the launch of yet another Amazing Amy sequel. Real Amy is and always was jealous of Amazing Amy's adventures and accomplishments. Even though Amy seems to literally "have it all" and is indeed the picture of idealized femininity (whiteness, class and sexual privilege, an elite education), she sees herself as falling short. The real Amy is always measured against the achievements of Amazing Amy, the myth that structures and haunts the real woman's experiences. While the myth affects Amy directly, the rest of the country's women do not escape unscathed: a female detective, Rhonda Boney, informs her younger male colleague that Amy is the "star of a book series every woman in the country read as a kid." Like most girls subject to the demands and expectations of myths crafted under patriarchy, Amy longs to get married. As Beauvoir ([1949] 2011, 429) so poignantly says, "The destiny that society traditionally offers women is marriage. Even today, most women are, were, or plan to be married, or they suffer from not being so. Marriage is the reference by which the single woman is defined, whether she is frustrated by, disgusted at, or even indifferent to this institution." Amy doesn't escape this fate, and in fact suffers keenly from it: "With me—regular, flawed, Real Amy—jealous, as always, of the golden child. Perfect, brilliant Amazing Amy. Who is getting fucking married!" As Amy explains, her parents "improved upon" her childhood and then "peddled it to the masses." At the launch party for the book, whose plot finds Amazing Amy enjoying her big, fat, white wedding, the real Amy is accosted by reporters inquiring about her own (lack of a) wedding. Amy avoids the humiliation of telling the reporters the truth, that she is a thirty-something *single* woman, when Nick proposes to her that very night. He is her knight in shining armor, or, at least for a while, her "great, gorgeous, sweet, cool-ass guy."

The film's politics are ambiguous at best, misogynist at worse. Viewers are left guessing whether Nick really is a "sweet, cool-ass guy" or neglects, ignores, and ultimately abuses his wife. About midway through we learn that Nick is innocent (of domestic abuse) and Amy has constructed an alternative reality wherein he is guilty. Out of jealousy and desire for revenge for Nick's having cheated on her, Amy leaves behind pieces of damning evidence that she knows will land Nick in jail: a faked positive pregnancy test, clues in a demented treasure hunt that uncover further false evidence of Nick's guilt, evidence of her abuse manufactured by splashing her blood around the house, and a diary full of lies.

After viewing *Jeanne Dielman* and reading *The Second Sex*, however, we can interpret Amy's actions in a new way: as a perverse form of protest rather than a dangerous psychotic break or the demented actions of a manipulative, powerful witch. The film offers several clues to what motivates Amy's seemingly crazy behavior—something far short of domestic violence but a form of violence nevertheless. In a voice-over Amy explains that she embraced one of femininity's tried and true roles in order to be attractive to Nick. Amy was "Cool Girl": "Cool Girl is fun. Cool Girl is game. Cool Girl is hot. Cool Girl never gets angry at her man. She only smiles in a chagrined, loving manner and then presents her mouth for fucking. Go ahead! Cum on me! I don't mind. I'm a Cool Girl. The window dressing varies. The personality's the same. Cool Girl likes what he likes and puts him first and does it all with a fucking smile." Rebelling at her own embrace of the misogynist Cool Girl image, Amy takes revenge on Nick and on herself, hitting herself in the face with a hammer (figure 6.6).

Looking closely we find narrative and formal features of the film that challenge the misogynist view of Amy's behavior. The cuts that move between Amy's faked escape, her manufactured diary entries, and the seemingly frank recollections of how she molded herself into the perfect woman for Nick add up to an alternative interpretation of her story. Moreover there are moments

FIGURE 6.6. Amy hitting herself with a hammer in *Gone Girl*.

FIGURE 6.7. Amy killing Desi with a box cutter in *Gone Girl*.

when there is hope that Amy will form a genuine bond with another woman and get a new perspective born of female friendship. But the woman Amy begins to trust betrays her and steals Amy's money for herself and her boyfriend. Out of money and out of options, Amy calls an old boyfriend, Desi (played by Neil Patrick Harris), who traps her in his fortress-like lake house, expecting her to play her role as Amazing Amy. She ends up murdering him with a box cutter during sex (figure 6.7).

Amy's behaviors and actions turn pathological as her self is increasingly erased. Nevertheless the film dishes up a hefty dose of skepticism for patriarchal myths: that marriage is fulfilling; that happiness is a destiny for women who follow patriarchal rules; that beauty protects women, or makes them powerful because it gives them something to sell; that women can ever be saved from undoing and destruction by acting in accordance with the demands of femininity. Even though Amy lived up to the myth and did everything right, she was denied all pleasure, and experiences only jealousy, paranoia, and a desire for revenge. An excerpt from the filming script describes the ending of *Gone Girl* this way: "They lie down side by side on the marital bed. Nick is staring at the back of Amy's head, just as in the opening. NICK (O.S.) What are you thinking? How are you feeling? What have we done to each other? What will we do? Amy turns, and gives him a haunting SMILE. * FADE TO BLACK.*"

At the end of the film Amy lands back where she started: trapped in marriage and expecting a child. What happens to the woman who insistently refuses all false promises? In Lars von Trier's *Nymphomaniac*, Joe's emotions and actions resist recuperation into any of our familiar lexicons on female sexuality, agency, or desire. Like Jeanne and Amy, Joe lives at the apex of danger and pleasure. Her story, however, offers an even more exemplary case of a woman's refusal.

FUCKING

There are a few sorceresses, some old women who wield formidable power in stories . . . but they are not attractive characters. More seductive are the fairies, mermaids, and nymphs who escape male domination. —SIMONE DE BEAUVOIR, *The Second Sex*

When we first see Joe (played by Charlotte Gainsbourg, with Stacy Martin as the younger Joe), she is lying, beaten and bruised, in an alleyway behind the house of Seligman (Stellan Skarsgård). Seeing her distress, Seligman, a solitary, elderly, and (as we learn later) celibate man, offers to call an ambulance or the police, but the only help Joe will agree to is an invitation into Seligman's house for a cup of tea. Lying in a spartan narrow bed in the house, Joe tells Seligman her story. The narrative moves back and forth between the Joe-Seligman conversation, intercut with flashbacks to Joe's sexual (mis)adventures and Seligman's far-fetched and far-flung connections to Joe's stories. Seligman constantly appropriates Joe's story to offer his own interpretations, sometimes extending her story by relating it to random objects in the room and linking it to long discourses on the history of science, botany, mathematics, medicine,

FIGURE 6.8. Young Joe lifted to the heavens by her orgasm in *Nymphomaniac*.

Jewish mysticism, anti-Zionism and anti-Semitism, fly fishing, polyphonic music, classical painting, and more. He also constantly interrupts her; at one point Joe flatly retorts, "I think this was one of your weakest digressions."

Were we to ask the usual questions about desire, agency, pleasure, and danger, we would want to know the following: Does Joe, the nymphomaniac whose story from birth to age fifty is told in two cinematic volumes by Lars von Trier, escape male domination through her sexual prowess, or is she its ultimate victim? Does Joe's extrapatriarchal pleasure place her out of the grasp of dangerous traps—love, marriage, and motherhood—or has she succumbed to one of patriarchy's despicable stereotypes, the insatiable whore? Maybe Joe, even more than my earlier examples, inhabits a liminal space between these poles. My reading of *Nymphomaniac* will show that Joe's agency best demonstrates how pleasure and danger are always joined. To begin to move beyond the danger of getting trapped in dead-end fantasies of escape or victim-centered acceptance of perpetual abuse, we should avoid moralistic solutions that force us to choose between and then celebrate either sexual liberation (pleasure) or sexual victimhood (danger).

In the epigraph to this section from *The Second Sex* Beauvoir refers to the nymph as the mythical and beautiful maiden; she is close to nature; drawn to rivers, fields, forests of flowers; and not exactly human. The nymph, however, is also the immature form of an insect, one that does not change much physically as it grows, such as a dragonfly or locust. Joe is both of these in von Trier's film. She is the mermaid and mystical girl-woman who seems more than or not quite human and can commune with nature: learning about

FIGURE 6.9. The nymph as a lure in *Nymphomaniac*.

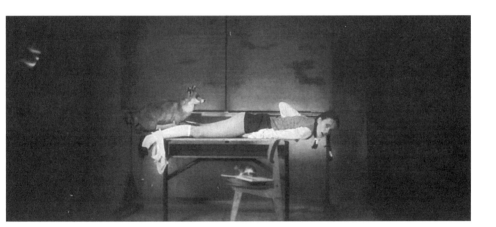

FIGURE 6.10. Young Joe as a schoolgirl Lolita in *Nymphomaniac*.

leaves and trees and flowers relaxes her; she says that when she was only a little girl, she discovered her "cunt"; and as we learned in chapter 3, when she was about twelve she experienced such a strong orgasm lying supine in a field that she was lifted up to the heavens (figure 6.8).

In this version Joe's voracious desire for sex seems to be authentic and for herself, although it could be that with this image von Trier is poking fun at what Lynne Huffer (2015) calls Andrei Tarkovsky's "spiritual, Tarkovsky-esque levitations." With a group of young girlfriends—and here we see the beginnings of sororal solidarity—Joe forms "the Little Flock." The activities of this proto-feminist girls' club include destroying all manifestations of institutional romance, worshipping their girl parts, and making a pledge to never have sex more than one time with any man.

Seligman, however, compares Joe to the other kind of nymph, the insect at the end of a fishhook that might lure men away from their patriarchal responsibilities (figure 6.9). In Seligman's imagination, Joe is a Lolita figure, a dangerous whore (figure 6.10).

Joe gives oral sex to a much older stranger on a train, even though be begs her not to as he is returning home to his wife. But Joe insists. Her motivation? Joe and her friend together stage a contest to win a bag of "sweeties" that will go to the girl who fucks more random strangers on the train. Joe juggles so many relationships at once that she has to keep notes. She tells each of the men that with him, and him only, she has experienced an orgasm for the first time. She breaks up families. In one of the funniest scenes in volume 1, a distraught and crazed Uma Thurman comes with her three young boys to Joe's apartment to show them their father's "whoring bed." Joe tells all these stories to Seligman with a mix of guilt and disgust, saying that her lust is dangerous and destructive. Seligman, in his best liberal feminist guise, tries to convince Joe that though she is indeed a nymph who, with her sexual prowess, lures men from their better judgment, she is also a victim of patriarchal hypocrisy.

Significantly, however, and almost dogmatically, Joe deems herself a *nymphomaniac*, a woman with a too big appetite for sex, always wanting more pleasure, never feeling satiated. In an early point in the film Joe tells Seligman, "Perhaps the only difference between me and other people is that I've always demanded more from the sunset . . . more spectacular colors when the sun hit the horizon; that is perhaps my only sin." Much later, telling Seligman of her experience at a self-help group for sex addicts, rebelling from its strictures and its twelve-step program, Joe proclaims, "I am a nymphomaniac and I like myself for being one. Above all I love my cunt and my dirty, filthy lust!" (figure 6.11).

Huffer (2015) asks, "What are we to make of this nasty girl declaration of sexual agency?" Rejecting readings of *Nymphomaniac* that reduce it to "flat realist terms," Huffer links the film's "passionate ambivalence" to Bonnie Honig's agonistic politics, seeing what I call Joe's obstructed and perverse form of agency as alerting us to the "feel of the agon." Following Huffer, I argue that the film makes us feel something new; but even more powerfully than *Jeanne Dielman* or *Gone Girl*, that feeling reveals how pleasure and danger are never separated, are indeed always ambivalently joined, in women's ex-

FIGURE 6.11. "I love my cunt and my dirty, filthy lust!" says Joe in *Nymphomaniac.*

perience. *Nymphomaniac* also shows us that if we are to take up a feminist politics that can speak to current conditions—rather than fantasize a future of empowerment or remain trapped in conditions of victimhood—we cannot disavow the ambivalence of the twinned conditions of pleasure and danger that shape sexuality and violence for female subjects.

The end of the two-volume film antagonizes and divides spectators. As I noted, volume 1 begins with Joe looking like a victim, bruised and helpless in a dark alley. So far, so good; we know how to feel and what kind of film we are viewing. Quickly, however, our feelings become increasingly complicated: Is Joe a bad person, as she seems to insist? Should we feel bad for her? Is sex fulfilling, or is it dangerous? Does she have a grip on her own desire, and does she even know what she wants? Volume 2 ends with Joe shooting Seligman in response to his attempting to rape her. Significantly, however, unlike in *Jeanne Dielman* or *Gone Girl*, spectators don't see the violence; we only hear the gunshot off-screen. This turn of events, both the attempted rape and the gunshot, takes us by surprise since slowly but surely we were (maybe some of us only almost) lured into thinking Seligman was a sensitive, liberal, helpful older man—not the "sweet, cool-ass guy" that Nick appeared to be but another, way less threatening, certainly not dangerous type. But true to form as a well-intentioned liberal who misreads Joe's promiscuity (just as he repeatedly misreads her story), Seligman turns out to just not get it. Surprised at Joe's refusal, Seligman says, "But you've fucked thousands of men!" Fucking thousands of men, however, does not mean that Joe wants to fuck one more, nor this particular one, nor one not of her own choosing. To escape Seligman's grasp she has to shoot him. The screen turns black; we hear the gunshot, the slammed door, the departing footsteps; and the credits roll. With the credits we hear Charlotte Gainsbourg, not as Joe but as Charlotte Gainsbourg the recording artist, singing, "Hey Joe, where are you going with that gun in your hand?"

Where is Joe going with that gun in her hand? Rosalind Galt (2015) reads the ending of *Nymphomaniac* as Joe's exit from the world of patriarchal representation: "Throughout *Nymphomaniac*, Seligman articulates a liberal optimism that Joe can be rehabilitated, folded back into the world despite her unruly actions. But social conformity offers no cure and the radicality of the film's ending is not to kill her but to allow her to exit the picture." Unlike *Jeanne Dielman*, in which viewers must sit and watch Jeanne in her living room, or *Gone Girl*, for which viewers must suffer through Amy's return to Nick still wearing her signature smile, with Joe in *Nymphomaniac* we hear the gunshot, the slamming door, and Joe's footsteps rushing away, but the screen is black. As another complementary interpretation, we might read *Nymphomaniac*, volumes 1 and 2, as mimicking *The Second Sex*, volumes 1 and 2. In volume 1 men give their views on women (Seligman tries to steal Joe's story), and in volume 2 women come to consciousness and take matters into their own hands. Joe kills Seligman, an act of individual rather than collective resistance; but even though Beauvoir advocates collective resistance, I would venture that she still may applaud Joe's actions. Either way, Joe is left with a gun in her hand. Where does she go next?

PLEASURE, DANGER, AND COLLECTIVE RESISTANCE

There is much feminine behavior that has to be interpreted as protest.
—SIMONE DE BEAUVOIR, *The Second Sex*

What does it mean to think of negativity not as an effect of bad power but as a way of being critical without consciousness? —LAUREN BERLANT, "Critical Inquiry, Affirmative Culture"

Where Joe, Jeanne, and Amy go next is the question at the heart of feminist politics. As we have seen, the heroines in these films live fully within the victim/agent, danger/pleasure dynamic. They have a lot of ugly feelings but are able to lodge only perverse forms of protest against the conditions of their lives. At least, unlike Fanon's colonial Algerians who lash out at each other, the women depicted here do not become violent against other women. While there is a distinct failure in these films to make connections between women that might foster collectivity, and though they can't find allies or make friends, at least they know who their enemies are.

Reading Beauvoir side by side with Lauren Berlant we might say, contra Berlant, that these forms of negativity *are* an effect of bad power or, as Beauvoir would put it, a response to situation, but that at the same time we can read them as a way of being "critical without consciousness," even "as protest." Might we include these perverse forms of protest, the complex feelings that enliven them, and the ambiguity they express as a form of agonistic action? They stop short of freedom in encounter, but at least their protests allow these women to act.

Rather than subscribe to a subjective account of pleasure and danger wherein all actions and their motivations are located within either active consciousness or unconscious repetition of individual psychic structures, Beauvoir's account of bodies and situation in *The Second Sex* helps us understand the relationships among power, sexual difference, perverse and pleasurable feelings, individual acts of violence, and potential collective protest. As I have shown here and in the earlier conversation with Fanon, Beauvoir's somatic and affective orientations help us see that protest may be registered without consciousness or on bodies experienced as uncomfortable feelings and perverse behaviors, and it may even erupt at a moment of unexpected pleasure. Beauvoir argues that because women live "life's becoming" they are "suspicious of the principle of identity" and the "notion of causality." Due to their situation and experiences, women are poised to grasp something that men cannot: "the ambiguity of all principles, of all values, of all that exists" ([1949] 2011, 651). Having lost the possibility of acting and living in conditions of freedom and reduced solely to immanence, women unconsciously register resistance in affects, behaviors, and symptoms that we can certainly read as critique and potentially register as pointing toward an alternative. Beauvoir sees diverse women's experiences of ambiguity themselves as a somatic protest or a feeling of disruption that might move us to feel something or want something new. This was my wager in chapter 3, where I argued that SHE especially and von Trier's women more generally (and here we can add Joe) encourage us to feel our way beyond patriarchy. These feelings themselves destabilize the taxonomies that rule our currently bifurcated existence: we are either victim or agent, immanence or transcendence, feeling or thinking.

Beauvoir's insights take us further, helping us to see key differences in what appears to be a repetition of affects and behaviors in these three films. We move from a story of complete isolation in *Jeanne Dielman* to an attempt at sororal membership in *Gone Girl*, when Amy hopes for friendship on the run but is betrayed by heteronormative loyalty, to the incomplete and failed attempt at woman-to-woman friendship and solidarity as represented by Joe's membership in the Little Flock and her desire to nurture a relationship with P, her younger protégée. Jeanne is the most isolated, never able to even make an attempt to form collective bonds. In one scene she stands at the door listening to an off-screen female neighbor talk about the price of meat and the difficulty of putting food on the table that the family will eat and enjoy, but Jeanne barely responds and the exchange goes no further. Amy manipulates the other women in the suburbs, making them pawns in the plan to frame her husband, and her one attempt at solidarity ends in her betrayal. Joe enjoys membership in the Little Flock, but her "sisters" end up falling into the trap of romance and love, and P (a daughter, apprentice, sister, and lover for Joe) ends up betraying Joe with Joe's ex-husband.

In *The Second Sex* and several of her works of fiction Beauvoir explores the themes of women's feelings toward their oppressors, as well as their often negative feelings toward each other. In *The Woman Destroyed* ([1967] 1969), for example, the heroine, Monique, is betrayed not only by her adulterous husband but by her husband's girlfriend and her own friends, whose gossip and advice mislead her and add salt to her wounds. While Beauvoir always is careful to situate women's feelings in response to context and particular scenarios and examples, at the same time she indicates that were women to take the risk of turning to each other in collectivity rather against each other in envy and jealousy, revolutionary change would be possible. Another possibility, one that Fanon charts in his attention to movement and shifts in situation that characterized the Algerian War for Independence, is that circumstances themselves shift to reveal an opening. In the chapter "History" in *The Second Sex*, Beauvoir discusses how various contingencies, changes, and encounters provide opportunities to seize greater freedom for women as a collectivity, although these possibilities can also be ignored or denied. As we saw in Beauvoir's conversation with Richard Wright, she is cognizant of the fact that "lack of solidarity and collective consciousness" leave women workers "disarmed in front of the new possibilities available to them" ([1949] 2011, 134). She also notes that "a deeper consciousness of the situation is necessary so that blacks and whites, women and male workers, form coalitions rather than opposition" (135). The formation of any collectivity, including feminist collectivity, is a process involving agonistic and negative bonds—in other words, a *political* process. It is far better to avow rather than to dismiss or belittle antagonisms as a critical force for agency toward transformation (Marso 2010).

Do Jeanne's, Amy's, and Joe's complicated feelings and violent actions and Joe's failed attempts at community call out to us, as viewers, in ways that might encourage collective action? Even if, as Mulvey contends, films are produced through a male gaze, they might still be interpreted through a feminist lens. For such an interpretation we need to seek out moments and spaces for resistance, a practice that Beauvoir has expressly prepared us for in *The Second Sex*. When we see their actions as perverse protests, we see Jeanne, Amy, and Joe making attempts, albeit doomed (because they are alone), to alter the conditions of their lives. The fact that these women embody the most desirable forms of femininity should further alert us to the many ways less privileged subjects express their anger and dissatisfaction with oppressive conditions.[12]

We cannot know what sexualities and agencies look like outside patriarchy's vision. But we do know that alongside danger and victimhood there is resistance, action, agency, and pleasure. As we saw in the conversations between Beauvoir and Arendt, von Trier, Fanon, and Wright, we ignore the latter, even when it takes perverse forms or erupts into acts of violence, at the peril of losing the ability to press on the need for collective forms of agency, to seize freedom in encounter, and to find and nurture diverse paths toward resistance. I suggest the practice of feminist friendship based on new conversations might portend a different future.

UNBECOMING WOMEN WITH VIOLETTE LEDUC, RAHEL VARNHAGEN, AND MARGARETHE VON TROTTA

In *Jeanne Dielman* Jeanne talks to an unnamed and unseen woman behind the door (the voice of Akerman) concerning what to buy for dinner.[1] In *Gone Girl* Amy makes a desperate attempt to reach out to another woman when she is on the run, but that woman betrays her. In *Nymphomaniac* Seligman completely misunderstands Joe, tries to envelop her actions into one of his several wacky theories, and in the end treats her simply as a sexual object. With the Little Flock, with her protégée P, and with her unnamed friend with whom she stages the contest for "sweeties" on the train, Joe tries but fails to enter into female friendship.

Although these films appear to fail the Bechdel rule, they also surely pass its interpretive task. They fail the rule in the sense that they do not deliver on female friendship: the women appear to be relating to other women in a genuine way, but betrayal is in the offing. The films, however, pass the interpretive task in the sense that they depict the lives of women on their own terms. They are struggling with patriarchal demands, and not, I would argue, through the male gaze. In a sense, then, maybe the point of the Bechdel rule is not to apply it faithfully but rather to heed its warnings about female isolation and the relative obscurity of women's lives under patriarchy.[2]

In this chapter I continue my work with the Bechdel task,[3] turning to one (auto)biography and two biopics. While autobiographies, biographies, and biopics are sometimes elevated in intellectual and cultural status by the quality of their authors or directors or the stature of their subject, these related life genres are often denigrated as lowbrow precisely because of their too close connection to a life. Like all feminized genres (melodrama, soap opera, the women's weepie), female biopics in particular are cheapened by their proximity to women's lives.

Beauvoir takes the opposite view. As she sees it, in novels and in narrative film, plots are often overconstructed, episodes *too full of meaning* ([1966] 2011, 291). Autobiographies, biographies, and biopics, in contrast, might be free to be more *like art*—in other words, able to show the contingency, the facticity, the nonnecessity of life's experience. Expressing a life, an artwork must be a "communication of the inexpressible, of the incommunicable, a communication through non-knowledge" (292). In life, as in art, nonknowledge, nonsovereignty, obscurity, and nonnecessity are the only rules. What we make of these experiences, how we make connections with each other, *whether* we do, and how we talk about them is the stuff of politics (or at least the stuff of politics with Beauvoir).[4] Beauvoir speaks to this as she confides the aspirations she has for her own writing: "By the tone, the style, by the way in which I speak and tell a story, I must charm, win over and retain the [viewer's or] reader's freedom; he must freely remain there listening to me, and for his part, carrying out this work of creation which belongs to him" (294).

Bechdel's seemingly simple rule helps us see anew several features of popular culture's impact on how we narrate women's lives and agency and how women absorb or struggle with these stories. Is it possible that by making a simple, clear, and inherently political demand—that at least two named women on screen must speak to each other about something other than men—the rule asserts something more profound, and far more queer, than making sure we see *more* women on screen? Named women must be on screen; women must talk to each other; they must talk about something other than men. Is that all? It turns out that is quite a lot. Does this demand create new women? Does it generate new conversations among them, not only on-screen but off-screen as well?

When women fail to come together as women, or when they do come together but talk only about men, they often remain trapped in patriarchal logics of desire. But when women come together to talk about something other than men (a dynamic between Violette Leduc and Beauvoir and between Arendt and Rahel Varnhagen), or maybe when women come together to talk about men in different ways (as in the conversation between Mary McCarthy and Hannah Arendt portrayed by Margarethe von Trotta), new dynamics are put in motion and things begin to change. Or else something has already changed and that is what makes these conversations possible. Their conversations may not be very pleasant; sometimes they are not suited for "polite" company and are in most cases relegated to the realm of the apolitical. But these intimate moments are infused with the play of power and agonism that structures the public sphere. In both form and content these conversations restructure and reanimate our usual conceptions of what is proper, polite, and political. These depictions of women's lives show feminist politics as energized by new forms and subjects of conversation.

VIOLETTE EXCEEDS THE RULE

Depicting the life of Violette Leduc (played by Emmanuelle Devos) in the 2014 film *Violette*, director Martin Provost features several encounters between Leduc and Beauvoir. The film unfolds as a nonnarrative, encounter-based, sovereignty-challenging story of two women talking to each other but not about men.

What *Violette* shows most powerfully at the diegetic level is how the lives of Leduc and Beauvoir intersected. The film reveals the anger, bitterness, rejection, sexual energy, and depression that saturated Leduc's emotional life, fueled her creativity, and dominated her writing. It also tells the story of macro social forces and how they were rebuffed, or at least held at bay to an unknown but still palpable extent, by two women sharing their experiences in conversation.

At first glance *Violette* seems to follow a traditional narrative arc, featuring a clichéd frustrated writer who is long-suffering but eventually vindicated. This interpretation is undermined or challenged, however, by several choices in the film's aesthetics, including visual and narrative choices. Narratively the film is sprawling, visceral, and unnerving, and the woman at its center is difficult and often unsympathetic. The poverty is grueling, the writing comes at great cost, relationships are fragile; Leduc herself is often unwise, clingy, and irresponsible. But by the end of the film it is not the wherewithal of Leduc but rather encounters with several people, most importantly Beauvoir (played by Sandrine Kiberlain), that free Leduc to live on her own terms. The film's complicated and compelling choices demonstrate what another film might have betrayed: the world shapes our destiny and choices, but freedom, while in no way redemptive and always contingent, might still be grasped. The film makes clear that that experience happens through Leduc's encounter with Beauvoir.

When we first see Leduc she is smuggling black market goods at the end of

World War II somewhere in rural France. She is living with the writer Maurice Sachs (played by Olivier Py), who relies on her to read his manuscripts and give him writing advice but refuses to sleep with her. When he abandons Leduc for good, he sneaks out in the middle of the night, hoping to avoid her desperate pleading. When she hears him leaving and runs after him to claw at his back and beg him to love her, we get the feeling that this tawdry incident is but one in a long series of personal rejections. Having feelings much like those Arendt recorded for Varnhagen, Leduc writes, "Ugliness in a woman is a mortal sin," and "My mother never took my hand." But Sachs did do one thing for Leduc: he urged her to write.

Leduc's penchant for writing draws her to Beauvoir, and their encounter is the film's heart. It is depicted as happening completely by chance, or to put it more accurately, Leduc discovers Beauvoir's writing by chance and subsequently seizes every opportunity to draw herself into Beauvoir's orbit (figure 7.1). Delivering black market goods to a bourgeois client, Leduc discovers a book by Beauvoir on a table (she is impressed by its length and the sex of the author, whose name she does not recognize) and slips it into her purse. The book is *She Came to Stay*, the bold story of a ménage à trois in which a woman's feelings, desires, anxieties, and emotions are at the center. Completely seduced by the book and its author, Leduc seems to feel she has found her everything in Beauvoir: soul mate, role model, lover, and friend. This is repeated in the Arendt-Varnhagen chance encounter: Arendt discovers Varnhagen almost by chance and seizes onto her life and experiences as if they were her own.

After stalking Beauvoir in a café, through the streets, and back to her apartment, Leduc shoves the manuscript for *In the Prison of Her Skin* into her hands. Several conversations ensue. Up to (and exceeding) the Bechdel test, the film features two named women talking, not about men, at the center (figure 7.2).

Later in the film, Beauvoir summons Leduc back to her apartment, where she praises her work: "You talk about female sexuality like no woman before you; with poetry, honesty, and more besides. Go further! Tell it all: trafficking, love lives, the abortion; you'll be doing women a favor." Moreover, with Beauvoir's help Leduc starts to see connections between her own and other women's lives. For example, Leduc comforts Beauvoir after Beauvoir confides that her mother has just died (figure 7.3).

Having witnessed several confusing and painful scenes between Leduc and her mother, we see that Leduc intuitively understands Beauvoir when she says that though she felt only ambivalence toward her mother in life,

FIGURE 7.1. Violette Leduc looking through her mirror at Simone de Beauvoir in *Violette*.

FIGURE 7.2. Leduc and Beauvoir in *Violette*.

FIGURE 7.3. Leduc and Beauvoir speaking about mothers in *Violette*.

her mother's too-sudden death has affected her profoundly. Between Leduc and Beauvoir in this scene is the risk of a dependent relationship between two women constituted by their ambivalence to their own mothers. It is to some extent a healing of prior wounds, and in another very different sense, notwithstanding Beauvoir's mentorship of Leduc, a manifestation not of the vertical mother-daughter bond but of the bond that feminism mandates: the horizontal sororal bond, or the feminist friendship.

Themes of affinity, friendship, and bonds of situated oppression between women are central to the film. Most remarkably it instances solidarity between women across class lines, something feminist films and writing often neglect to do. A comfortable woman allows herself to be drawn to one who is discomforting (Arendt will do the same with Varnhagen). There is no moral to the story in *Violette*; this is one of the film's great strengths. These episodes make it clear, however, that Beauvoir's influence on Leduc made her the writer she was and helped Leduc to find the meaning in her work and even her afflictions. We don't learn very much about the content or style of Leduc's writing from this film about her life, and this does seem odd. But perhaps the point is to look away from the product and understand the encounter that germinated it.[5] We do learn that Beauvoir read and edited all Leduc's manuscripts; she encouraged her to travel, to feel and explore nature and the countryside; she pays for her stay in a mental hospital, visiting and sustaining her there; and always she urged her to take up her pen: "Screaming and sobbing won't get you anywhere; writing will!" In addition Beauvoir wrote a preface to *The Bastard*, an act that may have finally propelled Leduc to fame in 1964. In this preface Beauvoir introduces Leduc to a reading public. The film captures that act of friendship by depicting Beauvoir giving an interview about Leduc's book.

To foreground the relationship between Beauvoir and Leduc, as I have done here, is to risk erasing Leduc, as others have done. She is sometimes neglected in the presence of Beauvoir's reputation. Sophie Lewis (2014), the translator of a 2015 edition of *Thérèse and Isabelle*, Leduc's iconic lesbian tale of adolescent sexuality set in a convent, warns of the difficulty: "Leduc is in the difficult position of belatedly, posthumously indeed, coming out from the shadow of Simone de Beauvoir's championing of her. Beauvoir did what she could to help Leduc towards independence as a writer, but Leduc remains in the shadow of a hugely celebrated, dominant feminist icon."

The film shows, though, that Leduc is both in Beauvoir's shadow and also successful because of her support. And because of her own talent. The encounter with Beauvoir moves Leduc toward some measure of freedom. While we cannot know what would have happened to Leduc's writing had she not encountered Beauvoir, we can say that Beauvoir was in a position to introduce her writing to a larger public, given that "she was refused publication by some of the male editors at Gallimard who were equally celebrated as avant-garde writers" and "her story as a writer is one of suppression and blocking at many points, including by an avant-garde that rapidly moved to exclude her in favour of establishment standards" (Lewis 2014).

The ideal of feminist friendship is equality. It seems out of reach in a friendship that crosses class and in which one party is so dependent on the goodwill of the other. But that is the problematic the film invites us to explore. Showing this complexity is, to my mind, one of the film's successes. The other aspect that shows this film exceeds the Bechdel task is formal: the meaning Beauvoir gleans from Leduc's writing, that a singular woman's lived experience is important for all women, is felt bit by bit through the film as sensation revealed through language and image, calling out to spectators to feel it too. Both the camera perspective and the structure of the film are from Leduc's subjective view. Several of the other characters appear flat, almost comic, because everything is presented through Leduc's senses. We can almost *feel* the physical sensation of love between young girls, of the sun on one's face, of poverty, of Leduc's late-term abortion and its aftermath, of having to fight and traffic for food during the war, of being unloved and unwanted, of never having one's hand held, of never hearing god's voice. We feel *with* Leduc that life is always too much, too volatile, too pressing, too close, too painful or pleasurable, unable to be understood, and too intense. Leduc's subjective position, reinforced by the structurally nonnarrative way events unfold, practically undoes us as viewers. The film techniques depict sensations as lived through the body, absent the typical clarity of the biopic, and this makes it feel more like an experience to live through rather than a story to view and evaluate. In these ways the film does what Beauvoir says novels should do but rarely do: communicate through "non-knowledge, through the lived." As she puts it, "In life, there is this share of non-sense, of contingency—one writes a novel to present together the contradictions, difficulties and ambiguities at the heart of an object which does not speak, a silent object" ([1966] 2011, 289).

By drawing us to the impact of sensation as framing life's experiences, the role of the several swerves and failures of this woman's life, and presenting the "de-totalized" nature of existence (Beauvoir [1966] 2011, 289), the film makes clear that there is no *message* in *Violette*—it is, as any life is, a "multifaceted object (a silent object) that can never be summed up, which does not put forth any definitive word" (289). In *The Second Sex* and elsewhere Beauvoir asks us to experience a life both as a singular life and as refracting social forces. At the same time that she reveals and critiques the structures that bind and oppress women, she also affirms the struggle to live and thrive, the pleasures of nature or the beauty of a moment, and the surprising sources and locations of resistance. Beauvoir's critical attention to bodily sensation and to the importance of feeling and emotions for politics are present in the film's depiction of Leduc's experiential world—being female, lonely, loveless, and deemed ugly.

RAHEL VARNHAGEN PASSES

Hannah Arendt's friendship with Rahel Varnhagen was not the same sort as that shared by Leduc and Beauvoir. Arendt never met Varnhagen, who died long before Arendt was born; Arendt wrote about her and thus is analogically closer to the director of *Violette* than she is to Beauvoir. But we have reason to think of these two women as friends. Arendt even referred to Varnhagen as "my closest friend even though she has been dead some 100 years" (Young-Bruehl 1982, 56). In *Rahel Varnhagen: The Life of a Jewess* (2000), sometimes read as Arendt's own autobiography, Arendt reads her own life through the letters of the nineteenth-century *salonnière*. Doing so she links her life with Varnhagen's across time. Calling Arendt's work an "intellectual biography," Seyla Benhabib (2000, 8) nevertheless affirms, "In telling Rahel Varnhagen's story, Arendt was engaging in a process of self-understanding and self-redefinition as a German Jew. . . . Ironically, it is [Arendt's] perspective 100 years later, and her 'awareness of the doom of German Judaism' that allows her to tell Rahel's story in a way in which Rahel could not but might have told it."

We learn from Arendt that one version of Varnhagen's life story is that of a woman out of control; this is mostly due to social and political circumstances (the anti-Semitism and sexism of nineteenth-century German society) but also because of Varnhagen's deep need for love and acceptance by others. Attracted to this story for political, social, and maybe emotional and psychological reasons, Arendt traces Varnhagen's life through her letters. She hopes to bring Varnhagen's life into a new view and also to seize control of the record of her life from Varnhagen's husband, who, Arendt says, imposed a false narrative. The husband's version of Varnhagen's life made her "appear less Jewish and more aristocratic" and showed her "in a more conventional light, one more in keeping with the taste of the times" (Arendt [1933] 2000, 80).

In contrast to Varnhagen's husband's view, Arendt (2000, 81) says she wants to "narrate the story of Varnhagen's life as she herself might have told it." And yet Arendt has some criticisms of how Varnhagen saw her own life: "To live life as if it were a work of art, to believe that by 'cultivation' one can make a work of art of one's own life, was the great error that Rahel shared with her contemporaries" (81). Arendt elaborates that Varnhagen chose to expose herself so completely that life would confront her "like a storm without an umbrella" (81). Varnhagen sought to add up all her experiences, sift through them, and display them as a curator might. But Arendt shows that the world can be stubbornly resistant to an individual's desires. She shifts our focus from Varnhagen's self-crafting to Varnhagen's *world*. In Arendt's story Varnhagen was never a free agent or a sovereign individual; her desperate attempts to be at home in the world were always beyond her reach due to specific political facts of her existence: she was impoverished, a female, and a Jew. Until she married.

In Arendt's hands Varnhagen's is still a singular life, but played out against a backdrop beyond any single individual's control, a world that no amount of "self-thinking" can banish. Although Varnhagen might have hoped to eradicate the fact of being born a Jew, "it remained a nasty present reality as a prejudice in the minds of others" ([1933] 2000, 90). Translating Varnhagen's life story by linking it to her own, Arendt gives Varnhagen's suffering new meaning. She becomes a female version of Arendt's (1944, 107) "conscious pariah," one who translates exclusion from society and the sense of not being at home in the world into "terms of political significance."[6] The "conscious pariah" accepts her outsider status rather than, like the parvenu, seeking to pretend otherwise and assimilate. Thus Arendt (2000, 85) opens her biography with Varnhagen's late-in-life revelation: "What a history!—A fugitive from Egypt and Palestine, here I am and find help, love, fostering in you people. With real rapture I think of these origins of mine and this whole nexus of destiny, through which the oldest memories of the human race stand side by side with the latest developments. The greatest distances in time and space are bridged. The thing which all my life seemed to me the greatest shame, which was the misery and misfortune of my life—having been born a Jewess—this I should on no account now wish to have missed."

Arendt maintains that avowing her Jewishness was Varnhagen's first and final triumph. Had it come earlier, all might have been different. Disavowing her history, or the history of her country and its relationship to its Jews, was to Arendt's mind a key reason for Varnhagen's lifelong flailing. Her desire to assimilate often appeared desperately tragic; at the very least it caused her undue unhappiness and heartache. In society's eyes Varnhagen was ill-prepared for success as an individual: "Not rich, not cultivated and not beautiful—that meant that she was entirely without weapons with which to begin the great struggle for recognition in society, for social existence, for a morsel of happiness, for security and an established position in the bourgeois world" ([1933] 2000, 88).

Most promising for feminist politics in Arendt's narrative of Varnhagen's life is how Arendt, although not especially or specifically interested in women's lives or known for feminist proclivities,[7] not only notices how Varnhagen's being a female, a Jew, and poor affected her reception in society but makes this central to her account of Varnhagen. In criticizing Varnhagen's "self-thinking," her Romantic introspection, Arendt distinguishes between public and private; she offers not an antifeminist rendering of the private as apolitical but rather a way to see how what is seemingly private is shaped by public perception, that being a "Jewess" is a social fact that Varnhagen needed to acknowledge and affirm in order to discover a route toward the world. No matter how hard she tried, Varnhagen could not think away in private the public prejudices against her: "Introspection accomplishes two feats: it annihilates the actually existing situation by dissolving it in a mood, and at the same time it lends everything subjective an aura of objectivity, publicity, extreme interest. In mood the boundaries between what is intimate and what is public become blurred; intimacies are made public, and public matters can be experienced and expressed only in the realm of the intimate—ultimately in gossip" ([1933] 2000, 99). By observing that the lines between public and private should not be blurred in this way, Arendt calls attention to how the public inexorably affects and shapes the private, even seemingly the most private affectations and emotions.

Reminiscent of the way the "stern" and "aloof" Beauvoir allows herself to be drawn into the orbit of the impoverished, clearly damaged, and emotionally out-of-control Leduc,[8] Arendt is also drawn to Varnhagen's feelings—her suffering, her melancholy, her messy and overwhelming desire for love—and spends pages detailing them, even deciphering her dreams in the chapter titled "Day and Night." It is as if Arendt really does crawl into Varnhagen's skin, and a transformed Varnhagen, but also a transformed Arendt, emerges. Is this text evidence of Arendt's feminist unconscious? She disavowed feminism repeatedly when asked, later in life.[9] And she is famous for denying the liminal spaces between bodies and proper politics (the field of action) in all her subsequent texts (and, as I noted in chapter 2, in her reading of Eichmann). But in her 1933 work on Varnhagen, Arendt lavishes attention on the "facts" of bodily existence and experience and sees that they are shaped and maybe even partially determined by perception of the body in public space, having a profound effect on one's personal, private, and even dream experiences. But she goes only so far. In the chapter "Day and Night," for example, diagnosing Varnhagen's repetitive dreams (there was one she had for ten years), Arendt ([1933] 2000, 186) says, "It is terrible when something that was once of the day assumes the featurelessness and eternal repetitiousness of the night . . . terrible when peace is transformed into consuming, hopeless yearning." In the first of the dreams, one that supposedly dogged her for ten years, Varnhagen is in a shimmering palace with distinguished people, whose identity she cannot make out (they are far away and have their backs to her), and she is befriended by a strange creature, reminiscent of the "foreign existences" Beauvoir cautioned us to acknowledge and von Trier made material (although in a more grotesque version) in *Antichrist*. Here is Varnhagen's description of the animal:

> There appeared, in the room in which I was, an animal that I could not name, because its like did not exist in the world; of the size of a sheep, though rather thinner than sheep usually are, pure and white as untouched snow; half sheep, half goat, with a sort of angora pelt; pinkish snout like the purest, most delightful marble—the color of dawn—the paws likewise. This animal was my acquaintance. I did not know why, but it loved me *tremendously*, and knew how to tell me and show me

that it did; I have to treat it like a human being. . . . I called this loving darling my pet; and whenever I was there I asked for it, for it wielded a great power over me and I do not recall having felt during my whole waking life so powerful a stirring of the sense as the mere touching of hand with this animal gave me. But it was not this alone which defined my attachment; it was also an overflowing of the heart in sympathy; and that I alone knew that the animal could love and speak and had a human soul. (Arendt [1933] 2000, 187)

This goes on for some length, and later we learn that in the dream the animal (harboring a secret Varnhagen longs to possess) is revealed (to her horror) to be only a pelt, a dead thing that lies flat. Arendt ([1933] 2000, 189) interprets the dream:

> The torment of such dreams does not lie in the clarity of their inter-pretation. What, after all, can a dream make clear but something that the day clarifies anyhow? That Rahel always found herself in a world more distinguished than the one in which she belonged, but which always turned its back to her or permitted her only to peer through the cracks. That her lovers had only kept her farther removed from the great world, prevented her from entering it. That in the eyes of society her lovers, whom she had always tried to introduce into her society, were mere "animals," but for that reason of tremendous importance to her—namely, gifted with human voice and as animals therefore rep-resenting the natural, in contrast to the social, and hence what was essentially human.

Arendt says what was most shattering to her in the dream was how the sym-bolism of the animal erupted into what she calls "ghostly realism" (189), re-vealing the clarity of the world.

We could say more about the dream, but it is, notably, the repetition of the dream that both Varnhagen and Arendt emphasize. And we might well observe that Beauvoir, and certainly Akerman, instance the theme of repe-tition in women's lives. Repetition was a key conversation topic for Beauvoir and Fanon in chapter 4, as both worried about the links between lives of forced immanence, their repetitive cycles, and how to break out of them. But in chapter 6 we saw how repetition can accumulate to become difference, and how repetition and immanence themselves become a form of pleasure, even a resource (rather than a constraint) for politics. Read with *Jeanne Diel-man,* Beauvoir's analysis of housework brought the theme of repetition and its sensual pleasures to our attention as well as a new relationship to time. This, and more, is present in Varnhagen's dream world, were she only to read it in encounter with others. But while Arendt ([1933] 2000, 193) seems close to this position in 1933, she says, "Only the night, only the despair which had taken refuge in the night revealed in its depths what the day had tried to circumvent, to improve, or to distract her attention from." By the time she wrote *The Human Condition* (1958), Arendt assigned repetition to Labor, as it is focused on survival and subject to cyclical time. In *The Human Condition*'s lexicon, immortality and singularity are accorded to Action's linear time. But Akerman, Beauvoir, and the younger Arendt navigate a different relationship to repetition. With them we see the limits of our attachment to linear notions of history and progress (the teleology of which Arendt herself would continue to strongly repudiate consistently across her writings).

To bring one more connection between Arendt and Akerman into view, Akerman's 1991 film *Night and Day* (a reversal of Arendt's chapter "Day and Night"), turns to dream time and the darkness and repetitions of the night for a critique of the linearity of the day. Pulled into what Arendt calls "consuming, hopeless yearning," Julie, *Night and Day*'s heroine, wanders the streets of Paris at night with one lover and stays in bed all day in an apartment with the other. In an obvious gesture to the similarities of men and their repetitive behaviors in relationships with women, the two men, Jack and Joseph, are nearly indistinguishable; they even share a job driving a cab, one on the day shift and one on the night shift. This circular series is broken only when Julie decides to leave them both.

In contrast to Akerman, Arendt cannot fully see the pleasure and perversity in repetition. (She would be more likely to see it as a pathology hidden by the day's more rational view.) What she does see (maybe her feminist unconscious coming through) is that Varnhagen is situated to approach the world only in the specific and limited ways open to women: the section headings of the chapter "Into the World" are "By Marriage" and "Through Love." If Varnhagen's life is, for Arendt, exemplary of the nature of the political features of the world, it is not exemplary in the usual ways for which Arendt has become famous. Benhabib (1995, 91) writes, "Romantic inwardness displays qualities of mind and feeling that are the exact opposite of those required of political actors and that Arendt highly valued."

For Benhabib, Varnhagen's potential for feminist politics is connected to her role as a salonnière: she was known to her peers not only as a Jew but also for her conversation, her wit, her sociability, and her judgments. Her salon was central to her sense of self and her crafting of her appearance to and with others, mostly through her letters. Benhabib (2000) thus describes the salon as an alternative feminized social space that emerges within modernity as potentially political and world building. But knowing the fate of German Jews in the twentieth century, Arendt is relentlessly negative about the salon's ability to recognize equality or erase the pernicious effects of social difference. Benhabib insists, though, that *today* we might see a feminist alternative in the salons that Arendt failed to see and hence read Arendt's condemnation of the "social" in her political theory differently.

I interpret Arendt's intervention into Varnhagen's life story in yet another way. While Arendt condemns the space of the social as a route to political action, she nevertheless offers Varnhagen a *different path toward the world* through a new interpretation of the meaning of her life. We might even go so far as to say that Arendt's analysis of Varnhagen's romanticism, in the way she condemns it but at the same time is so clearly drawn to it, is a form of feminist consciousness-raising that extends an explicit appeal to readers of this text. By showing us that the attributes and feelings Varnhagen saw as private, idiosyncratic, and able to be thought or wished away were actually formed, circulated, and constituted in public and replicated in the social space of the salon, Arendt makes clear that she could have become a conscious pariah. Although Varnhagen did not reconcile herself to her destiny until moments before her death, her story might have been different had she met Arendt or been drawn into a similar female friendship or collective space of politics.

Arendt changes the story and meaning of Varnhagen's life by breathing new life into her biography. This is a kind of friendship. Arendt's extension of friendship to Varnhagen, the gift of a new perspective on her story, is the gift of feminist friendship at the heart of the book. It is two women talking to each other, across time, about something other than men, something other than the usual topics consigned to women. It is not pleasant talk, and it definitely breaches the boundaries of bourgeois respectability so valued in the salons. It also breaches the boundaries of the public and private rules that Arendt valued.

A negative review of the *Rahel Varnhagen: The Life of a Jewess* characterized it in this way: "Slow, cluttered, static, curiously oppressive; reading it feels like sitting in a hothouse with no watch. One is made to feel the subject, the waiting, distraught woman; one is made aware, almost physically, of her intense femininity, her frustration" (Bedford 1958, quoted in Benhabib 1995, 86).[10] From Akerman's perspective, this sense of stultification is itself a feminist genre! It takes romanticism's love of the interior and turns it inside out. What we see is the gendered fatigue and overwork of just being in the world.[11] What Arendt talks about with Varnhagen is the lived experience of being women, Jewish, poor, cast out of the world. Arendt helps us feel the experience of Varnhagen as a Jew, and she restores the absent collectivity to Varnhagen's story. As Arendt narrates this story, talk among women about something other than men could be lifesaving, possibly even world-saving in the life of a Jew, just as the chance encounter with Beauvoir became a key life- and world-saving intervention in the life of Leduc.

HANNAH ARENDT REWRITES THE RULES

Another way to think about Arendt's narration of Varnhagen's life is to say that by rewriting Varnhagen's story, Arendt enacts the vital significance of the in-between. Emphasizing across her oeuvre that politics exists only in action with others, Arendt consistently lauds the potential and priority of plurality, intersubjectivity, and the worldly in-between. The in-between is what brings people together: it is the space between people in their distinct difference each from all, or what she calls plurality; objects or things, like her famous table, that both separate and bring people together; and ideas—the political meaning of bodily facts, policies, or goals—people come together to talk about. This is politics for Arendt: distinct, unique individuals coming together to talk, interact, debate, argue, and act. When people gather in this fashion, the "what" of their identity is left behind in revelation of the "who" of their subjectivity. The "who" is discovered in relationship to others pursuing or arguing over something in the world.

What is remarkable about the *Varnhagen* text considered in relationship to Arendt's other writings is that here Arendt recognizes that Varnhagen needed to acknowledge and affirm the "what" of her identity (the fact of being a Jew) in order to move from a false assimilation to an assessment of the political shaping of her subjectivity. She saw the issue in terms of anti-Semitism, not misogyny, but had Arendt been proficient in feminist theory she could have argued that this is the paradoxical place in which women often find themselves situated. Here we see Arendt and Beauvoir drawn together in encounter again, and in a new way. Seen as Woman, or what Beauvoir called the "essential feminine," women must struggle to assume their subjectivity beyond the male imagination. But to do this they must reckon with the fact of being a woman, an avowal that need not be a new form of essentialism, as Toril Moi (1999), reading Beauvoir, has demonstrated in several iterations. Without affirming her role as a conscious pariah, Varnhagen was confined to the paradoxical condition of being both too visible (as woman, as Jew) and invisible (as subject) at once. As we learn from Arendt's *Rahel Varnhagen*, by failing to notice pariah status, being a woman (or in Varnhagen's case a Jew) becomes simultaneously highly visible (the "what" of one's objectified body) and seemingly insignificant or invisible (a personal attribute).

Moving to a discussion of Margarethe von Trotta's film on Arendt, a film very different from *Violette* since it has a central narrative arc and a clear message to convey, I bring my focus back to the following question: How do different forms and thematic and aesthetic choices differently convey the experiences of women, instigating and extending conversations about feminist politics? In the early years of feminist film studies it was assumed that feminists should reject "women's films," often offered up as melodrama, and that narrative as an aesthetic choice more generally is indelibly linked with bourgeois ideology. For example, even narrative arcs that offer new and positive role models were seen as failing to fundamentally disrupt the male gaze and considered as conservative as what are sometimes disparagingly called "female victimology" biopics (Hollinger 2012, 160).

We should ask too: Is Bechdel's seemingly simple and baseline rule, to represent women speaking to each other about something other than men, a higher bar than it appears? Why is it of such great importance to bring two women *together* in a film rather than direct our vision to a singular exemplary heroine? Questions concerning sovereign power and sovereign rules anticipate the scenes of thinking about thinking in von Trotta's *Hannah Arendt*. The Arendt who learns on screen from Martin Heidegger that "thinking is a lonely business" has to question or at least think anew about how to think with others, why others do not want to think with her, and the several effects of different kinds of encounters that serve to somewhat undermine the confidence she may have had in the power of her individual thinking. I consider whether von Trotta's narrative of an agonistic heroine battling history, friends, and even the state of Israel and her aesthetic choices—the shots of Arendt (played by Barbara Sukowa) "thinking" while smoking and the look and feel of her New York City intellectual life—unwittingly replicate masculine perspectives on sovereignty, agency, and progress, or whether the film is up to the Bechdel challenge in another way, in the spirit if not the letter of the law.

Another way of approaching the question is to ask whether von Trotta extends feminist friendship to Arendt (or enacts the in-between) in the same way Beauvoir is seen extending it to Leduc. Von Trotta (2015, 70) herself describes her relationship to Arendt as an alliance, not a friendship: "Hannah Arendt is . . . not the only woman in my filmic life with whom I have tried to form an alliance. I certainly sensed from the very beginning that she would offer the most resistance to me." She anticipates this resistance due to Arendt's reputation for being "extremely reserved about her private life" and "almost never reveal[ing] her emotions to strangers" (71). But did she prefer to be alone? Von Trotta depicts Arendt, narratively and aesthetically, as the singular female heroine; evidence of this is that a good share of screen time is devoted to showing Arendt as the lonely thinker, the only one who could see the meaning of Eichmann's specific role in the Nazi horrors. Mostly abandoned by friends and colleagues and, most important, her circle of Jewish male friends, Arendt nevertheless mostly keeps her cool and keeps her distance. Bonnie Honig (2015) cleverly suggests Arendt's aloneness is the result of her own behavior, a kind of repetition compulsion. Honig describes Arendt "on the couch" in the film: thinking dangerously, precipitating a crisis, pushing people away, and then trying to move within the breach is a pattern born of Arendt's own experience of trauma.

However, through it all, her friend Mary McCarthy (played by Janet McTeer) and her assistant Lotte Kohler (played by Victoria Trauttmansdorff) are at her side. In real life Arendt and McCarthy wrote each other about everything under the sun. In the von Trotta film they mostly talk about men, but what they say is revealing. I contend that multiple conversations among women are initiated by the film: between von Trotta and Arendt; between Arendt and McCarthy; among Arendt, McCarthy, and Kohler; between and among spectators of the film.

Significantly, when Arendt is not alone thinking, typing, and smoking, she is depicted as engaged in conversation. In these shots, recalling her autobiographical double Varnhagen, Arendt is cast as the salonnière par excellence. She welcomes Jewish New York intellectuals into her home to share drinks, cigarettes, gossip, and philosophical, political, and literary conversation (figure 7.4). In 1982 Alfred Kazin recalled the scene:

> I met Hannah Arendt in 1946, at a dinner party given for Rabbi Leo Baeck by Elliot Cohen, the editor of *Commentary*. It was that long ago. She was a handsome, vivacious forty-year-old woman who was to charm me and others, by no means unerotically, because her interest in her new country, and for literature in English, became as much part of her as her accent and her passion for discussing Plato, Kant, Nietzsche, Kafka, even Duns Scotus, as if they all lived with her and her strenuous husband Heinrich Bluecher in the shabby rooming house on West 95th Street. (quoted in Weissberg 1997, 3)

They are a lively bunch, agonistic but mostly convivial. At the center is Hannah Arendt, the convener of minds, until the publication of her report on

FIGURE 7.4. Friends gathered in Arendt's apartment in *Hannah Arendt.*

Eichmann over which, as we learned in chapter 2, Arendt lost many of her friends.

Let me return to a line I already quoted from the film, presented as a key lesson that Arendt learns from Heidegger: "Thinking is a lonely business." In "Thinking and Moral Considerations," an essay Arendt (2003c, 165) wrote in response to the controversy over her report on the Eichmann trial, she confirms that thinking removes one's self from the world in that it deals with objects that are "absent, removed from direct sense perception." The "gift for dealing with things that do not appear has often been believed to exact a price—the price of blinding the thinker or the poet to the visible world" (167). Yet she also insists that thinking is an activity available to "everybody," not just to "professional" thinkers, and her model is Socrates, who engaged with others in conversation.

In "Thinking and Moral Considerations" Arendt (2003c) discusses the "two-in-one," or the "encounter of the self with the self," as the dialogue Richard III has with himself after committing a great number of crimes. She characterizes this encounter as meeting a "fellow" when one "leaves the marketplace" and goes home alone, but never quite alone since the "absent fellow" will be there waiting to begin the "soundless solitary dialogue we call thinking" (187). This is thinking characterized as the "difference given in consciousness," not just a "prerogative of the few but an ever-present faculty of everybody" (187). At the same time, though, it is also an "ever-present possibility for everybody" to "shun that intercourse with oneself whose possibility and importance Socrates first discovered" (188). This is what Eichmann did

FIGURE 7.5. Arendt smoking in *Hannah Arendt*.

FIGURE 7.6. Arendt at her typewriter in *Hannah Arendt*.

FIGURE 7.7. Arendt on the couch in *Hannah Arendt.*

when he failed to think, and thinking is what Arendt does, and what she is shown to be doing in von Trotta's film, when she is alone smoking, in front of her typewriter, and lying on her couch (figures 7.5–7.7).

Thinking is the activity that precipitates the loss of almost all her male friends in the film, although her female friends—McCarthy, Lotte, and Lore, the wife of the philosopher Hans Jonas—remain steadfast in their friendship with her (figures 7.8–7.10).

There is yet another way of thinking presented in "Thinking and Moral Considerations," maybe a complementary way, and that is the model of Socrates in the marketplace, speaking with his friends and his enemies, engaged with others in the world, talking about everyday concepts, the concepts that "arise whenever people open their mouths and begin to talk" (2003c, 171). In his roles as gadfly, midwife, and electric ray, as Arendt describes it, Socrates engaged with people in conversation, encouraging them to examine their lives, discard too simple answers, and stop and think, an activity that "cannot but look like paralysis from the outside and the ordinary course of human affairs, but is felt as the highest state of being alive" (175).

Von Trotta shows Arendt doing both kinds of thinking. She is often alone smoking, typing, and ruminating, but she is also often in dialogue and in conversation with enemies and friends. Sometimes the conversations get heated and Arendt's thinking produces results that defy the conventional wisdom on the nature of evil, the role of the Jewish councils, and the interest of the state of Israel in teaching moral lessons to young Israeli Jews rather than pursuing justice. That's when Arendt loses the majority of her male friends, but the

FIGURE 7.8. Arendt with Mary McCarthy in *Hannah Arendt*.

FIGURE 7.9. Arendt with Lotte Kohler in *Hannah Arendt*.

FIGURE 7.10. Arendt with Lore Jonas in *Hannah Arendt*.

women stick by her.[12] In fact they stand up for her. At the beginning of the film McCarthy and Arendt speak only about men, Arendt offering such gems as "Either you are willing to take men as they are or you live alone!" and "The men in your novels are not perfect. Why do you expect the real ones to be any better?" Ariella Azoulay (2015, 124) notes of this conversation, "Surprising as it may sound when voiced by a woman who, in the mid twentieth century, revolutionized political philosophy, a discipline ruled solely by men, it should astonish us less if we understand it as Arendt's way to survive in a world she shared with men, and which at that time was ruled exclusively by them." Azoulay also remarks that this is not a "superficial speech" but one rooted in Arendt's conception that love is a private matter, that it does "not partake in building a common world" (125).

But the film challenges the truism that conversations about love do not build a common world. Spectators are participants in the conversation too, and we might be persuaded that conversations about love and friendship between women on screen are as transformative as the ones between men about more narrowly political matters. In the film McCarthy is constantly bringing up private matters (a depiction that has been criticized as belittling her intellectual role in the mid-twentieth-century world of letters). To my mind, McCarthy and Arendt's conversations depict essential qualities of their friendship and show how this friendship changed both of them and their lives. At key points McCarthy is Arendt's champion; for example, late in the film McCarthy interrupts an all-male circle to defend her friend's ideas: "Isn't

FIGURE 7.11. A circle of men in *Hannah Arendt*.

FIGURE 7.12. Mary McCarthy breaking into the circle of men in *Hannah Arendt*.

it admirable that she is the only one who can discuss this topic without beating her breast?" (figures 7.11 and 7.12).

Another criticism of the depiction of McCarthy in von Trotta's film is that the feminist director introduced the friendship in the way she did because she is interested in sororal connections, the private lives of great feminist heroines, and she seeks to address her films to female viewers (Weigel 2013). In response I would ask: why is this a bad thing? The fact that this is a criticism speaks volumes about our expectations about male dominance in film and in politics. Even putting masculinist expectations aside, I see the depiction of the friendship between McCarthy and Arendt as much more expansive and transformative than these criticisms allow. Considering Arendt's own writing on thinking as both solitary and communal, I would argue that von Trotta was right to depict Arendt as engaged in conversation and also as needing to sometimes think alone. What is most remarkable about von Trotta's film is her featuring of female friendship, and women talking together, as central for Arendt's thinking in both modes.

Consider the substance of what women say to each other in the film and how and why these conversations are shown as sustaining and enabling Arendt's thinking. To do so, we might return to the context of the Bechdel rule. When the Bechdel rule is lifted out of its queer context, it seems to demand some very simple changes in film: to have two women speaking together about something other than men. But this is actually far more demanding, far more political than it initially seems! In the comic strip's queer context two dykes are speaking to each other, debating whether the two women in *Alien* talking to each other about the monster actually meets the rule of women talking to each other not about men. These are transformative encounters, both in and out of context! We have dykes speaking about a film that is about women speaking together about monsters and whether they are men. And out of context we see Arendt and McCarthy talking about Eichmann, considering whether he is a monster or just another man, a repetition (with a difference) of Beauvoir and Arendt talking about men as monsters in chapter 2. Their discussion of Heidegger too becomes a conversation about his monstrous actions. Other conversations about the usual topics for women, about marriage, about love, are also perverted in this film, often highlighting erotic and sororal attachments between women. Von Trotta's decision to continually highlight the role that Arendt's assistant Lotte and her friend McCarthy played in her life, particularly during the difficult time of the Eichmann controversy, shows Arendt as primarily moving within the world of men but enabled by conversations with women.[13] Interestingly von Trotta (2015, 71, 84) writes that although she initially tried to "form an alliance" with Arendt, Arendt "increasingly became a friend" to her.

In these several ways I have described it, von Trotta's film is up to the challenge of the Bechdel task, both in and out of context. Consider the two images that end *Hannah Arendt* and *Violette* (figures 7.13 and 7.14). In each our heroine is alone. This may seem surprising, and maybe disappointing, in terms of Bechdel's challenge for women to come together and start new conversations. Leduc is in the country, and Arendt is on the couch. Leduc is writing, just like a "sovereign on a hillside," as Beauvoir wrote,[14] and Arendt is smoking and

FIGURE 7.13. Arendt on her couch in *Hannah Arendt*.

FIGURE 7.14. Leduc in the countryside in *Violette*.

thinking. But although alone, each has been enabled by her conversational encounters with other women *to be alone*, to try to make feminist sense of her contingent, violent, oppressive experiences that are transformed from personal to political by a feminist textual encounter. Elena Ferrante (2016), the author of the "Neapolitan" novels, charting the friendship of two girls "unbecoming" women in Naples, says that even when alone, we are not alone:

> I can't even think without the voices of others, much less write. And I'm not talking only about relatives, female friends, enemies. I'm talking about others, men and women who today exist only in images: in television or newspaper images, sometimes heartrending, sometimes offensive in their opulence. And I'm talking about the past, about what we generally call tradition; I'm talking about all those others who were once in the world and who have acted or who now act through us. Our entire body, like it or not, enacts a stunning resurrection of the dead just as we advance toward our own death. We are, as you say, interconnected. And we should teach ourselves to look deeply at this interconnection—I call it a tangle, or, rather, *frantumaglia*—to give ourselves adequate tools to describe it. In the most absolute tranquility or in the midst of tumultuous events, in safety or danger, in innocence or corruption, we are a crowd of others. And this crowd is certainly a blessing for literature.

Together Arendt, McCarthy, Varnhagen, Leduc, Beauvoir, Ferrante's characters, and a host of others make feminist political sense of the world's terrors and life's contingencies, from the most seemingly private (being deemed ugly, aberrant, or unlovable) to the most public (marked for death by genocide).

What we learn too, seeing these women alone on screen after they were with others, is that the challenge of "unbecoming women" is to refuse the essentialist vision at the heart of the (mythic) collective. Being together, experiencing freedom in encounter, but only by preserving the in-between, makes visible the singularity that defines a woman's (anyone's) life. Indeed singularity of experience is made possible only by freedom in the encounter.

Hearing and seeing conversations between women on screen, just as we did in volume 2 of *The Second Sex*, new conversations can begin between readers and viewers, Maybe we too can start to move differently and orient ourselves toward freedom. These conversations transform the way we think about what women speaking together can help us see, help us imagine, and help us do.

CONCLUSION
A HAPPY ENDING

One diligent reader of this manuscript said of chapter 7 that my depiction of feminist friendship—between Violette Leduc and Simone de Beauvoir, Hannah Arendt and Rahel Varnhagen, Mary McCarthy and Hannah Arendt—all, in the end, seemed a "bit too rosy." As I revised the manuscript, particularly that chapter, this worry lodged in me and hung on. I looked for ways to complicate my picture. Was I making Beauvoir too rosy? What about all my encounters? As I looked back on the different sections of the book, now with this question in mind, I noticed I always close with a happy ending. I do not mean the orgasm ending the massage, although keeping the body center stage has been something this book has done all along. I also do not mean the Hollywood or fairy tale happy ending. I agree with Sara Ahmed (2010), who condemns versions of happiness that orient us on the "right" path or seek to guarantee a certain outcome. These redemptive happy endings close down the politics of the encounter that I have sought to open up for scrutiny. My happy ending embraces the *hap* in *happiness* that Ahmed points to: the chance, the contingency, the opportunity to grasp joy in a moment or freedom in the encounter.

My book starts with war trials (Brasillach's and Eichmann's) and moves to *Antichrist* (no one would call this a "happy" movie, but somehow I take a reparative message from it) in part I; from pathology (Fanon) to solidarity

(Wright) in part II; and from isolated women acting violently to feminist friendship in part III. The naming of my interlocutors repeats the movement toward happy endings: I start with enemies, make allies, and embrace friends. I move from isolation to conversation. Throughout I claim that encounters can be freeing. Being with others can save us; we can work together; we can move in new directions. Rosy? I have to say yes! There is no guarantee, though. If we do politics with Beauvoir, we see that freedom cannot be experienced other than in encounter, where it also risks destruction or diminution. We can fail, we can lose; tragic consequences can ensue. Or we may win.

Beauvoir's vision of politics, particularly her claim that we must grasp freedom to make it grow even in airless spaces, emerges only when we read her writings *themselves* in encounter. Her political thinking, contained in her recognized philosophical work but also in essays, novels, and her four-volume autobiography, is rooted in critical dialogue with her peers in response to events in her life, including the discovery that prompted her to write *The Second Sex*: that becoming a woman, and in particular being seen in the world as a woman, had affected her more than she had thought. Thus I have parsed her writing in conversation with contemporaries about the political events in their lives and extended these to explore the implications of their insights for contemporary contexts. This opens Beauvoir's work to new readings. I have also attended to those moments in her texts when she stages encounters of her own. Doing so I wanted to show that although *encounter* is not a central term in Beauvoir's lexicon, it was nevertheless her method of political thinking.

Carving up the world into enemies, allies, and friends—as I argue Beauvoir did, and as I do in this book—emphasizes the felt and lived intimacies of how politics happens (in addition to offsetting the still too central Schmittian distinction between friend and enemy). Politics with Beauvoir is never anything but up close and personal. Situating the body as the primary site where political freedom, as well as affect, violence, and destruction, are located and ideologies take hold, Beauvoir shows that what happens intimately, in agonism and affect, portends the world and is *the* site of politics. What is politics, Beauvoir makes us realize, but the site and shape of relationships, body to body. While she distinguishes among sexual, familial, racial, national, cultural, colonial, and textual encounters, her language of situation and ambiguity helps us decipher the interrelationships of various intensities and kinds of encounter, as well as judge and try to redirect their differing impacts on our emotions, our identities, and our potential collectivities.

Beauvoir's historical moment and her political commitments saturate and situate this book, as does the reception context of her texts. But the encounters staged here also moved beyond them. Several of my staged encounters were remarkably out of context. Adding the films of Chantal Akerman, Margarethe von Trotta, David Fincher, and Lars von Trier, as well as Arendt's writing about Eichmann and especially Rahel Varnhagen, to Beauvoir's universe of encounters was (likely) unexpected and (hopefully) instructive. Being open to the encounter mandates sensitivity to reception contexts that condition how we have seen a thinker or a text in earlier moments but also summons our willingness to resituate thinkers and texts in new contexts. This method dislodged previous scholarly investments in Beauvoir's feminism and the settled meanings of its relationship to her activism and her other writing so that I could analyze and reconfigure antiquated desires.

As I noted at the outset, Beauvoir is read as a feminist thinker, indeed as "our Beauvoir," who in a dizzying variety of interpretations has been blamed and venerated for feminism's flaws, insights, and achievements. This Beauvoir serves as the edifice for second-wave feminism's shortcomings and advantages and situates us, her contemporary readers, as having moved past her by adopting new and more progressive forms of feminisms in new waves, or as nostalgic for what now seems lost at a moment when feminist movements are not a primary site of collective action. I have shown, however, that Beauvoir need not be caught up in this outdated emotional and political nexus where she is forever trapped as our (difficult, disappointing, although sometimes wise) mother. These earlier interpretations certainly ignited feminist passions and arguments that were crucial to their moment, but the power of these readings continues to cast a spell in feminist theory that needs to be broken. Reading Beauvoir with new sets of questions and with an emboldened curiosity about her relevance for us today moves her feminism, and indeed her political thinking, beyond a set of commitments that need not and should not constrain us now.

Seeing Beauvoir as a theorist of freedom in the encounter illuminates her work as much richer in political promise than prior interpretations would lead us to believe. I have enlisted her method to take her out of context and inspire a return to her for political and feminist theory that can take new directions. Reading Beauvoir's work as I have done, with an eye for bodily abjection and degradation, for the mark of affects on bodies and ideology made material, and for new configurations of power that trouble rather than reinforce gender and other identities, introduces a Beauvoir who can speak to us now and inspire new directions in thinking feminism's enduring political significance.

What has emerged here by way of these encounters, and by way of her focus on freedom, is a Beauvoir who does not essentialize nor shy away from so-called ugly feelings. Instead we meet a Beauvoir who prizes the importance of reflective judgment and is willing to throw away the rules or experiment with new ones. With Beauvoir we risk ourselves, and our most entrenched truisms, to follow the swerve in the road. We are likely to end up in a different place. Taking a risk, facing the abyss, we might find freedom. This is a Beauvoir who, rather than always already knowing where we should look to find and condemn misogynist ideology and practices, for example, is willing to look elsewhere and move differently, as well as look in the same places but see new things. My Beauvoir helps us to see that von Trier's films take us close to the brink of reinforcing patriarchy's myths and that they have the power to take a turn in another direction. Enlisting "the feel of the agon" (Huffer 2015), our perception of foreign existences is heightened in *Antichrist*, and in *Nymphomaniac* we are moved to expand the range of what counts as female pleasure.

Reading Beauvoir *this* way I dislodged entrenched, iconic, and static visions of what her feminism looks like. Such encounters help us together imagine new ways to shatter the rules of patriarchy and reenvision the terms and practices of freedom. Theorizing freedom in encounter is itself a feminist project, as it insists we focus on bodies and their meanings to reject systems, mechanisms, and moments of oppression based in these meanings. The encounters in these pages are not abstract or heroic; they are messy, confusing, conflicted, surprising, and sometimes angry. Freedom springs up in unlikely places and is sometimes quashed where we expected it to thrive. We never know; we most often fail; and yet we continue to try. We muddle through, mired, as we so intractably are, in a world marked by absurdity, contingency, disgust, disappointment, violence, and deep sorrows, but also joys, hope, victories, friendship, and love.

It is within the world with others, body to body, that freedom is experienced, but this is possible only when the in-between is safeguarded so our unique selves might safely appear. The effacing of freedom in encounter is all but certain within ideologies, totalitarian movements, and fundamentalist religions. Rule following and hubristic denials of the future's unpredictability also portend danger for freedom in the encounter. On this question Beauvoir agrees with Arendt, although Arendt, incisively depicted by von Trotta as smoking and thinking on her couch alone, stages this exemplary encounter with the respected stranger as occurring within our heads (impossible for a camera to capture). In contrast the encounter Beauvoir stages within a single individual is, predictably for her, not in the head but in the body. Describing pregnancy, Beauvoir ([1949] 2011, 538) says it is above all "a drama playing itself out in the woman between her and herself; she experiences it both as an enrichment and a mutilation; the fetus is part of her body, and it is a parasite exploiting her." Will the baby become enemy, ally, or friend? All depends on situation, ambiguity, and encounter. For Beauvoir the child herself is an Other, and whether freedom will be enriched or denied in relationship with the mother depends on the appeal and what the two make of it. As she puts it, "I can invent the most urgent appeals, try my best to charm . . . but [the other] will remain free to respond to those appeals or not, no matter what I do" ([1944] 2004, 136). And in *The Second Sex* she adds, "The mother can have *her* reasons for wanting a child, but she cannot give to *this* other—who tomorrow is going to be—his own raisons d'être; she engenders him in the generality of his body, not in the specificity of his existence" ([1949] 2011, 539). If the other becomes so familiar that we think we can predict what she will say or do, the space of difference is disavowed and freedom is missed. As Beauvoir constantly warns, and as I hope I have modeled in my own encounter with her writing in these pages, we must avow the dissonance in our thoughts, our bodies, and our identities; bodies themselves must be visible and felt; bodily desires, longings, pleasures, perversions, destruction, and potentialities need to acknowledged; and the space *between* bodies has to be recognized and preserved.

As we have seen, politics with Beauvoir is not in our heads, nor does it unfold in idealized or abstract situations. Most important, politics with Beauvoir does not leave us lost and alone, trying to make our own solitary way through confusion, despair, ecstasy, chaos, and violence. Beauvoir was emphatic that we can choose and that we can carve out a small space for movement in even the most narrow and constricted spaces. She was also emphatic in her condemnation of the narrowness and constriction of such spaces. Her response was to urge us to make and answer appeals, to risk freedom in the encounter in conversation and action with others. Our actions always risk failure. Indeed it sometimes seems that we are trapped in the darkest of times or the absurdist of circumstances. To embrace politics with Beauvoir is to appeal, to answer, to argue, to move, to desire more, and to make more possible. This is freedom in the encounter. It's a happy ending.

INTRODUCTION

1. Yolanda Patterson (1986, 90) points out that Beauvoir "laughingly" dismissed the idea that feminists look to her as a mother figure, noting, "People don't tend to listen to what their mothers are telling them." Patterson writes that in spite of this, Beauvoir has been proclaimed the "mother of the women's movement, the mother of all liberated women, whether or not they knew her name or her work" (90). Sartre does not escape his duties as "father" either. Beauvoir and Sartre are scrutinized as "parental" figures of mid-twentieth-century left politics: their sexual proclivities and rules of romantic engagement as well as spheres of influence (on each other and subsequent political and theoretical camps) have been extensively, even exhaustively studied.

Often Beauvoir is reduced simply to the role of "exemplary woman" of second-wave feminism whose life lessons are to be followed or rejected. Her life is held up as an example to follow or, in versions where she is seen as the girlfriend of Sartre, to be avoided as deeply hypocritical. In *Feminist Thinkers and the Demands of Femininity: The Lives and Work of Intellectual Women* (Marso 2006), I also read Beauvoir as an exemplary feminist, but in conversation with other historical and contemporary feminist writers. I frame her work this way not to praise or criticize her choices and activities but rather to provide a genealogical perspective on the several ways diverse feminist thinkers recount their struggles with gender expectations.

2. Beauvoir's existentialist emphasis on existence as action and activity and her focus on the ways structural and psychological limitations impose constraints on individual women direct our attention to individuals situated in relationship to structures of oppression (sometimes as oppressors, sometimes as the oppressed, even both at once, depending on the context) and habits of unfreedom. But to say Beauvoir is concerned primarily with individual women or, as is sometimes said, concerned primarily with white privileged women is to misread her diagnosis and her political commitments.

3. Some decry Beauvoir's embrace of communism instead of praising (or lamenting) her attention to liberal individualism. These interpretations are closer to the mark in terms of Beauvoir's political commitments, but still not quite right. Beauvoir ([1963] 1992, 12) explains her and Sartre's early but transforming political project: "In our youth, we had felt close to the Communist Party insofar as its negativism agreed with

our anarchism. We wanted the defeat of capitalism, but not the accession of a socialist society which, we thought, would have deprived us of our liberty."

4. In this context the new wave of Beauvoir scholarship that has been produced in the past two decades is particularly welcome, although it is mostly in the fields of literature and philosophy. This scholarship takes Beauvoir seriously as a thinker worthy not only of historical but also contemporary feminist interest, one who is not surpassed by contemporary feminist work but rather anticipates and informs it. In particular Bauer 2001; Deutscher 2008; Kruks 2012b; Moi 1999.

5. As Margaret Simons notes in the introduction to Beauvoir (2004, 2), the postwar popular press called Beauvoir "la grande Sartreuse" and "Notre-Dame de Sartre." Corrections of this position are offered by Simons 1981; Fullbrook and Fullbrook 1994; and most recently Daigle and Golomb 2009.

6. See Spelman (1988), as one example; there are many from this historical moment (late 1980s and throughout the 1990s).

7. In the second volume of *The Second Sex*, Beauvoir offers a descriptive phenomenology of female embodiment, or what she calls women's "lived experience." Because some of this experience is of shame or of horror (in part or whole due to women experiencing their body as an object of the male gaze) much of what Beauvoir says about women's experience is cast, at best, in an ambivalent light. Her work is the inspiration for Iris Marion Young's (1990, 2005) writing on female body experience with menstruation, having breasts, and aging, and yet Beauvoir's writings sit somewhat uncomfortably with "sexual difference" feminists such as Rosie Braidotti (1994) and Elizabeth Grosz (1994), who argue that women's otherness is unrepresentable within the male symbolic.

8. Beauvoir and Sartre never married and never became biological parents. Both decisions were deliberate. Beauvoir ([1960] 1992, 78) explains why she chose not to become a mother in *The Prime of Life*: "Maternity itself seemed incompatible with the way of life upon which I was embarking. I knew that in order to become a writer I needed a great measure of time and freedom. I had no rooted objection to playing at long odds, but this was not a game: the whole value and direction of my life lay at stake. The risk of compromising it could only have been justified had I regarded a child as no less vital a creative task than a work of art, which I did not."

9. For a reading that puts Beauvoir into the same space as feminists such as Irigaray and Cixous, see Emily Zakin's essay, "Beauvoir's Unsettling of the Universal," in Marso and Moynagh (2006).

10. In the introduction to *Transfeminist Perspectives in and beyond Transgender and Gender Studies*, A. Finn Enke (2012, 1) argues that the essays in this (edited) volume build on Beauvoir's insight, emphasizing that "there is no natural process by which *anyone* becomes woman and also that *everyone's* gender is made."

11. Beauvoir is rarely considered a political thinker. Important recent contributions in this vein are Kruks 2012b; Marso and Moynagh 2006. Deidre Bair (1990), author of Beauvoir's definitive biography, considers why Beauvoir's relationship to politics is so often mischaracterized: "She has never written anything exclusively devoted to the explication of a personal political credo, and has always denied in the strongest

language any interest or involvement in politics per se. Still, the curious thing about all her seemingly contradictory statements is how political they are and always have been. Hers is a political rhetoric that has sometimes led to charges that she advocates social anarchy, is clearly a misogynist, and has even lost touch with the realities of contemporary life for most of the women in the world" (Bair 1986, 150).

For most of her life, Beauvoir was a very political person. She admits that prior to the Occupation, she didn't pay much attention to politics, but living under Nazi domination changed all that. Characterizing Sartre's and her own feelings of responsibility after World War II, in *Force of Circumstance* Beauvoir ([1963] 1992, 12) writes, "Politics had become a family matter, and we expected to have a hand in it. 'Politics is no longer dissociated from individuals,' Camus wrote in *Combat* at the beginning of September, 'it is man's direct address to other men.' We were writers, and that was our job, to address ourselves to other men. . . . I knew then that my destiny was bound to that of all other people; freedom, oppression, the happiness and misery of other men was a matter of intimate concern to me."

Reflecting their new political awareness, in 1945 Beauvoir and Sartre founded *Les Temps Modernes*. Beauvoir remained active on the journal's board until her death in 1986. The monthly journal, and Beauvoir and Sartre particularly, were at the center of French intellectual life for several decades. Included in the journal, for example, were essays on race relations in the United States, articles condemning the French war in Algeria, analyses of life in the Soviet Union and the Eastern bloc, contributions of authors from the former colonies on race, colonialism, and oppression, and analyses of the Arab-Israeli conflict. *Les Temps Modernes* was the most important intellectual gathering place for political debates and conversations on the noncommunist Left during much of Beauvoir's lifetime, although after 1968 existentialism, particularly Sartre's intellectual dominance on the Left, was significantly challenged and the journal's influence waned. Nevertheless, directing the business of the journal and meeting activists and writers kept politics, narrowly defined, prominent in Beauvoir's activities and focus. In addition to traveling all over Europe to meet with important leftist thinkers and leaders, she spent extended periods of time in the United States, Mexico, the Soviet Union, North Africa, Cuba, Brazil, China, Japan, Egypt, and Israel. In their travels Sartre and Beauvoir met with everyone from government officials to dissident groups. Often, in each of these places, she also met independently with women's groups and feminist associations inspired by *The Second Sex*.

Given this very active life focused on politics (in its narrow definition), it is really quite remarkable that Beauvoir is not more widely recognized as deeply engaged with and directly influenced by political issues and questions. This oversight might be attributed, at least in part, to the dominance of *The Second Sex* in the reception of her writings and the unfortunate and ingrained habit of failing to see feminist theory *as* political theory.

12. *The Beauvoir Series*, published by the University of Illinois Press, edited by Margaret A. Simons and Sylvie Le Bon de Beauvoir, comprises seven volumes and is an especially important contribution that will certainly bring attention to Beauvoir's diverse writings. Also important is the 2011 Constance Borde and Sheila Malovany-

Chevallier translation of *The Second Sex*. Problems with the H. M. Parshley translation are legion, but the new translation, although it restores Beauvoir's philosophical language as well as all the excised portions, still has some problems. See Moi's (2010) essay in the *London Review of Books* for important corrections to passages in the new translation where Beauvoir's philosophical meaning is changed or missed. My references throughout this book are to the Borde and Malovany-Chevallier translation, with Moi's corrections noted when appropriate.

13. Sartre might say that women remain trapped by the male gaze because they don't look back.

14. In a compelling exposition of the way both Sartre and Beauvoir take up Hegel's Master/Slave dialectic, Nancy Bauer (2001, 149) argues that Beauvoir is able to transform it from within: "Put otherwise, the Other's freedom is to be seen as not just a threat to my subjectivity but a necessary condition of its being regularly exercised. That there is something positive about the Other's freedom is a possibility never raised by the Sartre of *Being and Nothingness*. That Beauvoir thinks we might see it this way is a function of her figuring my actions not as attempts to freeze the Other, along with his threats in my world, but as 'calls' or 'appeals.'"

15. Encounters occur within natural processes and material life (atoms move against other atoms, species within and against species, rivers meet oceans), between people and nature or other animals, between people and objects and nonorganic forces and materials, between nations and states, among people (self against other, group against group, class against class), and within the self (experienced consciously and unconsciously as divided desires, conflicted loyalties, bodily symptoms rebelling against conscious will). But only human beings choose. While some complex confrontations do not involve conscious willing people (in nature, between and within processes, and even in unconscious or habitual interactions between humans), what we make of them is a political question.

16. Sonia Kruks's (2012b) important book *Simone de Beauvoir and the Politics of Ambiguity* thoroughly explains how ambiguity features in Beauvoir's writings in several registers and compares this approach to rationalism, liberalism, and poststructuralism. I focus on encounter to capture a different dynamic in Beauvoir's work, one that highlights her struggle with others (enemies, allies, and friends) and helps us see why and how the Self/Other dynamic not only played out between subjects but in other ways too (with objects, with history, in nature, between more than two subjects) is a political dynamic that makes freedom possible.

17. I discuss Beauvoir's work on racism and colonialism in part II, on Fanon and Wright. While her anti-imperialism comes out in several contexts, one key example of this commitment was her membership in the 1966 Russell Tribunal, organized by Bertrand Russell and Sartre. The Russell Tribunal (a citizen's court, a performance of what justice would look like) investigated war crimes and acts of genocide by the U.S. government in Vietnam, although it did not have the power to impose sanctions.

18. In a letter to the journalist Samuel Grafton, Arendt writes: "When, many years ago, I described the totalitarian system and analyzed the totalitarian mentality, it was always a 'type,' rather than individuals, I had to deal with, and if you look at the

system as a whole, every individual person becomes indeed 'a cog small or big,' in the machinery of terror. . . . In other words, I wanted to know: Who was Eichmann? What were his deeds, not insofar as his crimes were part and parcel of the Nazi system, but insofar as he was a free agent? . . . And it is for this reason that the whole small cog theory (the theory of the defense) is quite irrelevant in this context. . . . I have been thinking for many years, or to be specific thirty years, about the nature of evil. And the wish to expose myself—not to the deeds, which, after all, were well known, but to the evildoer himself—probably was the most powerful motive in my decision to go to Jerusalem" (quoted in Berkowitz 2016).

19. Casting Beauvoir into another all too familiar box, that of Sartre's girlfriend (a demeaned version of "our Beauvoir"), Arendt dismisses Beauvoir as just another woman—beautiful, and thus not very smart. In response to the *Partisan Review* editor William Phillips's complaints about Beauvoir and the "endless nonsense" she spoke about America when she visited in 1947, Arendt is said to have replied, "The trouble with you, William, is that you don't realize that she's not very bright. Instead of arguing with her, you should flirt with her" (quoted in Brightman 1995, xiii).

20. *Politics, Theory, and Film: Critical Encounters with Lars von Trier*, edited by Bonnie Honig and Lori Marso (2016b), showcases interpretations of several of von Trier's films that challenge the picture of von Trier as only misanthropic and misogynist. In the introduction, focusing in particular on the claim that von Trier is a misogynist, we argue that von Trier intensifies the "clichés of our times" in ways that direct our political energies toward apprehending and repairing a shattered world.

21. Doing so I take Beauvoir's texts out of their contexts as well as reading them within historical context. Here I follow the practice of political theory exemplified in Honig (2013) and Martel (2013).

22. In *She Came to Stay* (Beauvoir [1943] 1984), for example, the heroine murders her nemesis at the end of the novel as a result of the fear that she has lost herself in their encounter.

23. See "Right-Wing Thought Today," an essay Beauvoir ([1955] 2012) published in two parts in *Les Temps Modernes* in 1955.

24. In 1963 Beauvoir ([1963] 1992, 75) reflected, "Of all of my books, it is the one that irritates me the most today." She felt the book was too abstract, too idealist, when in fact she had been trying to refute "Kantian maxims" as well as the "delusion of the *one* monolithic humanity used by Communist writers" (75). Upon reflection her judgment is that, "like Sartre," she was "insufficiently liberated from the ideologies of my class; at the very moment I was rejecting them, I was still using their language to do so" (77). Yet despite this harsh judgment of her own work, what still emerges very clearly from *The Ethics of Ambiguity* is her commitment to reject all metaphysical explanations and meanings, to show the failures, antinomies, and complications of action, and present "collective reality against the interiority of every being" (76).

25. Thinking of Beauvoir in this register, she would be a productive conversation partner with the work of Jacques Rancière. In Jason Frank's review of some of Rancière's recently translated writings (written between 1975 and 1985 and responding to the events of May 1968), Frank argues against what he calls the "eventual" reading

of Rancière's work, which is focused on the exception, the revolutionary, and the rupture. As Frank (2015, 259) puts it: "What the works reviewed here most clearly reveal, and that the dominant reception in political theory obscures, is Rancière's distinctive approach to the politics of the ordinary. In contemporary political theory, the politics of the ordinary is usually associated with theorists influenced by ordinary language philosophy and Stanley Cavell, on the one hand, or those taking up Foucauldian or Deleuzian investigations into 'micropolitics' on the other (or some combination of the two). Rancière belongs to this contemporary theoretical constellation as much as he does with the one preoccupied with 'the axioms of rupture,' emergency, or the 'supposedly radical experience of the heterogeneous.'"

26. See "An Invitation from Lars von Trier—Transcript of the First TV Interview Since the Cannes Press Conference, with Martin Krasnik, Danish Journalist, Translation by Troels Skadhauge, Lars Tønder," in Honig and Marso 2016b.

27. See Patchen Markell's (2014) reading of Arendt's critique of "cultured philistinism" in the 1961 essay "The Crisis in Culture." Along with that essay Markell wrestles with Arendt's unique take on Kant in order to show how she "resist[s] the collapse of aesthetic judgment back into rule-governed morality" (68).

28. See Gordon's (2015, 32) *What Fanon Said*, wherein he laments the fact that Fanon "failed to articulate his indebtedness to Beauvoir": "Beauvoir not only offered much intellectual sustenance for Fanon's thought but he . . . was also well aware of at least two of her major contributions at the time of writing *Black Skin, White Masks*, as the presence of these books in his home library attests."

29. Bonnie Honig is the exemplar of this practice, asking why we see a text in a certain way and drawing our attention to what we don't see. In much of Honig's work, particularly in *Antigone, Interrupted* (2013), she makes us query why and how some of our most cherished works of political theory have a particular grip on us and why we can't see them in other ways. Then she opens up a new reading. This is my goal for *The Second Sex* and for reading Beauvoir's politics as encounter.

CHAPTER 1: (RE)ENCOUNTERING *THE SECOND SEX*

1. I argue that drawing an affective response from readers is a result of the formal features of Beauvoir's text but that it doesn't always work; it is an appeal to do so that emerges from the formal mechanisms of the conversations that Beauvoir introduces in her text. In these ways my reading of *The Second Sex* is in keeping with the kind of work Eugenie Brinkema (2014, xv–xvi) argues is needed as an intervention into debates on affect: "A consequence of decoupling textuality and theory—which I will argue comes from the tradition of arguing for affect by arguing against reading for form—is a suffocating dearth of material with which a theorist can press on affect in a text and an almost nonexistent ability to let affect press back against theory. The loss works both ways, for not only do critics fail to find in the details the workings of violence or intensity, but such a reading strategy closes down the paths by which textual specificity might speak back to, challenge, undermine—or perhaps radically revise— the very theory at stake in any argument."

2. Reading Frederick Douglass's Fourth of July address, Jason Frank (2010, 211, 219) attends to its "dramatic *staging* of the address itself," arguing that "his enactment of the people would radically change the very people in whose name it is enacted." I attend to similar features of *The Second Sex*, particularly in this chapter and in chapter 5, where I argue that Beauvoir and Wright together stage the conditions of solidarity by bringing a new coalition into being where it previously had not existed.

3. In her introduction to "Right-Wing Thought Today" in its new translation, the Beauvoir scholar Sonia Kruks (2012a) argues that this piece employs a rather uncharacteristic (for Beauvoir) and vulgar form of Marxism. She says that Beauvoir was persuaded by Sartre to be a "staunch fellow traveler in her own right" with the French Communist Party from 1952 to 1956 and the Soviet invasion of Hungary, a position evidenced by this essay. Kruks laments that its argument is limited to "a striking Manichaeism: either one is with the Communists, or one is against them" (109). Spoiler alert: Beauvoir is with the communists, at least until 1956. But while Kruks laments Beauvoir's too apparent Marxism, saying it elides her usual penchant to embrace ambiguity and highlight situation, I see this essay differently, as an exemplar of Beauvoir's conversational method and her complex articulation of stylistic relations between form and technique, and substantively between materialism, experience, and affect. When we focus on form, technique, and affect in this text, it resists a reading that reduces it to system or structure. *The Second Sex* and "Right-Wing Thought Today" have been read as confirming Beauvoir's politics as antipatriarchy and anticapitalist (but also sometimes pro-individualist in a way that sits uncomfortably with her collective feminist and left politics). Changing the interpretive lens through which we view these texts allows us to see that although Beauvoir is indeed against both patriarchy and capitalism and decries the ways these structures oppress individuals, she offers a much more sophisticated theory of the way individuals and structures interact than these characterizations of her work allow. In fact, as I will show, Beauvoir's politics are not best captured by those who see her as embracing the methods of structuralism or as promoting freedom as the affirmation of ambiguity, although both these features are strong in her work. I will argue, in contrast, that Beauvoir is attentive to bodies, affect, experience, and materiality in a way that defies these too neat categorizations of her thought.

4. One passage where Beauvoir specifically uses the term *enemies* is not in reference to right-wing thinkers or to male thinkers defining Woman. It is instead a term hurled at her by a young black girl in the United States in reference to Beauvoir herself. The incident is recounted in *America Day by Day* (Beauvoir 2000), published just before *The Second Sex*, documenting her several-months trip through the United States. Here she recounts her consciousness of being white, a consciousness of racial marking similar to that she had learned from Richard Wright as the constant awareness of being black. However, the lived experience of racial identity is not one that Beauvoir had encountered before being among blacks in America: "With every step, our discomfort grows. As we go by voices drop, gestures drop, smiles die: all life is suspended in the depths of those angry eyes. The silence is so stifling, the menace so oppressive that it's almost a relief when something finally explodes. An old woman glares at us in

disgust and spits twice . . . a tiny girl runs off crying, 'Enemies! Enemies!'" (236). One thing we might note from this passage, balanced by an earlier part describing white hatred of blacks, is that one is not made an enemy by personal hatred or personal experience but rather by social and political situation. This accords with Beauvoir's theorization of "enemies" in "Right-Wing Thought Today," although there she specifically focuses on the intellectuals who purposely seek to justify bourgeois class privilege as a universal or human stance, which Beauvoir claims is an impossible task.

5. Francine du Plessix Gray, "Dispatches from the Other," *New York Times*, May 27, 2010, http://www.nytimes.com/2010/05/30/books/review/Gray-t.html?pagewanted =all.

6. Excessive historicizing may be a result of its strong links with inspiring women's liberation movements in the late 1960s and early 1970s in the United States, in France, and across the globe, and the pronounced tendency within feminist movements to conceptualize time as unfolding either in a linear and progressive improvement narrative (wherein the text would be seen as long surpassed) or as tinged by nostalgia for the past and disappointment about the failure to deliver a promised future (wherein the text would be read nostalgically or in anger). I diagnose stances toward feminist time and the labeling of the waves in the generational model to make a political argument for reading feminism as genealogy in Marso (2010).

Emily Apter (2013, 171) has diagnosed how the philosophicality of Beauvoir was lost in translation for English-speaking feminists and suggests that we can see philosophical untranslatability as a way to "pose the problem of sexual difference to ontology."

7. Widely different interpretations of Beauvoir's writings abound precisely because it is sometimes frustratingly unclear where she stands in relation to the conversation she stages. In addition to defying all disciplinary boundaries (engaging the fields of history, literature, biology, psychology, theology, sociology, anthropology, politics, classics) she employs techniques of mimicry and parody, and she never outright tells us what to think or the final meaning we should take from any encounter.

8. Beauvoir is often misread as endorsing opinions that denigrate female biology. For example, see O'Brien (1981). For a more recent discussion of the interpretation of Beauvoir's views on biology and reproduction that mark her as "masculine" in comparison to French writers on "feminine specificity" (Cixous, Irigaray, Kristeva) see Kaufmann 1986.

9. I borrow this language from Lauren Berlant (2008, viii), who defines an "intimate public" thus: "Its consumer participants are perceived to be marked by a commonly lived history; its narratives and things are deemed expressive of that history while also shaping its conventions of belonging; and, expressing the sensation, embodied experience of living as a certain kind of being in the world, it promises also to provide a better experience of social belonging—partly through participation in the relevant commodity culture, and partly because of its revelations about how people can live."

10. I explore these at length in Beauvoir's oeuvre in Marso 2006.

11. I have changed Borde and Malovany-Chevalier's translation (Beauvoir [1949] 2011) of this important line in light of Moi's (2010) critical review. Moi is correct in noting that their translation "one is not born, but becomes, woman" rather than "one

is not born, but becomes, a woman," it makes it sound as if a girl grows up to be the incarnation of the male myth of Woman rather than one woman among many but still subject to women's situation.

12. Repudiating the contention that Beauvoir created a sex/gender duality, Sara Heinämaa (1997) has documented that the sex/gender distinction first arose in the beginning of the 1960s in work by American psychoanalysts.

13. For Beauvoir the facts of biology are simultaneously ontological and political creations subject to interpretation. Rather than depicting sex as natural and gender as cultural, she analyzed the body as somatic, active, and affective, as well as created by and interpreted and lived through situation. For an excellent analysis of the role of bodies in Beauvoir's aesthetic theory see Moskowitz (2014).

14. On the subject question, see Marso 2015. Beauvoir ([1949] 2011, 4) writes, "The truth is that anyone can clearly see that humanity is split into two categories of individuals with manifestly different clothes, faces, bodies, smiles, movements, interests, and occupations; these differences are perhaps superficial; perhaps they are destined to disappear. What is certain is that for the moment they exist in a strikingly obvious way." See Moi 2010.

15. See, as another example, the seemingly benign act of a woman keeping a man waiting. Beauvoir ([1949] 2011, 650) reads this as a "protest against the long wait that is her life."

CHAPTER 2: "AN EYE FOR AN EYE" WITH HANNAH ARENDT'S
EICHMANN IN JERUSALEM

1. It is remarkable that the work of Arendt and Beauvoir has rarely been compared or studied together. This is quite striking given the common phenomenological tradition out of which each works, as well as the recent resurgence in scholarship on Arendt by political theorists and on Beauvoir by feminist philosophers. At the very least historical circumstances bring them together. During their lifetimes they witnessed the rise of fascism and communism, the emerging prominence of the United States and the Soviet Union as competing world powers, the Algerian and Vietnam wars, and, at the end of their lives, the origins of the New Left, the counterculture, and the women's and black power movements as potentially democratic alternatives brought forth by coalitions of workers and students. Yet they are never thought of together, and rarely even brought into the same intellectual conversations.

Maybe this can be explained by the very different intellectual company they kept: Arendt, a German Jew, emigrated to the United States in May 1941, and her work became known mostly by American intellectuals and scholars, while Beauvoir was most famous in Europe as a novelist, the lifelong partner of Sartre, and the author of The Second Sex. It could also be that their differing political visions and sympathies make it seem that they are worlds apart: Arendt's most famous work, The Origins of Totalitarianism (1966), includes the Soviet Union alongside Nazi Germany as a totalitarian state, while Beauvoir was criticized, along with Sartre, for not breaking political ties with the French Communist Party and the Soviet Union clearly and soon enough.

On this point see Judt (1994). While Arendt was writing her penetrating critique of totalitarian states, Beauvoir ([1954] 1999) was writing *The Mandarins*, wherein she fictionalizes her and Sartre's agony and initial disbelief on learning of Stalin's extensive crimes. Also, while Beauvoir has become most well regarded posthumously for her contribution to feminist debates, Arendt's reception by feminists has always been controversial. For work in English that brings Beauvoir and Arendt into conversation, see Blanchard 2004; Shelby 2006; Veltman 2010.

2. Although there has been a resurgence of work in political theory that explores the implications of Kantian reflective judgment for politics, there is a stunning lack of literature on the actual practice of judging hard cases. Authors exploring Kantian reflective judgments, particularly as glossed by Arendt, agree that once we abandon the universe of cognitive truth or rule-governed activities and the subjective basis of judgment is acknowledged, it becomes quite difficult to find firm ground for judgment. When we explore actual trials raising complex and unprecedented issues, difficult judgments are illuminated as located at the heart of politics. For recent work on reflective judgment and its political implications, see Beiner and Nedelsky 2001; Ferrara 2008; Kohn 2003; Marshall 2010; Zerilli 2005. See Berkowitz (2010b) and Culbert (2010) specifically on the practice of judging hard cases and events.

3. In *The Prime of Life* Beauvoir ([1960] 1992, 434) recounts a conversation with Sartre during the war in which she challenged his commitment to the radical and unrestrained freedom of the individual: "I maintained that from the angle of freedom as Sartre defined it—that is, an active transcendence of some given context rather than mere stoic resignation—not every situation was equally valid: what sort of transcendence could a woman shut up in a harem achieve? Sartre replied that even such a cloistered existence could be lived in several quite different ways. I stuck to my point for a long time, and in the end made only a token submission. Basically I was right."

4. De Gaulle refused to grant the pardon, and Brasillach was executed by firing squad on February 6, 1945. For a fascinating in-depth account of Brasillach's trial, see Kaplan (2000). Kaplan explores accusations that Brasillach was singled out as a suspected homosexual and asks whether it was right that he was executed when others, such as real killers and economic collaborators, went free. Rubenstein (1993) looks specifically at the way intellectual collaborators were treated in postwar France. She points out that Brasillach's was the "quintessential show trial" and lasted only five hours; it began at 1 p.m. and by 6 p.m. he was sentenced to death.

5. For context on the controversy and Arendt's response to it, see Kohn 2003.

6. Ian Buruma (2011, 17) observes that before the Occupation of France even began, Germans were cultivating French public figures, such as Brasillach, who were part of the anti-Semitic Right: "The journalist Robert Brasillach, among others, was invited in 1937 to attend the Nazi rally in Nuremberg, and came back so impressed with all the drum-beating, flag-waving, goose-stepping Hitler-worship that he compared the event to the Eucharist."

7. See Maxwell (2014) for an important reading of how Arendt's narrative works as a political claim of democratic failure to solicit a new public to act on behalf of them. She writes, "Arendt's claim of democratic failure in *Eichmann in Jerusalem* thus

challenges Israel's claim of justice done, but not because she believes the verdict is wrong. Rather, her claim interrupts nationalistic, state-based, and popularly sanctioned understandings of justice, which she sees as masking a failure to do full justice to Eichmann's unprecedented crimes against humanity" (5).

8. Beauvoir ([1963] 1992, 29) writes in *Force of Circumstance*, "To me, it seems utterly unjust that economic collaboration should have been passed over, but not that Hitler's propagandists in this country should have been so severely dealt with."

9. This is a simplified summary of the various positions taken against judgment, all for complex reasons and by different constituencies. Beauvoir discusses these controversies and arguments against judgment both in *The Prime of Life* ([1960] 1992) and *Force of Circumstance* ([1963] 1992) and fictionalizes these issues in *The Mandarins* ([1954] 1999); Arendt discusses these controversies as they pertain to the Eichmann case in "Personal Responsibility under Dictatorship" (2003b) and "Collective Responsibility" (2003a).

10. "For the life of a man to have a meaning, he must be held responsible for evil as well as for good, and, by definition, evil is that which one refuses in the name of the good, with no compromise possible. It is for these reasons that I did not sign the pardon petition for Robert Brasillach when I was asked to" (Beauvoir [1949] 2004, 257).

11. "I had somehow taken it for granted that we all still believe with Socrates that it is better to suffer wrong than to do wrong. This belief turned out to be a mistake. There was a widespread conviction that it is impossible to withstand temptation of any kind, that none of us could be trusted or even be expected to be trustworthy when the chips are down, that to be tempted and to be forced are almost the same" (Arendt 2003b, 18).

12. Arendt (2003b, 21) argues, "Where all are guilty, no one is": "What I wish to point out, in addition to these considerations, is how deep-seated the fear of passing judgment, of naming names, and of fixing blame—especially alas, upon people in power and high position, dead or alive—must be if such desperate intellectual maneuvers are being called upon for help." She adds that "under conditions of terror most people will comply but some people will not" (1963a, 233). In like manner Beauvoir ([1949] 2004, 257) argues, "Certainly, man is wretched, scattered, mired in the given, but he is also a free being [and] he can reject the most urgent temptations." To hold the collectivity or history or god responsible is to fail our human responsibility to judge.

13. For more on Beauvoir and judgment, see Kruks 2005, 2012b.

14. Shoshana Felman (2002, 140) argues that Arendt "reserves some of her harshest language and fiercest irony in *Eichmann in Jerusalem* for the description of K-Zetnik's unsuccessful court appearance." K-Zetnik (a pseudonym, a slang word for a concentration camp inmate; his real name was Yehiel Dinoor) was a writer who began chronicling his experience in Auschwitz soon after he was liberated. He was called to testify at Eichmann's trial as the only eyewitness for Eichmann, but he collapsed on the stand before he could make an identification. Felman reads the incident as a confrontation between the "legal" apparatus and the truth that cannot be conveyed in its legal language. She sees Arendt's frustration with any and all survival testimony as Arendt's conservative philosophy of law.

15. Beauvoir ([1949] 2004, 258) writes, "Only [an embodied desire for vengeance] bites into the world." The passing of time, she acknowledges, makes the satisfaction of punishment of these criminals much more difficult, but even if exacted as vengeance in the moment, punishment often fails to satisfy. "[When reading the articles in *Je suis partout*,] we said to ourselves in an outburst of anger, 'They will pay.' And our anger seems to promise a joy so heavy that we could scarcely believe ourselves able to bear it. They have paid. They are going to pay. They pay each day. And the joy has not risen in our hearts" (246).

In the heat of the moment, at the time of struggle, vengeance inspired by ha-tred seeks to directly punish the individual responsible for suffering. But since the punishment seeks to "compel a freedom," as Beauvoir puts it, to make the torturer understand the injustice of acting as a tyrant by being the victim of violence himself, the punishment always misses its mark. It is impossible to make the tyrant feel the abomination of his crime. He might suffer with "a sense of irony, with resistance, with arrogance, with a resignation lacking remorse" and so "punishment suffers a defeat" ([1949] 2004, 250). How, then, do we compel the lessons we want the tyrants to learn? While the "affirmation of the reciprocity of interhuman relations" is "what vengeance strives to reestablish in the face of a tyranny that wants to be sovereign" (249), be-cause control of an other's consciousness is always out of our reach, there is no way to establish justice on the level of the particular. If we turn the tables and torture the torturer, he becomes "nothing more than panting flesh—torture misses its aim" (249), failing to reestablish human ambiguity and instead demolishing it by enacting the punishment. Moreover vengeance committed by individuals runs amok: "One act of revenge calls for another act of revenge, evil engenders evil, and injustices pile up without wiping one another out" (251). So the question for Beauvoir becomes whether we can possibly enact justice on the level of the general. As she admits, "In renouncing vengeance, society gives up on concretely linking the crime to the punishment" (254). Moreover "the official tribunals claim to take refuge behind an objectivity that is the worst part of the Kantian heritage. . . . They want to be only an expression of imper-sonal right and deliver verdicts that would be nothing more than the subsumption of a particular case under a universal law" (258). In Beauvoir's estimation justice seems to fail on both levels, the concrete and the general. And yet she names Brasillach's crime and seeks his punishment. Despite the fact that we cannot establish justice on the level of the general, we can affirm political community and affirm the embrace of freedom in making such a judgment.

16. For the most influential article on Arendt's thinking about embodiment and its relationship to political questions, see Zerilli (1995). As Zerilli puts it, the body, "often figured as ravenous and oral, poses an immanent threat to Arendtian plurality" (171). Zerilli claims these symptomatic fears, while indicating a displacement, also make visible the sheer "terror of having a body, an anxiety about mortality and loss of symbolic mastery that, on [Arendt's] account, haunts every speaking subject in Western culture" (174). Moreover, as Zerilli indicates, Arendt recognizes the injustices and violence of the borders that separate those in the realm of necessity from those in the realm of politics; she also seeks to transgress them, noting that in ancient Greece

the slave "stood as the disavowed, embodied part of the free (masculine) subject" (179). But yet her worry to preserve a common world and the boundaries that would secure it push her to maintain the public space where she claims people can disclose the "who" of their being beyond the "what" of our body. It is this "who," the speaking and acting citizen, that is unique and distinct, while the "what" links us in common (bodily) traits with others, even though, as Arendt recognizes, we are uniquely different in our given bodies as well.

17. What Arendt fails to mention here, when speaking about the possibility of politics, is that the acting "who" is dependent on, or made possible by, the labor of the people who are disallowed from disclosing themselves beyond the "what" of their existence. We might argue that in *The Human Condition* Arendt is delineating and describing segregated dimensions of human activity, but politically it is too often the case that these segregated dimensions map all too clearly onto different people and populations. For Beauvoir the phenomenon whereby some people are destined to labor in the realm of necessity while others are free to transcend is called oppression, while Arendt sees it as part of the human condition inherent in the nature of labor itself. See Arendt 1958; Veltman 2010.

18. Documenting the conditions of French Jews in 1940, Beauvoir ([1960] 1992, 458–59) writes, "The note 'Out of Bound[s] to Jews' began to appear in the windows of certain shops. *Le Matin* published a muckraking article on 'the Ghetto,' demanding its abolition. Vichy Radio was busy denouncing the 'renegade Jews' who had left France in the lurch, and Pétain repealed the law forbidding anti-Semitic propaganda. Anti-Jewish demonstrations were whipped up in Vichy, Toulouse, Marseille, Lyon, and on the Champs Elysées, while a large number of factories fired all 'Jews and foreigners' among their workers."

19. In a *New York Times* article the philosopher George Yancy describes a series of troubling verbal attacks that he received after publishing an article entitled "Dear White America":

> Words do things, especially words like "nigger," or being called an animal that should go back to Africa or being told that I should be "beheaded ISIS style." One white supremacist message sent to me ended with "Be Prepared." Another began with "Dear Nigger Professor."
>
> The brutality and repetitiveness of this discursive violence has a way of inflicting injury. Given the history of the term "nigger," it strikes with the long, hate-filled context of violence out of which that term grew. This points to the non-spectacular expression of violence. The lynching of black people was designed to be a spectacle, to draw white mobs. In this case, the black body was publicly violated. It was a public and communal form of bloodlust. There are many other forms of violence that are far more subtle, non-spectacular, but yet painful and dehumanizing. So, when I was called a "nigger," I was subject to that. I felt violated, injured; a part of me felt broken.

This incident hauntingly recalls not only Brasillach's crimes but also the context in which they took place. The difference is that Brasillach was the editor of a paper in a position to cause widespread damage. Yancy's experience, however, pointedly informs us of the way words can wound, particularly when embodiment has taken on political meanings reaching back to slavery, lynching, and Jim Crow. Brad Evans, "The Stone: The Perils of Being a Black Philosopher," interview with George Yancy, *New York Times*, April 18, 2016, http://opinionator.blogs.nytimes.com/2016/04/18/the-perils-of-being-a-black-philosopher/?action=click&pgtype=Homepage&clickSource=story-heading&module=opinion-c-col-right-region&region=opinion-c-col-right-region&WT.nav=opinion-c-col-right-region&_r=0.

20. Julie Bindel, in Xan Brooks, "*Antichrist*: A Work of Genius or the Sickest Film in the History of Cinema?," *Guardian*, July 15, 2009.

CHAPTER 3: THE MARQUIS DE SADE'S BODIES IN
LARS VON TRIER'S *ANTICHRIST*

1. She says this: "We could say, parodying Claudel," that is to say, Paul Claudel (1868–1955), brother of Camille Claudel, whom he had committed to a mental hospital. Paul Claudel was a right-wing Catholic poet and dramatist who was horrified by claims portending a random, mechanized, material universe. Beauvoir was deeply fascinated by Claudel's writing when she was young and refers frequently to his work in her early diaries.

2. See, for example, Xan Brooks, "*Antichrist*: A Work of Genius or the Sickest Film in the History of Cinema?," *Guardian*, July 15, 2009.

3. Noting that Beauvoir is a particularly productive interlocutor in helping us to read von Trier's images, my reading of *Antichrist* is informed by an aesthetic and narrative conceptual framework that features Beauvoir as a film theorist. Her attention to the active, affective, sensorial, and visceral body within systems, structures, and ideologies navigates political terrain that captures both somatic and structural dimensions of experience. Her work on the body as an object within systems, her attention to lived corporeality as fleshy, sensual, and affective, and her aesthetic sense of image and language as material forces help us navigate toward an alternative model of film analysis that moves beyond the dichotomies that pit narrative meaning against discontinuity, images, and perception. Beauvoir wrote explicitly on film and film images in only two essays, on Brigitte Bardot (1959) and Claude Lanzmann's *Shoah* (1985).

4. For many French people, Charlotte Gainsbourg will always be thought of as the daughter of Serge Gainsbourg, one of the greatest and most "libertine" songwriters of the twentieth century. (Her mother was the great actress Jane Birkin, Serge's lover and muse.) In 1984 Serge recorded a song with Charlotte, who was twelve at the time, that alludes to an incestuous love between father and daughter ("Lemon Incest"). In 1986 Serge cast fourteen-year-old Charlotte in the provocative film *Charlotte for Ever*. There is obviously a clear link between Serge Gainsbourg and Sade, in the simple sense that they both enjoyed shocking the bourgeoisie, often by exploiting sexual themes. When asked who he would have liked to be if he were not himself, it is rumored that Serge responded "Sade." And to make one more connection, at Lincoln Center's January–February 2016 film retrospective featuring the work of Jane Birkin

and Charlotte Gainsbourg (titled "Jane and Charlotte Forever"), Charlotte remarked that she loves to work with Lars von Trier because, in so many ways, he reminds her of her father.

5. In fact the words and theme of the Handel aria give away some of von Trier's preoccupations. Almirena, who sings the aria, is an innocent, virtuous, ideal woman who is Rinaldo's wife-to-be. She is abducted by a sorceress-witch called Armida and is kept in captivity in a magical garden. Armida is the opposite of Almirena, a nemesis of sorts: she is evil, sexually promiscuous—she falls in love too quickly—and above all she is anti-Christian. There are many other binaries at play here: good/evil, natural/artificial, reason/passion, East/West. In the aria Almirena laments her captivity. The theme is a desire for freedom even when one is surrounded by beauty. She sings, "Let me weep over my cruel fate and that I long for freedom!" This can be read as a cry for freedom in the face of the suffocating artificial beauty of the bourgeois household and the patriarchal order that sustains it. I thank Çiğdem Çıdam for seeing this connection.

6. Rosalind Galt (2015) moves beyond the interpretation of this film as misogynist. She explores how von Trier's films affect the spectator such that we don't really know how to feel; he makes us both complicit with and resistant to misogynist moves. I argue that taking on SHE's perspective in *Antichrist* accomplishes the queering of subjectivity that Galt says disorders our accustomed ways of being. Through SHE we feel our way toward rejecting patriarchy and desiring something else, a politics wherein we can truly acknowledge foreign existences such as the grotesque feminine.

7. See Mandolfo (2010) for a fascinating reading of the sacrifices of Bess and Selma in *Breaking the Waves* and *Dancer in the Dark* as read against Grace's revenge in *Dogville*. Also see essays by James Martel, Victoria Wohl, and Paul Apostolidis in Honig and Marso (2015).

8. We will see that von Trier plays with the trope of bad mothers as freaks of nature in making his females grotesque. I argue, however, that his female grotesque reveals the inadequacies of the patriarchal lexicon rather than buttressing it.

9. Power should have noted von Trier's *Medea* in her essay, as this too is a film about maternal infanticide that ends with the mother freed of her husband and his betrayal. We might even say that *Antichrist* is a reception of *Medea*, von Trier's own and that of Euripides. See Leonard (2016) on how events look from the different perspectives of Medea's two children.

10. The name *Justine* for the main character in *Melancholia* is likely a nod to Sade, who was known for a time mostly as "the author of *Justine*," his most scandalous novel before the publication of *120 Days of Sodom*.

11. There are a number of instances of gender reversal in the film wherein HE is out of control and SHE is cool and collected. Although von Trier portrays HE as trying to hang onto the male role of rational actor or contained sovereign, HE is not successful.

12. HE is a spectator to subsequent events, just as the spectators are. Although we uncover the horrors of Eden with HE, as documented in the next section, it is not grounds for solidarity with his experience; instead we are encouraged to identify with SHE.

13. Language and literary compositions, such as the essay, can also be included in

the tradition of the grotesque to associate its effects with a "playfulness that rescues us from a kind of nihilism that imagines death as an insurmountable nothingness," as well as "all the qualities of becoming that Bakhtin attributes to early grotesque imagery" (Panagia 2006, 99).

14. This image is a copy of Victorian painter John Everett Millais's *Ophelia* (1851), which itself is a comment on Victorian social oppression.

15. In her analysis of *Nymphomaniac*, Lynne Huffer (2015) notices von Trier's several references to the filmmaker Andrei Tarkovsky that point to the friction between a kind of "empty freedom" and (as I suggest in this chapter and in chapter 6) what von Trier warns can happen when women miss freedom in the encounter. Huffer might say these two screen shots I feature from *Nymphomaniac*, of Joe being lifted to the heavens, are cast as a slightly ironic nod to "spiritual, Tarkovsky-esque levitations."

16. I thank Torrey Shanks for this observation.

17. Reading the ending of *Antichrist* as an affirmation of the viewer's alignment with SHE rather than as an elimination of female subjectivity and celebration of the triumph of HE is a refusal to read through the male lens, which has been discredited throughout the film. This reading of *Antichrist*'s ending recalls my reading of Rousseau's novels (Marso 1999) as affirming the perspective of his female characters Julie and Sophie in spite of, even in light of, their deaths.

18. Brooks, "*Antichrist*: A Work of Genius or the Sickest Film in the History of Cinema?" The first comment is by Brooks; the second by Julie Bindel; the third by Jane and Louise Wilson.

19. In the "Myths" section of *The Second Sex*, Beauvoir says male ideologues portray female sexuality and Mother Earth as immanent, unknowable, chaotic, in short, as embodying the *absolute Other*, as a result of male fear, anxiety, disgust, horror, and embarrassment (all Beauvoir's terms) in the face of finitude, mortality, and carnal contingency. Associating women with magic, witchcraft, the immanence of nature and the cosmos, the mysteries of sexuality and reproduction makes men feel better, more in control. But it also disallows women from embracing freedom and transcendence, confines women only to repetition and the reproduction of life, and makes women only the mirror of men rather than affirming women as foreign subjectivities in their own right. Beauvoir writes, "Man wants to assert his individual existence and proudly rest on his 'essential difference,' but he also wants to break the barriers of the self and commingle with water, earth, night, Nothingness, with the Whole. Woman who condemns man to finitude also enables him to surpass his own limits: that is where the equivocal magic surrounding her comes from" ([1949] 2011, 167).

20. This is not, then, typical horror or pornography wherein women are depicted as alluring but dangerous. When images traffic in horror or pornography, they often reproduce and justify fear of the feminine. In horror films, for example, often women's bodies are a threat to patriarchy, but in the end patriarchy is applauded. Analyzing the monstrous feminine in several horror films, Barbara Creed (1993) says that typically woman terrifies due to a fear that she might castrate. In films depicting women as archaic mother, monstrous womb, vampire, witch, possessed body, monstrous mother, and castrator, Creed argues, horror operates through fear of woman's generative

powers reproducing and enhancing those fears rather than subverting them. Likewise while pornography can be a transgressive genre (Zolkos 2011), in order to transgress the images must defy voyeurism and titillation. For example, Siri Husvedt (2014) articulates Susan Sontag's (1964) contribution to theorizing pornographic literature that does more than replicate the same economy of gender hierarchy: "The flayed, abused, pierced and violated victims of Sade don't really suffer. They are creatures of endless repetition—more machine than human. The form creates a democratization of the text's landscape, in which human beings and things mingle without defined borders in an abstract, unfeeling world."

21. Geoffrey Macnab, "*Nymphomaniac*, Film Review: Despite the Surreal Sex Scenes This Is a Serious Drama," *Independent*, December 17, 2013, http://www.independent .co.uk/arts-entertainment/films/reviews/nymphomaniac-film-review-despite-the -surreal-sex-scenes-this-is-a-serious-drama-9011438.html.

22. Thanks to Perry Moskowitz for putting it this way.

23. Eugene Hernandez, "Von Trier: 'I Am the Best Film Director in the World,'" *Indie Wire*, May 18, 2009, http://www.indiewire.com/article/von_trier_i_am_the_best _film_director_in_the_world.

PART II: ALLIES

1. Prompted by these conversations and concerns, in 1955 Beauvoir wrote "Right-Wing Thought Today."

2. See Camus, *Algerian Chronicles* ([1958] 2013), his writings on the situation in Algeria from 1939 to 1958.

3. My references to Boupacha are based on Beauvoir and Halimi (1962), which includes Beauvoir's preface, her *Le Monde* article, and a complete account of the events of Boupacha's capture, torture, and trial. Beauvoir's preface has been retranslated and published in Beauvoir (2012), with a very informative introduction by Julien S. Murphy.

CHAPTER 4: VIOLENCE, PATHOLOGIES, AND RESISTANCE IN FRANTZ FANON

1. Fanon and Beauvoir use psychoanalysis against itself. They each know full well that psychoanalysis as a discipline is patriarchal and misogynist in its conception of subjectivity as Western, male, and white, articulated against a background of the primitive, black and brown, and female, and that its methods of therapy help individuals accept the status quo. But Fanon and Beauvoir reconfigure the politics of psychoanalysis to use to their own ends. As I will show, they incorporate key psychoanalytic insights that help us read behavior and affects as wounds reflecting a collective political unconscious that internalizes dominance and submission. Moreover Fanon argues that these wounds are only capable of healing in a transformed society.

2. There are several approaches to theorizing affect on view in Gregg and Siegworth

(2010), and this collection is a good place to start if one wants to understand the debates among these theorists and the several ways of understanding human emotions, drives, and instincts in relation to our social and political environments. Most of the essays in this volume recognize that the separation between nature and nurture is a false one. The editors claim in the very first paragraph that affects arise in the midst of "in-between-ness," in the "capacities to act and be acted upon" (1), and they seek to theorize the links between biology and the social or political.

3. Relatedly Beauvoir is attentive to how she (and others) might deploy their structural privilege to transform politics. Kruks (2012b, 93–123) discusses how Beauvoir saw and seized the opportunity to use her privilege as a well-known French intellectual (able to gain the attention of the public) to intervene in Boupacha's case.

4. These behaviors "are not dictated to woman by her hormones or predestined in her brain's compartments: they are suggested in negative form by her situation" (Beauvoir [1949] 2011, 638).

5. It is fascinating that Beauvoir also offers a positive and sophisticated interpretation of *candomblé* when she witnesses several ceremonies in Bahia, Brazil, in 1959. In contrast to Fanon, who seems to see only alienation in such voodoo practices, Beauvoir ([1963] 1992, 240–41) says: "Forced to bow before the strength of the Western world, the Negroes of Bahia, once slaves, now an exploited class, live in a state of such oppression that they can scarcely call their lives their own; to preserve their customs, their traditions, their beliefs is not a sufficient defense; they also cultivate those techniques which will help them attain a state of ecstasy and so tear themselves free of the falsely earthly manifestation in which they have been imprisoned. At the moment when they seem to lose themselves in the dance, they in fact find their true selves; they are possessed, yes, but by their own truth. Even if the *candomblé* does not change men into gods, at least it uses the mediating action of imaginary spirits to restore their humanity to a group of men who have been forced to the status of cattle. . . . The supreme moment of her individual life—when she is transformed from pancake vendor or dishwasher in Ogun or Yemanja—is also the one in which the daughter of the saints becomes most closely integrated with the rest of the community."

CHAPTER 5: IN SOLIDARITY WITH RICHARD WRIGHT

1. Wright's address to the Paris Congress is discussed by Diawara (1998) and Iton (2008).

2. Wright was involved in founding the journal in 1947; it was devoted to advancing the work of black writers on oppression, colonization, and the black diaspora.

3. See Moskowitz (2016) for a rich discussion of the problems with the idea of (black) authorship as collective representation of blacks.

4. Bigger's individual acts of resistance include killing a white woman and a black woman.

5. Singh (2004, 176) briefly discusses Wright's address to the Paris Congress, noting that Wright advocated for U.S. blacks and colonized peoples to act with the Bandung participants to find a "third way" between the "monopoly capitalism of the West"

and the "political and cultural totalitarianism of the East. " Here Singh quotes from Wright's *The Color Curtain*.

6. The work from Ghana, Indonesia, and related lectures are collected in Wright (2008). Also in this collection is *The Color Curtain*, Wright's report from the 1955 Bandung Conference. See Roberts and Foulcher (2016) for a wonderful set of documents on the "Asian-African encounter" and "transnational crosscurrents" put in motion by Wright's three-week visit to Bandung for the meeting of twenty-nine Asian and African countries. This collection gives Indonesians the opportunity to talk back to Wright, to challenge what, following Roland Barthes, the editors call the "mythology" of the Bandung Conference that evokes a commonality of experience between Asian and African participants and positions at the conference. These documents extend my argument about what we might discover in encounter, even long after the historical moment of the original encounter has passed.

7. In particular Alioune Diop of Senegal, founder of *Présence Africaine* who spoke the opening remarks at the Congress, as well as Aimé Césaire of Martinique and Léopold Sédar Senghor of Senegal.

8. There are no comments on women recorded in the version of Wright's speech to the Congress printed in *Black Power*, but in the complete proceedings printed in a special issue of *Présence Africaine*, it is recorded that Wright said the following: "I don't know how many of you have noticed it there have been no women functioning vitally and responsibly upon this platform helping to mold and mobilize our thoughts . . . When and if we hold another conference—and I hope we will—I hope there shall be an effective utilization of Negro womanhood in the world to help us mobilize and pool our forces . . . we cannot afford to ignore one half of our manpower, that is, the force of women and their active collaboration. Black men will not be free until their women are free." A PDF is available here: http://www.freedomarchives .org/Documents/Finder/Black%20Liberation%20Disk/Black%20Power!/SugahData /Journals/Presence.S.pdf.

9. Kelley (2000) informs us that *négritude* had many faces. The version articulated by Aimé Césaire was not strictly identified with racial essentialism; in fact Kelley describes it as "future-oriented and modern" (23).

10. This opening is not included in the version of the essay published in *White Man, Listen!*, but Diawara (1998) references it as present in the original version.

11. Wright would agree with Fanon's emphasis on the peasantry as a potential revolutionary class; he had seen Nkrumah trying to mesh tradition and modernity. In fact Wright had seen peasants and market women as the real heroes in revolutionary Ghana. He would also have agreed with Fanon's analysis and critique of *négritude* as a "racialization of thought" (Fanon [1963] 2004, 150).

12. The quote is from Marable (2011, 315) discussing Malcolm's 1964 trip to Accra.

13. Al Jazeera, "Africa: The First Fifty Years," September 18, 2010, http://www .aljazeera.com/indepth/2010/09/20109189268906591.html.

14. As Jane Gordon pointed out to me in conversation, there of course could be a different explanation for this resilience that stems neither from an essential quality to blackness or simply from oppression. Instead, these elements describe distinct ways

communities forge shared collective worlds. The elements that remain are those that they find continue to have meaning or salience under new circumstances. But since Wright was trying to understand what, if anything, black people shared from the African to other continents, he saw traditions that did not conform to modern ways as a product of marginalization. Beauvoir also talks about what are considered to be distinctly feminine traits (being coy, demure, restrained) as forged in close relationship to the experience of the denial of freedom. These are formed in conditions of oppression and a way to create a shared world, all at the same time. When shared they are called the "female complaint." What Beauvoir is not willing to say, and here she agrees with Wright about blackness, is that traits of femininity are themselves attached to female bodies. They are a response to situation, and that situation is unfreedom.

15. Gilroy (1993, 148) demonstrates how Wright links the black vernacular to an "emergent, global, anti-imperialist and anti-racist" politics.

16. Many of the photos that Wright took with Russell Lee, a photographer in Chicago, did not make it into 12 Million Black Voices, but are included in Stange (2004).

17. These images are not published but are available, many online, in the Beinecke Collection at Yale.

18. I owe this insight partly to Allred (2006, 550), who calls attention to Wright's voice that "figures readers as pupils, insisting on their blinkered relationship to blackness and demanding that they recognize African Americans as a collectivity on the national and international stage."

19. Wright points out that not all blacks responded to the Depression by crossing the color line to join in solidarity with other oppressed groups. Some blacks still, *correctly*, Wright notes, saw whites as those to whom blacks must pay rent, from whom blacks receive education and health care, in other words as controlling central aspects of the lives of blacks. And yet, though they were correct in identifying a remaining and strong white supremacy, Wright ([1941] 2008, 145) says they reacted in the wrong way: filled with a "naïve and peasant anger," these "inarticulate black men and women" rioted in Harlem. Why does Wright condemn the Harlem riots of 1935? Described by Singh (2004, 64) as the first major urban property riot, this event was modern too. The property riot, like the picket line, the union, and engaging with the press, is a means of modern protest of the sort that Wright admires later in Ghana, not simply a result of "peasant" anger. A reader suggested that maybe Wright has this blind spot because of his high estimation of language. Property riots "smash and burn," are reactive rather than proactive, and do not require literacy. Unions, mass marches, demonstrations, picket lines, and forms of collective action that utilize language and communication are more modern in Wright's eyes. As we see in Wright's book on Ghana, transforming peasants into political actors is what most impressed him about Nkrumah's form of politics.

20. What should we make of the fact that Beauvoir says "brotherhood" in this sentence? After so thoroughly dislodging the male universal, she slips back into the language of fraternity to make her appeal to solidarity. Is it that language betrays her, or is this a slip that portends something more troubling? Here is an example (a most

blatant one at that) of why Beauvoir's work continues to both attract and perplex, frustrating any final meaning of her feminism.

PART III: FRIENDS

1. Jon Nixon (2015) shows how Arendt's friendships illustrate her political thinking. One reviewer of Nixon's book explains: "Arendt saw friendship as a middle ground between the solitude and solipsism of internal dialogue, and the terror of the public square. It was a protected space in which ideas could be unveiled, sanded down, hardened, and polished. Her friends were her intellectual compatriots, and her boundless loyalty toward them was also an expression of her deep-seated appreciation for their kindnesses. Friendship was an intensely appealing concept for a woman who spent much of her life as a refugee among refugees, a Jew expelled from her country of birth, adrift in foreign countries. It was a protective amulet, as well as a symbol of the higher values crushed under the boot of totalitarianism. Nazism's mission was "to eradicate *totally* any trace of human freedom," and friendship's playfulness and compassion was a symbol of rebellion against fascism's inhumanity" (Austerlitz 2015).

2. As a recipient of the "Genius" grant, Bechdel and her rule for film might prompt one to consider the qualities of her queer genius with what Julia Kristeva (2001) deems to be Arendt's "female genius" in *Hannah Arendt*, volume 1 of her series called *Female Genius: Life, Madness, Worlds*.

3. For an exemplary reading of the promise in the "much-maligned genre of melodrama," see Honig (2013, 80) on Fassbinder's segment in Kluge's film *Germany in Autumn*: "Melodrama, with its emphasis on isolation, paranoia, affect, and suspicion, provide Fassbinder with the perfect generic frame with which, first, to contest the goings-on and then, second, to depict the collapse of democratic citizenship under conditions of real or contrived emergency."

CHAPTER 6: PERVERSE PROTESTS FROM CHANTAL AKERMAN TO LARS VON TRIER

1. See Honig and Marso (2015) for recent essays addressing von Trier's gender politics. See Emine Saner, "The *Gone Girl* Backlash," *Guardian*, October 7, 2014, http://www.theguardian.com/film/2014/oct/07/gone-girl-backlash-david-fincher -misogynist-feminist for a summary of several articles about *Gone Girl*'s relationship to various forms of feminist politics. All references to *Jeanne Dielman* are to the Criterion Collection edition; references to *Gone Girl* are from the DVD and shooting script accessed online; references to *Nymphomaniac* are to the Director's Cut DVD.

2. Sianne Ngai (2005) has written about the ugly feelings expressed by women characters in literature and film. According to Ngai, ugly feelings arise from situations of obstructed agency; women's feelings are often *especially* dangerous as they are "always easily prone to turning ugly" (33).

3. Each film intensifies and exaggerates situations, pressing in on both the everyday

and the extreme of these women's experience. The films also direct us to consider new ways of thinking both sexuality and action by opening ourselves up to something much more ambiguous than full sovereignty but less bound to fantasy and the thwarted, probably misguided desire to invert agency in both sex and politics.

4. What new thinking, action, and agency would open up were we to free female sexuality from heterosexual, bourgeois, and capitalist mechanisms? This question is bracketed in my essay as we cannot know *now* what female sexuality and agency could become in the future. Catherine MacKinnon's (1989, 325) assertion that "that which is called sexuality is the dynamic of control by which male dominance—in forms that range from intimate to institutional, from a look to a rape—eroticizes as man and woman, as identity and pleasure" disallows any form of agency or authentic sexual desire for women, closing off any possibility for finding something new or moving somewhere else. What these films offer instead is a sensual and emotional vista of a few key instances of specific (white, heterosexual) women's experience of sexuality and agency under current conditions of patriarchy. What is made visual and sensual on screen, available for our viewing pleasure, is the look and feel of distorted forms of agency.

5. In the one essay on visual culture in Vance (1989), Bette Gordan discusses the situation in which agency is inverted. She writes, "In this case, the traditional male role (male as voyeur, woman as object) is reversed, positing the woman as voyeur, in an attempt to locate female desire within a patriarchal culture" (191).

6. Mulvey (1989, 112) published "Feminism, Film, and the Avant-Garde" in 1979, writing, "Feminists have recently come to see the modernist avant-garde as relevant to their own struggle to develop a radical approach to art. . . The avant-garde poses certain questions which consciously confront traditional practice, often with a political motivation, working on ways to alter modes of representation and expectations in consumption. These questions arise similarly for women, motivated by a history of oppression and motivation for change."

7. In an interview included with the Criterion Collection release of the film, Akerman says she wanted to portray the rituals of housework that she witnessed her mother and aunts performing as a sort of replacement for the Eastern European Jewish rituals destroyed during World War II that they longed to replicate.

8. See Ortner's (1974) classic essay on how cooking shows that women are not just immanence or nature but mediate between nature and culture in the act of cooking.

9. Akerman, from an interview on the Criterion Collection DVD.

10. See Williams (2014) for an analysis of this film as a feminist classic that anticipates *Jeanne Dielman*.

11. Saner, "The *Gone Girl* Backlash."

12. Working within queer theory and black feminism, Cathy Cohen (2004, 29, 33) has written about the "deviance" of "those who stand on the (out)side of state-sanctioned, normalized, White, middle- and upper-class male heterosexuality" to find that this deviance is itself a form of defiance or resistance: "Not only do these individuals daily act in opposition to dominant norms, but they also contradict members of Black communities who are committed to mirroring perceived respectable behaviors and hierarchical structures."

CHAPTER 7: UNBECOMING WOMEN WITH VIOLETTE LEDUC, RAHEL VARNHAGEN, AND MARGARETHE VON TROTTA

1. The topic of conversation passes the test (it's not about a man), but the other woman is unnamed, so the film fails. Each of these brief conversations is conducted in flat, almost monotone voices and seems to suggest the interlocutors are unable to connect in any real way. If we compare these conversations in *Jeanne Dielman* (1975) with those in Akerman's 1988 film, *Histoires d'Amérique: Food, Family, and Philosophy*, the close links between Akerman's modernist sensibility and her Jewish identity come sharply into focus. The later film defies categorization—it looks and seems in part like a documentary, although it is staged; it plays with time, moving from pogroms to the aftermath of the Holocaust; and it frustrates our ability to locate its images in an ethnic type even though it trafficks in clichés—and reaches back to *Jeanne Dielman* not only in its use of repetition and its playfulness with time, duration, and history but also in the way it shows life and its meanings to be absurd, contingent, and ultimately unknowable.

2. Bonnie Honig and I (2016a, 10–11) write in "Lars von Trier and the Clichés of Our Times":

> In *Nymphomaniac*, Joe's early experiences with female friendship are like a deliberately cartoonish effort to fail the Bechdel test outright. She and her friend engage in a very adult rivalry, the prize for which is a child's treat. The girls compete with each other for who can seduce the most strange men on a train (a theme reprised in comic form here from a more tragic version of it in [von Trier's] *Breaking the Waves*, where the men are on ships). But even in the midst of this competition, men seem to be irrelevant. Joe shows far more enthusiasm for the candy she wins at the end of the evening than she does for the men she lures into sexual contact. The film shows how irrelevant men can be even when they and their desires are set at center stage. Though the two girls on the train seem to relate only through men, they are clearly affectively unengaged by those men and delight only in each other's company. They replay the game of Hollywood homoeroticism, in which men who desire each other are rendered safe for "mainstream" audiences by having the men compete for a woman's attentions. All they do is talk about the woman, try to impress the woman, put each other down for the woman, but none of it is about the woman. In fact, she couldn't be further from being the point.
>
> Watching Joe and her friend relate to each other through men, we do not feel comfortable and unthinking (as we would do, say, at a standard romantic comedy) because the relations they are having and the context for them are outlandish. We move past the questions of where are the women and what do they talk about, and we are pressed to ask how are they affectively experiencing and expressing the impact on them of patriarchal structures coursing through their lives, soaking into their pores? What are the limitations of female friendship in patriarchal settings? Can the women withdraw, distance themselves from, or ironize such deformational pressures? How do they try? How do they fail? How

are their efforts and failures depicted in the film? As moral justice? Tragic tales? Personal failures? Structural symptoms?

3. As I mentioned in the introduction to this section, applying the Bechdel rule too strictly—as a measurement of female presence or absence in a film talking together about a subject other than men—may in some cases only have the effect of buttressing the rules of liberal representation. Maybe, with Beauvoir and Arendt who cautioned that the application of rules erodes our capacity for reflective judgment, we should heed the rule to the extent that its way of measuring helps us better recognize the failures of representation itself.

4. One of the key issues at the center of debates in feminist film studies, although it is not put quite this way, is that there is a conceit, mostly on the part of men—male artists, male directors, male producers, to *know* and, even worse, be able to *represent* the lives and desires of women. As I noted in chapter 6, beginning with Mulvey's (1989, 14) theorization of the male gaze in 1975, feminist film theorists have had to reckon with the claim that the cinema is the male mirror projected onto the screen. The film theorist Miriam Hansen, among others, challenges Mulvey by focusing on female spectators. Hansen (1986) insists that just because male-dominated cinema claims to know and represent the lives of women, this does not mean we should assume female spectators are passive consumers of the images we are fed. Hansen thus makes space for a "feminist counter-cinema" based on feminist interpretations of film as well as forms of "visual pleasure that are not totally claimed, absorbed, or functionalized by the conventions of classical narrative" (11). She alerts us to the importance of film *for*, *of*, and *as* politics, emancipating female spectators to be active participants in the conversation, active interpreters of film.

5. As Lynne Huffer (2013, 129) puts it in *Are the Lips a Grave?*, Leduc's narratives render an "abject but ultimately transformative corporeality." Huffer calls Leduc's writing in *La Bâtarde* a "queer feminist ethics of eros" (129). She adds, however, that Leduc "reconfigures the existentialist, humanist models of subjectivity with which Beauvoir is struggling: she juxtaposes, without resolving, the philosophical reductions through which selves acquire meaning in their transcendence with the self-undoing practices of bodies in their immanence" (129). My interpretation of Beauvoir's freedom in encounter challenges this reading of Beauvoir as overly invested in forms of freedom that give priority only to transcendence.

6. The male version is Bernard Lazare, depicted with Heinrich Heine, Charlie Chaplin, and Kafka in Arendt (1944).

7. See Honig (1995) for several essays exploring what feminists can learn from Arendt and how feminists have engaged with her work.

8. This description of Beauvoir is in Manohla Dargis, "A Difficult Woman, with a Past Worth Writing About," *New York Times*, June 12, 2014, http://www.nytimes.com/2014/06/13/movies/violette-about-the-french-author-violette-leduc.html.

9. Honig (2016) identifies the "Jewish" unconscious of *The Human Condition*, Arendt's most "Greek" text. Honig keeps her essay focused on the text, not on Arendt. But does Arendt have a feminist unconscious? When she writes about the "conscious

pariah" in *Men in Dark Times* (1955), she discusses four men, Heine, Lazare, Chaplin, and Kafka's K. Why not include Varnhagen, on whom she had written in 1933?

10. As Bonnie Honig remarked to me, this sounds like a negative review of an Akerman film! Is Arendt Akerman avant la lettre?

11. Women experience a range of emotions (even joy and exuberance) in Akerman's staged domestic spaces. And as Bedford notes, they do seem to be "sitting in a hot house with no watch." Akerman intercuts small suffocating spaces, explicitly marked as domestic, with city vistas, vast swaths of land, and sublime panoramas, making the quotidian seem even more so. Her interiorized focus on everyday, repetitive mise-en-scènes might make us think that these films have nothing to contribute to debates in democratic theory, but as I said of *Jeanne Dielman*, the new ways to move and act that we see in Akerman films refuse the transcendence-versus-immanence dynamic, belie the binaries of agent/victim and human/object, and offer us potentially different ways to come together, around and attached to different objects, desires, and projects.

12. As one example, Lore Jonas remains Arendt's friend although Hans Jonas does not.

13. Kathleen B. Jones (2013) writes:

In a recent post on "Page-Turner," *The New Yorker*'s online book blog, Michelle Dean complained that the image of Arendt's friendship with McCarthy in von Trotta's film was a "flat portraiture." Dean argued that it represented the conversations between these two "ferocious minds" as if they had been dominated by exchanges "about men and love." In reality, she contended, their friendship formed a "close intellectual bond," serving as a "bulwark against their naysayers." All this is true; but it underplays the complexity and intimacy of Arendt's relationship with McCarthy. In an age when, as Dean notes, "women hunger for models of intellectual self-confidence," the pair's friendship can be a source of inspiration, an exemplar of women talking "about ideas among themselves."

In a book on Arendt's politics of friendship Nixon (2015, 7) writes, "That is why Arendt sees friendship as allied to politics: not as a substitute for politics, nor as a way of doing politics, but as a condition necessary for the survival of politics as she understood it. Friendship is what lies between the private world of familial, tribal and religious affiliation, and the political world of institutional and associative affiliation based not on family, tribe or religion but on equality." Nixon's parsing of Arendt's politics of friendship is right, but this is different from the importance Beauvoir gives to friendship in politics. Beauvoir would say that friendships, like love, are political spaces. She theorizes the intersections of various kinds and instances of relationships for politics rather than keeping one space separate as politics.

14. "Slave to her husband, children, and home, she finds it intoxicating to be alone, sovereign on the hillside; she is no longer spouse, mother, housewife, but a human being. . . . In front of the mystery of water and the mountain summit's thrust, male supremacy is abolished; walking through the heather, dipping her hand in the river, she lives not for others but for herself" (Beauvoir [1949] 2011, 657).

Abu-Lughod, Lila. 2002. "Do Muslim Women Really Need Saving? Anthropological Reflections on Cultural Relativism and Its Others." *American Anthropologist* 104, no. 3:783–90.

Ahmed, Sara. 2004. "Affective Economies." *Social Text* 79, no. 22:117–39.

———. 2010. *The Politics of Happiness*. Durham, NC: Duke University Press.

Akerman, Chantal, dir. 1975. *Jeanne Dielman, 23 quai du Commerce, 1080 Bruxelles*. Cinéart. Film.

———, dir. 1991. *Night and Day*. International Film Circuit, Inc. Film.

Akerman, Chantal, and Angela Martin. 1979. "Chantal Akerman's Films: A Dossier." *Feminist Review* 3:24–47.

Allred, Jared. 2006. "From Eye to We: Richard Wright's 12 Million Black Voices, Documentary, and Pedagogy." *American Literature* 78, no. 3:549–83.

Apter, Emily. 2013. *Against World Literature: On the Politics of Untranslatability*. London: Verso.

Arendt, Hannah. [1933] 2000. *Rahel Varnhagen: The Life of a Jewess*. Translated by L. Weissberg. Baltimore: Johns Hopkins University Press.

———. 1944. "The Jew as Pariah: A Hidden Tradition." *Jewish Social Studies* 6, no. 2: 99–122.

———. 1955. *Men in Dark Times*. New York: Harvest Press.

———. 1958. *The Human Condition*. Chicago: University of Chicago Press.

———. 1963a. *Eichmann in Jerusalem: A Report on the Banality of Evil*. New York: Viking Press.

———. 1963b. *On Revolution*. New York: Viking.

———. 1966. *The Origins of Totalitarianism*. New edition. New York: Harcourt, Brace and World.

———. 1981. *The Life of the Mind*. New York: Harcourt Brace Jovanovich.

———. 1992. *Lectures on Kant's Political Philosophy*. Edited by Ronald Beiner. Chicago: University of Chicago Press.

———. 2003a. "Collective Responsibility." In *Responsibility and Judgment*, edited by Jerome Kohn, 147–58. New York: Schocken.

———. 2003b. "Personal Responsibility under Dictatorship." In *Responsibility and Judgment*, edited by Jerome Kohn, 17–48. New York: Schocken.

———. 2003c. "Thinking and Moral Considerations." In *Responsibility and Judgment*, edited by Jerome Kohn, 159–89. New York: Schocken.

Austerlitz, Saul. 2015. "The Hannah Arendt Guide to Friendship." *New Republic*, March 9. https://newrepublic.com/article/121245/jon-nixons-hannah-arendt-and -politics-friendship-review.

Azoulay, Ariella. 2015. "Arendt's Guide for a Fictionalized Cinematic Portrait." *differ- ences* 26, no. 2:121–31.

Azoulay, Ariella, and Bonnie Honig. 2016. "Between Nuremberg and Jerusalem: Han- nah Arendt's *Tikkun Olam*." *differences* 27, no. 1:48–93.

Bair, Deidre. 1986. "Simone de Beauvoir: Politics, Language, and Feminist Identity." *Yale French Studies* 72:149–62.

———. 1990. *Simone de Beauvoir: A Biography*. New York: Summit.

Bakewell, Sarah. 2016. *At the Existentialist Café: Freedom, Being, and Apricot Cocktails*. New York: Other Press.

Baldwin, James. 1964. *The Fire Next Time*. New York: Dell.

Bauer, Nancy. 2001. *Simone de Beauvoir, Philosophy, and Feminism*. New York: Colum- bia University Press.

Beauvoir, Simone de. [1943] 1984. *She Came to Stay*. London: Fontana.

———. [1944] 2004. "Pyrrhus and Cineas." In *Philosophical Writings*, edited by Mar- garet Simons, 77–149. *The Beauvoir Series*. 7 vols. Urbana: University of Illinois Press.

———. [1945] 2004. "Moral Idealism and Political Realism." In *Philosophical Writ- ings*, edited by Margaret Simons, 175–93. *The Beauvoir Series*. 7 vols. Urbana: Uni- versity of Illinois Press.

———. [1948] 2000. *America Day by Day*. Translated by Carol Cosman. Berkeley: University of California Press.

———. 1948. *The Ethics of Ambiguity*. New York: Citadel.

———. [1949] 2004. "An Eye for an Eye." In *Philosophical Writings*, edited by Marga- ret A. Simons, 245–60. *The Beauvoir Series*. 7 vols. Urbana: University of Illinois Press.

———. [1949] 2011. *The Second Sex*. Translated by Constance Borde and Sheila Malovany-Chevallier. New York: Vintage.

———. [1952] 2012. "Must We Burn Sade?" In *Political Writings*, edited by Margaret A. Simons and Marybeth Timmermann, 44–101. *The Beauvoir Series*. 7 vols. Ur- bana: University of Illinois Press.

———. [1954] 1999. *The Mandarins: A Novel*. New York: W. W. Norton.

———. [1955] 2012. "Right-Wing Thought Today." In *Political Writings*, edited by Margaret Simons and Marybeth Timmermann, 113–93. *The Beauvoir Series*. 7 vols. Urbana: University of Illinois Press.

———. 1959. *Brigitte Bardot and the Lolita Syndrome*. London: New English Library.

———. [1960] 1992. *The Prime of Life: Autobiography of Simone de Beauvoir*. Eagan, MN: Group West.

———. [1963] 1992. *Force of Circumstance, II: Hard Times 1952–1962*. New York: Par- agon.

————. [1966] 2011. "My Experience as a Writer." In *"The Useless Mouths" and Other Literary Writings*, edited by Margaret A. Simons and Marybeth Timmermann, 282–301. *The Beauvoir Series*. 7 vols. Urbana: University of Illinois Press.

————. [1967] 1969. *The Woman Destroyed*. New York: Pantheon.

————. 1972. *The Coming of Age*. Translated by Patrick O'Brian. New York: Putnam. (Originally published as *Old Age*.)

————. 1984. *Adieux: A Farewell to Sartre*. New York: Pantheon.

————. 1985. Introduction to *The Complete Transcript of Claude Lanzmann's Shoah*, vii–xii. New York: Pantheon.

————. 2004. *Philosophical Writings*. Edited by Margaret A. Simons. *The Beauvoir Series*. 7 vols. Urbana: University of Illinois Press.

————. 2006. *Diary of a Philosophy Student, Volume 1, 1926–27*. Translated by Barbara Klaw. Edited by Barbara Klaw, Sylvie Le Bon de Beauvoir, and Margaret A. Simons. *The Beauvoir Series*. 7 vols. Urbana: University of Illinois Press.

————. 2008. *Wartime Diary*. Translation by Anne Deing Cordero. Edited by Margaret A. Simons and Sylvie Le Bon de Beauvoir. *The Beauvoir Series*. 7 vols. Urbana: University of Illinois Press.

————. 2011. *"The Useless Mouths" and Other Literary Writings*. Edited by Margaret A. Simons and Marybeth Timmermann. *The Beauvoir Series*. 7 vols. Urbana: University of Illinois Press.

————. 2012. *Political Writings*. Edited by Margaret A. Simons and Marybeth Timmermann. *The Beauvoir Series*. 7 vols. Urbana: University of Illinois Press.

————. 2015. *Feminist Writings*. Edited by Margaret A. Simons and Marybeth Timmermann. *The Beauvoir Series*. 7 vols. Urbana: University of Illinois Press.

Beauvoir, Simone de, and Gisèle Halimi. 1962. *Djamila Boupacha: The Story of the Torture of a Young Algerian Girl Which Shocked Liberal French Opinion*. New York: Macmillan.

Bechdel, Alison. 2006. *Fun Home: A Family Tragicomic*. Boston: Houghton Mifflin.

————. 2013. *Are You My Mother? A Comic Drama*. Boston: Houghton Mifflin.

Bedford, Sybille. 1958. "Emancipation and Destiny." *Book Notes*, December 12.

Beiner, Ronald, and Jennifer Nedelsky, eds. 2001. *Judgment, Imagination, and Politics: Themes from Kant and Arendt*. Lanham, MD: Rowman and Littlefield.

Bell, Vicki. 2000. "Owned Suffering: Thinking the Feminist Political Imagination with Simone de Beauvoir and Richard Wright." In *Thinking through Feminism*, edited by S. Ahmed, 61–76. London: Routledge.

Benhabib, Seyla. 1995. "The Pariah and Her Shadow." In *Feminist Interpretations of Hannah Arendt*, edited by Bonnie Honig, 83–104. University Park: Penn State University Press.

————. 2000. *The Reluctant Modernism of Hannah Arendt*. Lanham, MD: Rowman and Littlefield.

Bennett, Jane. 2010. *Vibrant Matter: A Political Ecology of Things*. Durham, NC: Duke University Press.

Bergoffen, Debra. 1996. *The Philosophy of Simone de Beauvoir: Gendered Phenomenologies, Erotic Generosities*. Albany: State University of New York Press.

Berkowitz, Roger, ed. 2010a. *Thinking in Dark Times*. New York: Fordham University Press.

———. 2010b. "Why We Must Judge." *Democracy: A Journal of Ideas* 18. Online.

———. 2011. "Bearing Logs on Our Shoulders: Reconciliation, Non-Reconciliation, and the Building of a Common World." *Theory and Event* 14, no. 1. Online.

———. 2016. "The Cynicism of Paraphrasing: A Review of 'Viva Activa: The Spirit of Hannah Arendt.'" *Amor Mundi*, April 10. https://medium.com/amor-mundi/the -cynicism-of-paraphrasing-a-review-of-vita-activa-the-spirit-of-hannah-arendt- 43b319826128#.rg8psqpxn.

Berlant, Lauren. 2004. "Critical Inquiry, Affirmative Culture." *Critical Inquiry* 30, no. 2:445–51.

———. 2008. *The Female Complaint: The Unfinished Business of Sentimentality in American Culture*. Durham, NC: Duke University Press.

Blanchard, Marc. 2004. "On the Style of the Coming Philosophy: 'Le style, c'est la femme.'" *MLN* 119, no. 4:696–717.

Boule, Jean-Pierre, and Ursula Tidd, eds. 2012. *Existentialism and Contemporary Cinema: A Beauvoirian Perspective*. New York: Berghahn.

Braidotti, Rosie. 1994. *Nomadic Subjects: Embodiment and Sexual Difference in Contemporary Feminist Theory*. New York: Columbia University Press.

Brightman, Carol, ed. 1995. *Between Friends: The Correspondence of Hannah Arendt and Mary McCarthy, 1949–1975*. New York: Harcourt Brace.

Brinkema, Eugenie. 2014. *The Forms of the Affects*. Durham, NC: Duke University Press.

Buruma, Ian. 2011. "Who Did Not Collaborate?" *New York Review of Books*, February 24, 16–18.

Butler, Judith. 2003. "Beauvoir on Sade: Making Sexuality into an Ethic." In *The Cambridge Companion to Simone de Beauvoir*, edited by Claudia Card, 168–88. Cambridge: Cambridge University Press.

Camus, Albert. [1958] 2013. *Algerian Chronicles*. Edited and introduced by Alice Kaplan. Translated by Arthur Goldhammer. Cambridge, MA: Belknap Press.

Césaire, Aimé. [1955] 2000. *Discourse on Colonialism*. New York: Monthly Review Press.

Cohen, Cathy J. 2004. "Deviance as Resistance: A New Research Agenda for the Study of Black Politics." *Du Bois Review* 1, no. 1:27–45.

Connelly, Frances. 2003. *Modern Art and the Grotesque*. Cambridge: Cambridge University Press.

Connolly, William. 2002. *Neuropolitics: Thinking, Culture, Speed*. Minneapolis: University of Minnesota Press.

———. 2011. *A World of Becoming*. Durham, NC: Duke University Press.

Creed, Barbara. 1993. *The Monstrous Feminine: Film, Feminism, Pyschoanalysis*. New York: Routledge.

Culbert, Jennifer. 2010. "Judging the Events of Our Time." In *Thinking in Dark Times*, edited by Roger Berkowitz et al., 145–50. New York: Fordham University Press.

Daigle, Christine. 2014. "*The Second Sex* as Appeal: The Ethical Dimension of Ambiguity." *philoSOPHIA* 4, no. 2:197–220.

Daigle, Christine, and Jacob Golomb, eds. 2009. *Beauvoir and Sartre: The Riddle of Influence*. Bloomington: Indiana University Press.

Deleuze, Gilles, and Felix Guattari. 1987. *A Thousand Plateaus: Capitalism and Schizophrenia*. Translated by Brian Massumi. Minneapolis: University of Minnesota Press.

Deutscher, Penelope. 2008. *The Philosophy of Simone de Beauvoir: Ambiguity, Conversion, Resistance*. New York: Cambridge University Press.

Diawara, Manthia. 1998. *In Search of Africa*. Cambridge, MA: Harvard University Press.

Enke, A. Finn, ed. 2012. *Transfeminist Perspectives in and beyond Transgender and Gender Studies*. Philadelphia: Temple University Press.

Fanon, Frantz. [1952] 1967. *Black Skin, White Masks*. New York: Grove.

———. [1959] 1965. "Algeria Unveiled." In *A Dying Colonialism*, 35–67. New York: Grove.

———. [1963] 2004. *The Wretched of the Earth*. New York: Grove.

Farred, Grant, ed. 2013. "Fanon: Imperative of the Now." Special issue of *South Atlantic Quarterly* 112, no. 1:1–4.

Federici, Silvia. [1975] 2012. "Wages against Housework." In *Revolution at Point Zero: Housework, Reproduction, and Feminist Struggle*, 15–22. Oakland, CA: PM Press.

Felman, Shoshana. 2002. *The Juridical Unconscious: Trials and Traumas in the Twentieth Century*. Cambridge, MA: Harvard University Press.

Ferguson, Kathy. 2011. *Emma Goldman: Political Thinking in the Streets*. Lanham, MD: Rowman and Littlefield.

———. 2012. "Simone de Beauvoir: Introduction." *Theory and Event* 15, no. 2. Online.

Ferrara, Alessandro. 2008. *The Force of the Example: Explorations in the Paradigm of Judgment*. New York: Columbia University Press.

Fincher, David, dir. 2014. *Gone Girl*. Twentieth Century Fox Home Entertainment. Film.

Frank, Jason. 2010. *Constituent Moments: Enacting the People in Postrevolutionary America*. Durham, NC: Duke University Press.

———. 2015. "Logical Revolts: Jacques Rancière and Political Subjectivization." *Political Theory* 43, no. 2:249–61.

Frank, Jill. 2014. "Circulating Authority: Plato, Politics, and Political Theory." In *Radical Future Pasts: Untimely Essays in Political Theory*, edited by Rom Coles, Mark Reinhardt, and George Shulman, 330–50. Lexington: University Press of Kentucky.

Fullbrook, Kate, and Edward Fullbrook. 1994. *Simone de Beauvoir and Jean Paul Sartre: The Remaking of a Twentieth-Century Legend*. New York: Basic Books.

Galt, Rosalind. 2015. "The Suffering Spectator? Perversion and Complicity in *Antichrist* and *Nymphomaniac*." In "Gender, Power, and Politics in the Films of Lars von Trier," edited by Bonnie Honig and Lori Marso. Special issue of *Theory and Event* 18, no. 2. Online.

Gana, Nouri. 2011. *Signifying Loss: Toward a Poetics of Narrative Mourning*. Lewisburg, PA: Bucknell University Press.

Gilroy, Paul. 1993. *The Black Atlantic*. Cambridge, MA: Harvard University Press.

———. 2005. *Postcolonial Melancholy*. New York: Columbia University Press.

Gordon, Bette. 1989. "Variety: The Pleasure in Looking." In *Pleasure and Danger: Exploring Female Sexuality*, edited by Carole S. Vance, 189–203. London: Harper-Collins.

Gordon, Lewis. 2015. *What Fanon Said: A Philosophical Introduction to His Life and Thought*. New York: Fordham University Press.

Gregg, Melissa, and Gregory J. Siegworth, eds. 2010. *The Affect Theory Reader*. Durham, NC: Duke University Press.

Grosz, Elizabeth. 1994. *Volatile Bodies: Towards a Corporeal Feminism*. London: Routledge.

Halberstam, Judith. 2011. *The Queer Art of Failure*. Durham, NC: Duke University Press.

Hansen, Miriam. 1986. "Pleasure, Ambivalence, Identification: Valentino and Female Spectatorship." *Cinema Journal* 25, no. 4:6–32.

Hawkesworth, Mary. 2010. "From Constitutive Outside to the Politics of Extinction: Critical Race Theory, Feminist Theory, and Political Theory." *Political Research Quarterly* 63, no. 3:686–96.

Heinämaa, Sara. 1997. "What Is a Woman? Butler and Beauvoir on the Foundations of Sexual Difference." *Hypatia* 12, no. 1:20–39.

Hesford, Victoria. 2013. *Feeling Women's Liberation*. Durham, NC: Duke University Press.

Hochschild, Arlie Russell. 2016. *Strangers in Their Own Land: Anger and Mourning on the American Right*. New York: New Press.

Hollinger, Karen. 2012. *Feminist Film Studies*. New York: Routledge.

Honig, Bonnie, ed. 1995. *Feminist Interpretations of Hannah Arendt*. University Park: Penn State University Press.

———. 2013. *Antigone, Interrupted*. Cambridge: Cambridge University Press.

———. 2015. "Arendt on the Couch." *differences* 26, no. 2:93–105.

———. 2016. "What Kind of Thing Is Land? Hannah Arendt's Object Relations, or: The Jewish Unconscious of Arendt's Most 'Greek' Text." *Political Theory* 44, no. 3: 307–36.

Honig, Bonnie, and Lori Marso, eds. 2015. "Gender, Power, and Politics in the Films of Lars von Trier." Special issue of *Theory and Event* 18, no. 2. Online.

Honig, Bonnie, and Lori Marso. 2016a. "Introduction: Lars von Trier and the 'Clichés of Our Times.'" In "Breaking the Rules: Gender, Power, and Politics in the Films of Lars von Trier," edited by Lori J. Marso and Bonnie Honig. Special issue of *Theory and Event* 18, no. 2. Online.

Honig, Bonnie, and Lori Marso, eds. 2016b. *Politics, Theory, and Film: Critical Encounters with Lars von Trier*. Oxford: Oxford University Press.

Huffer, Lynne. 2013. *Are the Lips a Grave? A Queer Feminist on the Ethics of Sex*. New York: Columbia University Press.

———. 2015. "The Nymph Shoots Back: Agamben, *Nymphomaniac*, and the Feel of the Agon." In "Gender, Power, and Politics in the Films of Lars von Trier," edited by Bonnie Honig and Lori Marso. Special issue of *Theory and Event* 18, no. 2. Online.

Hustvedt, Siri. 2014. "75 at 75: Siri Hustvedt on Susan Sontag." *Poetry*, March 6. http://92yondemand.org/75-at-75-siri-hustvedt-on-susan-sontag/.

Iton, Richard. 2008. *In Search of the Black Fantastic: Politics and Popular Culture in the Post–Civil Rights Era*. Oxford: Oxford University Press.

Jones, Kathleen. 2013. "Hannah Arendt's Female Friends." *Los Angeles Review of Books*, November 12. http://lareviewofbooks.org/essay/hannah-arendts-female-friends.

Judt, Tony. 1994. *Past Imperfect: French Intellectuals*. Berkeley: University of California Press.

Kaplan, Alice. 2000. *The Collaborator: The Trial and Execution of Robert Brasillach*. Chicago: University of Chicago Press.

Kaufmann, Dorothy. 1986. "Simone de Beauvoir: Questions of Difference and Generation." *Yale French Studies* 72:121–31.

Kelley, Robin D. G. 2000. "A Poetics of Anticolonialism." Introduction to *Discourse on Colonialism*, by Aimé Césaire, 7–28. New York: Monthly Review Press.

Khanna, Ranjana. 2003. *Dark Continents: Psychoanalysis and Colonialism*. Durham, NC: Duke University Press.

Kohn, Jerome, ed. 2003. Introduction to *Responsibility and Judgment*, vii–xxx. New York: Schocken.

Kristeva, Julia. 2001. *Hannah Arendt*. New York: Columbia University Press.

Kruks, Sonia. 1991. "Simone de Beauvoir: Teaching Sartre about Freedom." In *Sartre Alive*, edited by Ronald Aronson and Adrien Vandenhoven, 285–309. Detroit: Wayne State University Press.

———. 2005. "Living on Rails: Freedom, Constraint, and Political Judgment in Beauvoir's 'Moral' Essays and *The Mandarins*." In *The Contradictions of Freedom*, edited by Sally J. Scholz and Shannon M. Mussett, 67–86. Albany: State University of New York Press.

———. 2012a. Introduction to "Right-Wing Thought Today." In *Simone de Beauvoir: Political Writings*, edited by Margaret Simons and Marybeth Timmermann, 105–12. *The Beauvoir Series*. 7 vols. Urbana: University of Illinois Press.

———. 2012b. *Simone de Beauvoir and the Politics of Ambiguity*. Oxford: Oxford University Press.

Lagoia, Nicola. 2016. "'Writing Is an Act of Pride': A Conversation with Elena Ferrante." *New Yorker Magazine*. Online. http://www.newyorker.com/books/page-turner/writing-is-an-act-of-pride-a-conversation-with-elena-ferrante.

Leduc, Violette. 2003. *La bâtarde=The Bastard*. Translated by D. Coltman. Normal, IL: Dalkey Archive Press.

Leonard, Miriam. 2016. "'I Know What Has to Happen': Tragedy, Mourning, and Melancholia in Medea." In *Politics, Theory, and Film: Critical Encounters with Lars von Trier*, edited by Bonnie Honig and Lori J. Marso, 336–55. New York: Oxford University Press.

Lewis, Sophie. 2014. "On Violette Leduc: Interviewing Sophie Lewis." Interview by Eva

Richter. *Asymptote*, September 11. http://www.asymptotejournal.com/blog/2014/09
/11/on-violette-leduc-interviewing-sophie-lewis/.

MacKinnon, Catherine A. 1989. "Sexuality, Pornography, and Method: Pleasure under Patriarchy." *Ethics* 99, no. 2:314–46.

Mandolfo, Carleen. 2010. "Women, Suffering, and Redemption in Three Films of Lars von Trier." *Literature and Theology* 24, no. 3:285–300.

Marable, M. 2011. *Malcolm X: A Life of Reinvention*. New York: Viking.

Margulies, Ivone. 1996. *Nothing Happens: Chantal Akerman's Hyperrealist Everyday*. Durham, NC: Duke University Press.

———. 2009. "A Matter of Time." *Criterion Collection*. August 18. https://www
.criterion.com/current/posts/1215-a-matter-of-time-jeanne-dielman-23-quai-du
-commerce-1080-bruxelles.

Markell, Patchen. 2003. *Bound by Recognition*. Princeton, NJ: Princeton University Press.

———. 2014. "Arendt, Aesthetics, and 'The Crisis in Culture.'" In *The Aesthetic Turn in Political Thought*, edited by Nikolas Kompridis, 61–88. New York: Bloomsbury Press.

Markowitz, Sally. 2009. "Occidental Dreams: Orientalism and History in *The Second Sex*." *SIGNS* 34, no. 2:271–94.

Marshall, David. 2010. "The Origin and Character of Hannah Arendt's Theory of Judgment." *Political Theory* 38, no. 3:367–93.

Marso, Lori J. 1999. *(Un)Manly Citizens: J. J. Rousseau's and Germaine de Staël's Subversive Women*. Baltimore: Johns Hopkins University Press.

———. 2006. *Feminist Thinkers and the Demands of Femininity: The Lives and Work of Intellectual Women*. New York: Routledge.

———. 2007. "Feminism and the Complications of Freeing the Women of Afghanistan and Iraq." In *W Stands for Women: How the George W. Bush Presidency Shaped a New Politics of Gender*, edited by Michaele Ferguson and Lori J. Marso, 221–43. Durham, NC: Duke University Press.

———. 2010. "Feminism's Quest for Common Desires." *Perspectives on Politics* 8, no. 1:263–69.

———. 2012a. "Simone de Beauvoir and Hannah Arendt: Judgments in Dark Times." *Political Theory* 40, no. 2:165–93.

———. 2012b. "Thinking Politically with Simone de Beauvoir in *The Second Sex*." *Theory and Event* 15, no. 2. Online.

———. 2013. "Solidarity *sans* Identity: Simone de Beauvoir and Richard Wright Theorize Political Subjectivity." *Contemporary Political Theory* 13, no. 3:242–62.

———. 2015. "Feminism." In *Encyclopedia of Political Thought*, edited by Michael Gibbons. Hoboken, NJ: Wiley Blackwell. Online. http://onlinelibrary.wiley.com/doi/10
.1002/9781118474396.wbept0363/full.

Marso, Lori, and Patricia Moynagh. 2006. *Simone de Beauvoir's Political Thinking*. Urbana: University of Illinois Press.

Martel, James. 2013. *Textual Conspiracies*. Ann Arbor: University of Michigan Press.

Maxwell, Lida. 2014. *Public Trials: Burke, Zola, Arendt and the Politics of Lost Causes*. Oxford: Oxford University Press.

Mbembe, A. 2001. *On the Postcolony*. Berkeley: University of California Press.

McClintock, Anne. 1999. "Fanon and Gender Agency." In *Rethinking Fanon: The Continuing Dialogue*, edited by Nigel C. Gibson, 283–93. New York: Humanity Books.

McFadden, Cybelle H. 2014. *Gendered Frames, Embodied Cameras: Varda, Akerman, Cabrera, Calle, and Maiwenn*. Madison, NJ: Farleigh Dickinson University Press.

Moi, Toril. 1999. *What Is a Woman? and Other Essays*. Oxford: Oxford University Press.

———. 2010. "The Adulteress Wife." *London Review of Books* 32, no. 3. http://www.lrb.co.uk/v32/n03/toril-moi/the-adulteress-wife.

Moskowitz, Perry. 2014. "The Somatic Sex: Bodies in Simone de Beauvoir's Aesthetic Politics." Honors thesis, Union College.

———. 2016. "12 Million Dark Mirrors in Richard Wright's *12 Million Black Voices*." Unpublished manuscript.

Mulvey, Laura. 1989. *Visual and Other Pleasures*. Bloomington: Indiana University Press.

Murphy, Ann V. 2006. "Between Generosity and Violence: Toward a Revolutionary Politics in the Philosophy of Simone de Beauvoir." In *The Philosophy of Simone de Beauvoir: Critical Essays*, edited by Margaret A. Simons, 262–75. Bloomington: Indiana University Press.

———. 2012. *Violence and the Philosophical Imaginary*. Albany: State University of New York Press.

Murphy, Julien. 1995. "Beauvoir and the Algerian War: Towards a Postcolonial Ethics." In *Feminist Interpretations of Simone de Beauvoir*, edited by Margaret A. Simons, 263–98. University Park: Penn State University Press.

Narayan, Uma. 1997. *Dislocating Cultures: Identities, Traditions, and Third World Feminisms*. New York: Routledge.

Ngai, Sianne. 2005. *Ugly Feelings*. Cambridge, MA: Harvard University Press.

Nixon, Jon. 2015. *Hannah Arendt and the Politics of Friendship*. London: Bloomsbury Press.

"Nuremberg Trial Proceedings Vol. 1: Charter of the International Military Tribunal." Yale Law School: The Avalon Project. Lillian Goldman Law Library, 2008. http://avalon.law.yale.edu/imt/imtconst.asp.

O'Brien, Mary. 1981. *The Politics of Reproduction*. Boston: Routledge and Kegan Paul.

Oksala, Johanna. 2012. *Foucault, Politics, and Violence*. Evanston, IL: Northwestern University Press.

Ortner, Sherry. 1974. "Is Female to Nature as Male Is to Culture?" In *Woman, Culture, and Society*, edited by M. Z. Rosaldo and L. Lamphere, 68–87. Stanford, CA: Stanford University Press.

Ozon, François, dir. 2003. *Swimming Pool*. Focus Features. Film.

Panagia, Davide. 2006. *The Poetics of Political Thinking*. Durham, NC: Duke University Press.

————. 2009. *The Political Life of Sensation*. Durham, NC: Duke University Press.

Patterson, Yolanda. 1986. "Simone de Beauvoir and the Demystification of Motherhood." *Yale French Studies* 72:87–105.

Provost, Martin, dir. 2013. *Violette*. Doc and Film International. Film.

Rich, Nathaniel. 2016. "Inside the Sacrifice Zone." *The New York Review of Books*. November 10.

Roberts, Brian Russell, and Keith Foulcher, eds. 2016. *Indonesian Notebook: A Sourcebook on Richard Wright and the Bandung Conference*. Durham, NC: Duke University Press.

Rogat, Yosal. 1961. *The Eichmann Trial and the Rule of Law*. Santa Barbara: Center for the Study of Democratic Institutions.

Rubenstein, Diane. 1993. "Publish and Perish: The Épuration of French Intellectuals." *European Studies* 23:71–99.

Russo, Mary. 1994. *The Female Grotesque: Risk, Excess and Modernity*. New York: Routledge.

Sartre, Jean Paul. [1964] 2001. *Colonialism and Neocolonialism*. London: Routledge.

Schwarzer, Alice. 1984. *After The Second Sex: Conversations with Simone de Beauvoir*. New York: Pantheon.

Scott, Joan Wallach. 2007. *The Politics of the Veil*. Princeton, NJ: Princeton University Press.

Sedgwick, Eve Kosofsky. 2003. *Touching Feeling: Affect, Pedagogy, Performativity*. Durham, NC: Duke University Press.

Sedgwick, Eve Kosofsky, and Adam Frank. 2003. "Shame in the Cybernetic Fold: Reading Silvan Tomkins." In *Touching Feeling: Affect, Pedagogy, Performativity* by Eve Kosofsky Sedgwick, 93–121. Durham, NC: Duke University Press.

Shelby, Karen. 2006. "Beauvoir and Ethical Responsibility." In *Simone de Beauvoir's Political Thinking*, edited by Lori Marso and Patricia Moynagh, 93–108. Champaign: University of Illinois Press.

Simons, Margaret A. 1981. "Beauvoir and Sartre: The Question of Influence." *Eros* 8, no. 1:25–42.

————. 2001. *Beauvoir and The Second Sex: Feminism, Race, and the Origins of Existentialism*. London: Rowman and Littlefield.

Simons, Margaret A., and Sylvie Le Bon de Beauvoir, eds. 2004–15. *The Beauvoir Series*. 7 vols. Urbana: University of Illinois Press.

Singh, Nikhail. 2004. *Black Is a Country: Race and the Unfinished Struggle for Democracy*. Cambridge, MA: Harvard University Press.

Sinnerbrink, Robert. 2011. "Chaos Reigns: Anti-Cognitivism in Lars von Trier's *Antichrist*." In *New Philosophies of Film: Thinking Images*, 157–76. London: Continuum Press.

Sontag, Susan. 1964. "Notes on 'Camp.'" *Partisan Review* (fall): 515–30.

Spelman, Elizabeth. 1988. *Inessential Woman: Problems of Exclusion in Feminist Thought*. Boston: Beacon Press.

Spillers, Hortense. 1987. "Mama's Baby, Papa's Maybe: An American Grammar Book." *Diacritics* 17, no. 2 (summer): 64–81.

Stange, Maren. 2004. *Bronzeville: Black Chicago in Pictures, 1941–1943*. New York: New Press.

Thomsen, Bodil Marie Stavning. 2009. "*Antichrist—Chaos Reigns*: The Event of Violence and the Haptic Image in Lars von Trier's Film." *Journal of Aesthetics and Culture* 1:1–10.

Thurman, Judith. 2010. Introduction to Simone de Beauvoir, *The Second Sex*, ix–xxi. Translated by Constance Borde and Sheila Malovany-Chevalier. New York: Vintage.

Vance, Carole, ed. 1989. *Pleasure and Danger: Exploring Female Sexuality*. London: HarperCollins.

Veltman, Andrea. 2010. "Simone de Beauvoir and Hannah Arendt on Labor." *Hypatia* 25, no. 1:55–78.

von Trier, Lars, dir. 2009. *Antichrist*. IFC Films. Film.

———. 2011. *Melancholia*. Magnolia Pictures. Film.

———. 2014. *Nymphomaniac*. Magnolia Pictures. Film.

von Trotta, Margarethe, dir. 2012. *Hannah Arendt*. Zeitgeist Films. Film.

———. 2015. "My Approach to Biography: Rosa Luxemburg, Hildegard von Bingen, Hannah Arendt." *differences* 26, no. 2:70–85.

Weeks, Kathi. 2011. *The Problem with Work: Feminism, Marxism, Antiwork Politics, and Postwork Imaginaries*. Durham, NC: Duke University Press.

Weigel, Moira. 2013. "Heritage Girl Crush: On 'Hannah Arendt.'" *Los Angeles Review of Books*, July 16. https://lareviewofbooks.org/article/heritage-girl-crush-on -hannah-arendt/.

Weiss, Penny. 2009. *Canon Fodder: Historical Women Political Thinkers*. University Park: Penn State University Press.

Weissberg, Liliane. 1997. Introduction to *Rahel Varnhagen: The Life of a Jewess*, by Hannah Arendt, 3. Baltimore: Johns Hopkins University Press.

White, Rob, and Nina Power. 2009. "Antichrist: A Discussion." *Film Quarterly*. Dialogues: Web exclusives. http://www.filmquarterly.org/2009/12/antichrist-a -discussion/.

Williams, Tami Michelle. 2014. *Germaine Dulac: A Cinema of Sensations*. Urbana: University of Illinois Press.

Wollstonecraft, M. 2010. *Vindication of the Rights of Woman with Strictures on Political and Moral Subjects*. Auckland, NZ: Floating Press.

Wright, Richard. [1940] 2014. *Native Son*. New York: Harper Perennial.

———. [1941] 2008. *12 Million Black Voices*. New York: Basic Books.

———. [1945] 2007. *Black Boy*. New York: Harper Perennial.

———. 2008. *Black Power: Three Books from Exile: Black Power; The Color Curtain; and White Man Listen!* New York: Harper Perennial.

Young, Iris Marion. 1990. *Throwing like a Girl: And Other Essays in Feminist Philosophy and Policy*. Oxford: Oxford University Press.

———. 2005. *On Female Body Experience*. Oxford: Oxford University Press.

Young-Bruehl, Elizabeth. 1982. *Hannah Arendt: For Love of the World*. New Haven, CT: Yale University Press.

Zerilli, Linda M. G. 1991. "Machiavelli's Sisters: Women and 'The Conversation' of Political Theory." *Political Theory* 19, no. 2:252–76.

———. 1995. "The Arendtian Body." In *Feminist Interpretations of Hannah Arendt*, edited by Bonnie Honig, 167–93. University Park: Penn State University Press.

———. 2005. *Feminism and the Abyss of Freedom*. Chicago: University of Chicago Press.

———. 2012. "Feminist Theory without Solace." *Theory and Event* 15, no. 2. Online.

Zoladz, Lindsay. 2011. "Is *Melancholia* a Feminist Film?" *Salon*, November 23. http://www.salon.com/2011/11/23/is_melancholia_a_feminist_film/.

Zolkos, Magdalena. 2011. "Violent Affects: Nature and the Feminine in Lars von Trier's *Antichrist*." *Parrhesia* 13:177–89.

Page numbers followed by *f* indicate illustrations.

Bastard, The (Leduc), 181–82
Battle of Algiers, The (Pontecorvo film), 104, 118
battle of the sexes, 111–12
Bechdel, Alison, 6, 150f; feminist film rule, 15, 150, 151–52, 176–78, 191, 199. See also specific works
Bell, Vikki, 131
Ben-Gurion, David, 47, 49–50
Benhabib, Seyla, 183–84, 188–89
Berkowitz, Roger, 52
Berlant, Lauren, 29, 172, 216n9
biological data, 8–9, 21, 27, 109
biopics, female, 177
Black Boy (Wright), 14
blackness, 122, 125, 126, 129, 144, 228n18. See also African American experience; négritude
Blida Clinic (Algiers), 120
Borde, Constance, 25
Boupacha, Djamila, 2, 14, 94–95, 97, 105–6, 107, 118–19, 120–21
bourgeois taxonomies, 13, 39, 67, 86, 191
Brasillach, Robert, 5–6, 12; anti-Semitism of, 47, 50–51, 54, 57–58, 61–62; background, 37–38, 45–46, 54; as sub-man, 45, 56; trial, 38, 42, 44, 45–47, 49, 50–51, 56, 57–58, 65, 93
Breaking the Waves (von Trier film), 70
Butler, Judith, 52, 68

Camus, Albert, 46, 94, 211n11
candomblé, 226n5
Césaire, Aimé, 99, 106
Chagall, Marc, 130
citizenship, 60
collective action: freedom in, 100, 116, 144; vs. individual action, 118, 159; move toward, 13, 15, 34, 65, 100, 101, 121, 124, 137–38, 155, 159, 175–76; new forms of, 122, 127; risks of, 29
collective freedom: defense of, 38, 102; embodiment in, 56, 62, 100; encounters in, 3, 10, 16, 34; threats to, 12, 38, 56, 58–59, 62, 65
colonial trauma, use of term, 99
Color Curtain, The (Wright), 146
Combat (Camus), 211n11
Communist Party, 19
Connelly, Frances, 78
Connolly, Bill, 100
Convention People's Party, 126, 129, 130

Creed, Barbara, 224–25n20
"Crisis in Culture, The" (Arendt), 39
Critique of Judgment (Kant), 38

Dancer in the Dark (von Trier film), 70
death penalty, 51–53
Deutscher, Penelope, 114
Diawara, Manthia, 126, 130
Discourse on Colonialism (Césaire), 106
diversity, 5
Djamila Boupacha (Beauvoir/Halimi), 102
Douglass, Frederick, 215n2
Drieu La Rochelle, Pierre, 20
Dulac, Germaine, 161
Dying Colonialism, A (Fanon), 102, 106–7
Dykes to Watch Out For (Bechdel), 150f, 150–51

Eichmann, Adolf, 5–6; anti-Semitism of, 48, 50, 53; apprehension of, 49–50; background, 38, 47–48, 54; as sub-man, 45, 55; thoughtlessness of, 44, 54–55, 193–95; trial, 12–13, 38, 42, 44–45, 47–50, 52–54, 65, 93
Eichmann in Jerusalem (Arendt), 47–48, 51–52, 219n14
embodiment: in collective freedom, 56, 62, 100; in freedom, 44, 61; of inequality, 42, 63; of oppression, 42, 43, 60, 61, 63, 99, 101, 116, 120, 129, 140; in political theory, 43, 100, 205
emotions. See feelings/emotions
encounter(s): agency from, 4; ambiguity in, 7, 44, 65; in collective freedom, 3, 10, 16, 34; defined, 7–9; with enemies, 11, 12, 13–14, 93; everyday, 8; in feminist politics, 2–6; freedom in, 2–4, 8, 17, 30–31, 43, 94, 99, 113, 130–31, 201, 204, 206; historical events as, 5, 8; imagined, 6; individual subjectivity and, 4, 7, 36; language of, 3–4, 7–8; in political sphere, 63
enemies: collective, 116–17; encounters with, 11, 12, 13–14, 93; friend/enemy distinction, 11; judgment of, 41–42; of women, 17, 24–28
Ethics of Ambiguity, The (Beauvoir): on existentialism, 7–8; on humiliation of victims, 62; on justification of violence, 107; on political freedom, 47; on sub-men, 55

Huffer, Lynne, 169, 170, 232n5
Human Condition, The (Arendt), 8, 60, 149–50, 188

immanence, 3; duality with transcendence, 30, 33–34, 113, 157; as female, 27, 33–34, 113, 115, 136, 158
in-between, notion of, 7, 190, 206
incest taboo, 28
individual freedom, 22, 127
Indonesian Notebook, 146
inequality: conditions of, 18, 58, 65, 145; embodied, 42, 63; identity and, 147; justification for, 6, 19; self-interest and, 22
In the Prison of Her Skin (Leduc), 179
Israeli state, 50, 59

Jansen, G. H., 146
Jaspers, Karl, 20–21, 56
Jeanne Dielman (Akerman film), 15, 152, 153–55, 160f, 161f, 162f; household tasks in, 156–59; murder in, 159–63; overview, 156–57; pleasure/danger dynamic, 93, 155, 156, 158–59
Je suis partout (newspaper), 37–38, 46, 54
Jewish Council, 47
Jim Crow legislation, 15, 132–33
judgment, 37, 39, 41–42, 50–53, 58, 218n2
Judt, Tony, 46, 47, 56

Kant, Immanuel, 38
Kazin, Alfred, 192
kitchenettes, black lives in, 138–40
Kohler, Lotte, 192
Kovner, Abba, 54
Kruks, Sonia, 18, 56, 212n16, 215n3
Ku Klux Klan, 132

Lange, Dorothea, 133
Lanzmann, Claude, 14, 95
Lectures on Kant's Political Philosophy (Arendt), 55–56
Leduc, Violette, 5–6, 16, 152, 179. See also *Violette* (Provost film)
Lee, Russell, 133

Lewis, Sophie, 182
liberalism, 46–47, 56
Life of the Mind, The (Arendt), 44
Lumumba, Patrice, 127

MacKinnon, Catherine, 230n4
male gaze in cinema, 156, 175, 176, 191, 232n4
Malovany-Chevallier, Sheila, 25
Mandarins, The (Beauvoir), 19, 49
Mansfield, Katherine, 76
Margulies, Ivone, 158–59
Markell, Patchen, 39
marriage: as defining, 32, 75; instability of, 78
material reality, 6, 9, 10, 12, 22, 37
Maulnier, Thierry, 20
Mbembe, Achille, 146–47
McCarthy, Mary, 192, 197–98
McClintock, Anne, 104–5
Medea (von Trier film), 71
Melancholia (von Trier film), 69, 70, 72, 74f, 79f, 80f, 82, 84
melancholy: condition of, 32–33, 69, 75–76, 99, 186; as resistance, 33–34, 119
Men in Dark Times (Arendt), 41
Merleau-Ponty, Maurice, 20–21, 56
misogyny, 20, 27, 65, 68, 69, 76, 154, 163, 165
modernity: affirmation of, 125; freedom and, 144; oppressed subjects in, 135, 140–41; resistance to, 102; salons and, 189; tradition and, 129, 147
Moi, Toril, 190
Monde, Le (newspaper), 95, 97
Montherlant, Henry de, 20
Mormerot, Jules, 20
Moroccan-Algerian War (1963). *See* Sand War (1963)
motherhood, 136–37, 207
Mulvey, Laura, 156
"Must We Burn Sade?" (Beauvoir), 12, 39, 67

Native Son (Wright), 14
"Neapolitan" novels (Ferrante), 201
négritude, 15, 96, 125, 227n11
Neuropolitics (Connolly), 100
New Deal, 133
New Left, 94

New Yorker (magazine), 38, 42, 47

New York Times (newspaper), 25

Night and Day (Akerman film), 188

Nixon, Jon, 229n1

Nkrumah, Kwame, 15, 126, 127, 129, 130

nominalism, 30

nonreconciliation, 52

nymph, mythology of, 148–69

Nymphomaniac (von Trier film), 15, 57, 70, 73–75, 81f, 82, 89, 152, 153–55, 168f, 169f, 171f; overview, 167–68; pleasure/danger in, 167–68, 171–72, 206; shooting in, 171–72

On Revolution (Arendt), 60

On the Postcolony (Mbembe), 146

ontology: ambiguity and, 3–4; conditions of, 17, 108; of violence, 94, 101–2, 108–9, 112

oppression: acceptance of, 31; conditions of, 18, 30, 57, 58–59, 62–63, 65, 108, 154, 159; culture and, 142–45; defined, 62–63; embodied, 42, 43, 60, 61, 63, 99, 101, 116, 120, 129, 140; feelings as motivation for, 28–29; interdependence and, 63; justification for, 19, 109; materiality of, 136–38; under patriarchy, 30; plenitude and, 7; racial, 128, 130, 134; resistance to, 62–63, 98, 122, 124–25, 154; solidarity against, 53, 64, 130–41, 144–45, 181; violence and, 94

Origins of Totalitarianism, The (Arendt), 47, 64

otherness: as enemy, 14; in oneself, 2, 14; politics of encounter and, 44; subjectivity and, 157, 212n14; women's role, 31. *See also* Self-Other duality

Ozon, François, 86

Panagia, Davide, 100

Paris Congress speech (Wright), 122–23, 125

Parker, Dorothy, 76

Parshley, H. M., 25

Past Imperfect (Judt), 46

patriarchy: critique of, 76; on female sexual freedom, 82; instability of, 78; myth of femininity, 21, 23–24, 75, 98, 123–24, 136–37, 206; oppression under, 30; protest of, 34; of revolutionary militants, 118–19; secrets of, 67, 68; sexuality under, 230n4; trauma of,

99; violence of, 13, 102–6, 112; women's roles under, 32, 98

Patterson, Yolanda, 209n1

perverse protests, 14, 95, 119, 140, 155, 159–61, 165, 172–73, 175

pleasure/danger dynamic, 93, 155, 156, 158–59, 167–68, 170–71, 172–73

Plessix, Francine de, 25

plurality, 4, 38, 43, 44, 52, 58, 60, 64, 190

Political Life of Sensation, The (Panagia), 100

politics: action in, 13; agonism/affectivity in, 10–11; Beauvoir's interest in, 210–11n11; defined as encounters, 7–9; embodiment in, 43; freedom and, 9, 60–61. *See also* feminist politics

Pontecorvo, Gillo, 104, 118

Poplar, Ellen, 124

Powell, Adam Clayton, 96

Power, Nina, 70, 77

Prime of Life, The (Beauvoir), 46, 210n8, 218n3

privilege, 21–22

Promise of Happiness, The (Ahmed), 33

Provost, Martin, 6, 178–83. See also *Violette* (Provost film)

quietism, 21, 22

race and gender. *See* gender-race intersection

racism and oppression, 126, 128–29, 130, 134, 138–39

Rahel Varnhagen (Arendt), 16, 183–90; conscious pariah role, 184–86, 190–91; Jewish background, 184, 185; letters as basis of, 183–84; repetitive dreams, 186–87; *salonnière* role, 183, 188–89

Rancière, Jacques, 213–14n25

reconciliation, 52

repetition and time, 112–19

resistance: abandonment of, 103; Algerian, 97, 106–7; behaviors of, 107; collective action as, 100, 101, 118, 120, 154, 172–75; against colonization, 98, 119; embodiment and, 61, 99, 102; femininity as, 29; melancholy as, 33–34, 119; mobilization of affect and, 18; noncooperation as, 119–20; sovereignty and, 115; veiling as, 104; violent, 107, 110; of women, 118. *See also* perverse protests

"Right-Wing Thought Today" (Beauvoir), 11–12, 16, 18–24; on encounters with enemies, 20–21; on political freedom, 47

Rosskam, Edwin, 133

Sade, Marquis de, 5, 6, 38; on bourgeois ideology, 67, 86; on community and politics, 88; on eroticism in violence, 93; as misogynist, 12–13, 65, 68; trial, 12–13

salonnière role, 183, 188–89, 192

Sand War (1963), 94

Sartre, Jean-Paul, 130; on bad faith, 15; Beauvoir and, 1, 47; on communism, 19, 21; death, 9–10; explosion in apartment, 95; on individual freedom, 43

Schmidt, Anton, 54

Schmitt, Carl, 11

Scott, Joan, 102

Second Sex, The (Beauvoir): on biological data, 8–9, 21, 27, 109; critiques of, 24–25; de-sexing of, 34–35; encounters in, 6, 11, 24, 35–36, 174; on female independence, 78, 118; female voice in, 28; on feminine desires, 141; on freedom, 140, 144–45; on housework, 156, 157, 161; on lived experience of women, 210n7; male voice in, 26–27; on motherhood, 136–37, 207; mythology of nymph, 148–69; political theory in, 34, 36, 47; on politics of encounter, 17, 19; remaking femininity in, 28–34; on Self-Other duality, 2; textual strategies, 10, 16, 17–19, 24–27, 35, 37; translation debates, 25–26; on women as "we," 96, 135–37; women in stories, 167; on women's toilette, 163; on wounded subjects, 15; Wright's influence in, 14–15

Sedgwick, Eve Kosofsky, 101

Self-Other duality, 2–3, 157

Senghor, Léopold Sédar, 125

sexuality: female as unknowable, 224n19; nature and, 82, 87; normative, 39, 65, 230n12; under patriarchy, 230n4; pleasure/danger dynamic, 93, 155, 156, 158–59, 167–68, 170–71, 172–73; violence and, 88–89, 171

"Shame in the Cybernetic Fold" (Sedgwick/Frank), 101

She Came to Stay (Beauvoir), 179

Simone de Beauvoir and the Politics of Ambiguity (Kruks), 212n16

Simons, Margaret, 131

situation, 2–4, 30, 43, 56, 204

slavery/racial theories, 128

social contract theory, 109

solidarity against oppression, 53, 64, 130–41, 144–45, 174, 181

sovereignty: ambiguity and, 99, 121; female, 84, 115, 158, 178; logic of, 89; male, 3, 87, 111, 136, 191; mutuality and, 11; national, 94, 108, 129, 145; over nature, 115; unfettered, 6

Spillers, Hortense, 137

Stein, Gertrude, 130

Strangers in Their Own Land (Hochschild), 23

structure, 3; vs. agency, 16; existence of, 17; patriarchal, 24, 28–29, 32, 161, 215n3; protest against, 157

subjectivity: agency and, 131–32; anticolonial, 99, 102; arising from gender, 135, 190, 224n19, 225n1; collective political, 123–24, 130, 144, 146; as constructed, 131; encounters and, 4, 7, 36; erasure of, 34, 46, 103, 104, 121, 224n17; in judgment, 218n2; in oppression, 63, 136; otherness and, 157, 212n14; queering of, 223n6; violence and, 108

sub-men, use of term, 45, 55, 64

Tarkovsky, Andrei, 169

Temps Modernes, Les (journal), 18–20, 42, 45, 67, 94, 105, 211n11

Thérèse and Isabelle (Leduc), 182

"Thinking and Moral Considerations" (Arendt), 193

thoughtlessness, 54–55, 58

Tolstoy, Sophia, 33

Tomkins, Silvan, 101

transcendence, 3; ambiguity and, 57, 99, 121; duality with immanence, 30, 33–34, 113–14, 157; as male, 27, 87, 113, 136, 158

Trier, Lars von, 6, 12–13, 15, 152, 154, 167–72; aberrant women in films, 69–75, 206; Depression trilogy, 70, 72; on eroticism in violence, 93; female grotesque in films, 78, 84, 206. *See also specific films*

Trotta, Margarethe von, 6, 16, 56–57, 152, 191–201. See also *Hannah Arendt* (Trotta biopic)